T0344947

Agile Auditing

Founded in 1807, John Wiley & Sons is the oldest independent publishing company in the United States. With offices in North America, Europe, Asia, and Australia, Wiley is globally committed to developing and marketing print and electronic products and services for our customers' professional and personal knowledge and understanding.

The Wiley Corporate F&A series provides information, tools, and insights to corporate professionals responsible for issues affecting the profitability of their company, from accounting and finance to internal controls and performance management.

Agile Auditing

Fundamentals and Applications

Raven Catlin
Ceciliana Watkins

Copyright © 2021 by John Wiley & Sons, Inc. All rights reserved.

Published by John Wiley & Sons, Inc., Hoboken, New Jersey.
Published simultaneously in Canada.

No part of this publication may be reproduced, stored in a retrieval system, or transmitted in any form or by any means, electronic, mechanical, photocopying, recording, scanning, or otherwise, except as permitted under Section 107 or 108 of the 1976 United States Copyright Act, without either the prior written permission of the Publisher, or authorization through payment of the appropriate per-copy fee to the Copyright Clearance Center, Inc., 222 Rosewood Drive, Danvers, MA 01923, (978) 750-8400, fax (978) 750-4470, or on the web at www.copyright.com. Requests to the Publisher for permission should be addressed to the Permissions Department, John Wiley & Sons, Inc., 111 River Street, Hoboken, NJ 07030, (201) 748-6011, fax (201) 748-6008, or online at http://www.wiley.com/go/permission.

Limit of Liability/Disclaimer of Warranty: While the publisher and author have used their best efforts in preparing this book, they make no representations or warranties with respect to the accuracy or completeness of the contents of this book and specifically disclaim any implied warranties of merchantability or fitness for a particular purpose. No warranty may be created or extended by sales representatives or written sales materials. The advice and strategies contained herein may not be suitable for your situation. You should consult with a professional where appropriate. Neither the publisher nor author shall be liable for any loss of profit or any other commercial damages, including but not limited to special, incidental, consequential, or other damages.

For general information on our other products and services or for technical support, please contact our Customer Care Department within the United States at (800) 762-2974, outside the United States at (317) 572-3993 or fax (317) 572-4002.

Wiley also publishes its books in a variety of electronic formats. Some content that appears in print may not be available in electronic formats. For more information about Wiley products, visit our web site at www.wiley.com.

Library of Congress Cataloging-in-Publication Data

Names: Catlin, Raven, author. | Watkins, Ceciliana, author.
Title: Agile auditing : fundamentals and applications / Raven Catlin and Ceciliana Watkins.
Description: Hoboken, New Jersey : Wiley, [2021] | Includes bibliographical references and index.
Identifiers: LCCN 2021015254 (print) | LCCN 2021015255 (ebook) | ISBN 9781119693321 (hardback) | ISBN 9781119693482 (adobe pdf) | ISBN 9781119693468 (epub)
Subjects: LCSH: Auditing. | Agile project management.
Classification: LCC HF5667 .C325 2021 (print) | LCC HF5667 (ebook) | DDC 657/.45–dc23
LC record available at https://lccn.loc.gov/2021015254
LC ebook record available at https://lccn.loc.gov/2021015255

Cover Design: Wiley
Cover Image: © Casper1774 Studio / Shutterstock

SKY10027394_060121

We dedicate this book to our families and all auditors in search of knowledge and making the world a better place.

Contents

Tables and Figures

Foreword

Serving as a chief audit executive and then CEO of The Institute of Internal Auditors (IIA), I have strived to learn new concepts, develop new ideas, and advocate for new ways to approach challenges and opportunities. Continuous learning is what brings me to this book, *Agile Auditing: Fundamentals and Applications*, by Raven Catlin and Ceciliana Watkins, two remarkable individuals who epitomize the internal auditors of today and the future. In this book, Raven and Ceciliana offer a fresh approach to what our profession must do to become and remain relevant to our stakeholders by adopting an Agile mindset.

I have discussed the importance of being nimble and turning problems into opportunities over more than a decade, through my books, in presentations around the world, and in my weekly blog *Chambers on the Profession*. To implement Agile auditing, internal auditors must demonstrate intellectual curiosity and open-mindedness, two attributes discussed in my book *Trusted Advisors: Key Attributes of Outstanding Internal Auditors*. Additionally, Agile auditors must have the relational and professional attributes addressed in the book.

After reading *Agile Auditing: Fundamentals and Applications*, I gained new perspectives and reinvigorated my firm belief that, to be relevant, we must continuously evolve who we are as internal auditors and how we add value.

We are at a critical juncture in our profession. Being Agile also means being resilient amid every advancing risk. We must embrace fresh ideas and perspectives to execute bold, decisive, and Agile strategies to address the new frontier. Amid the COVID-19 pandemic, the need for social distancing around the globe challenged the management of audit activities, from risk assessments to testing, reporting, and the administration of the audit activity, including recruiting, retention, and training.

In a virtual environment, internal auditors face myriad challenges in how they address and complete their work, from different methods of communications to limitations on travel and physical access. The pandemic has certainly tested the concept of Agile auditing, but the good news is that, amid a changing risk landscape, we've learned that it actually can be most effective.

I met Raven Catlin in 2002 at The IIA's Volunteer Instructor Development Program. Raven stood out. She successfully completed the program and impressed me as a knowledgeable, articulate, experienced, and innovative auditor. As an instructor, Raven presents an effective method to deliver concepts and influence others to adopt new practices. This book showcases those attributes. It offers a framework for audit functions to add value and remain relevant. I find Raven and Ceciliana's Agile audit framework to be distinct in that it is not a method that simply provides ideas. It is truly a framework that's adaptable and allows audit teams to incorporate practices and tools into an Agile audit methodology they create and customize.

Moreover, the framework provides a structure and guidance for greater collaboration with audit customers/clients, a critical tenet of internal auditing. It integrates clients as members of the team from day one, and it acknowledges that, without this fully involved engagement, the audit cannot proceed as an Agile audit. Further, the framework focuses on creating value from the audit client's perspective. It centers the Agile audit on the value proposition, which makes achieving organizational objectives a foundation point.

It also helps organizations increase overall resiliency, which is critical in this new normal. The audit must deliver results more quickly and provide insights that will help reduce detrimental risks and achieve objectives. The flexibility provided by implementing this Agile approach helps management and auditors collaborate in risk identification, resulting in better-managed businesses and organizations. A vital aspect of this framework is that it uses a risk universe, rather than an audit universe, to determine priorities and an Agile audit plan.

As I have discussed in many of my blogs, tweets, and books, adapting and keeping an eye out for the most critical risk is crucial for our profession and our organizations. Continuous risk thinking is a lesson I learned early in my career and is vital to Agile auditing success. Conventional planning for internal auditing doesn't hold up in today's environment because it cannot deal with unexpected risks.

In 1990, I was in the middle of an old-school, annual plan as chief audit executive for the U.S. Army when Iraq invaded Kuwait. Risks that very few saw coming had suddenly appeared. I had to toss my annual audit plan and assess risks continuously, so that I could identify and reset our internal audit priorities. Traditional methods and routines of conducting audits based on plans that are six months to a year old are in the past. We need to assess risk continuously, and we must have new information to keep our audit plan up to date.

I wish that I had had this book back in 1990 as a guide not only for myself but also for my audit department and colleagues. The framework and information provided in this book provide the tools and ideas to spark your creative juices to make your audit activities successful today and in the future. In turn, it will allow you to continuously set your antenna high and be better prepared to address new risks as they emerge within our industry and in the overall economy.

Finally, one of the most valuable lessons you will learn in this book is to deliver focused results faster. As presented in the framework, auditors complete each Agile audit in short, two-week cycles – planning, performing, and communicating risk-focused results. Applying Agile auditing consistently and maintaining a tight delivery cycle require innovative thinking on audit processes and deliverables. It creates a baseline, so each auditor and each team can measure their performance and become better and stronger with every audit.

I highly recommended *Agile Auditing: Fundamentals and Applications* by Raven Catlin and Ceciliana Watkins whether you are a seasoned auditor, new to the profession, or even in a different domain unrelated to audit. You will find that the framework, lessons, and principles better equip you to meet new challenges. This book is one of few written by audit professionals to improve our audit services and value to our organizations by being more responsive and a better team player. Reading this book will prepare you with the knowledge and skills necessary to become an Agile auditor, implement Agile auditing in your audit activity, and deliver more value to the organizations you serve.

—Richard Chambers
President and CEO of The Institute of Internal Auditors (IIA)
January 2009 to March 2021
Author, *Lessons Learned on the Audit Trail* (2014),
Trusted Advisors:
Key Attributes of Outstanding Internal Auditors (2017), and
The Speed of Risk: Lessons Learned on the Audit Trail,
2nd edition (2019)

Preface

From the beginning, it seemed natural that Ceciliana Watkins and I would form a friendship. We think alike as auditors, respect each other immensely, and have a passion for learning and sharing knowledge, not to mention sharing a huge passion for cooking and experimenting with "recipes." On a warm summer night in 2011, just outside of Sacramento, California, we had dinner and talked about some of the pains and frustrations that we experienced in auditing. One of our frustrations is that many auditors work on multiple projects simultaneously and miss deadlines far too frequently. We continued our evening recognizing that we had to determine and fix the root causes of our problems, including audit clients (commonly referred to as "auditees") frequently failing to deliver evidence when needed, constant and often unconscious scope creep, excessive audit workpaper documentation, and wordsmithing masked as elegant writing consistently clouding the message we really need to deliver to add value, improve processes, and help our organizations accomplish their objectives.

Please understand, my friend and co-author Ceciliana is a life-long learner, creator, and challenger. She is a project management professional and has dedicated her professional life to auditing. She challenges others to think better and do more to help improve the audit profession. As we discussed many audit-related frustrations, my dearest friend asked, "have you ever researched Agile project management?" It was that dinner conversation, over home-cooked corn tortillas, ceviche, and watermelon-basil margaritas, that started my Agile auditing journey. On the plane back to Virginia, I started listing the problems faced in the audit process. The very next day, I purchased my first book on Agile and began learning about Agile, including Scrum and other frameworks. Moreover, I started tackling the list of frustrations and mapping Agile practices to the problems in a quest for solutions. I began the journey seeking answers to these questions:

- Can the auditing profession use Agile frameworks?
- How can auditing adopt Agile principles?

- How can Agile tools help fix our audit process problems?
- What needs to change in audit to be Agile?
- What is the root cause of the audit problems and frustrations?
- Can Agile frameworks and principles solve the root causes of our audit problems and symptoms?

I talked with Ceciliana about our journey, questions, and early conclusions. We realized that many of our problems are just symptoms of a root cause, poor audit client relationships. So, we looked for opportunities to use Agile frameworks to help resolve client relationship issues.

Since 2011, "I" became "we" as the Raven Global Training team expanded. Expert trainers joined, and courses increased, including courses on Agile auditing. Ceciliana was the first instructor we officially added to the team. We continually collaborate on many topics and bounce ideas off each other – it is a great partnership.

We concluded that the auditing profession can, and should, use Agile frameworks and that doing so can solve the root cause of many problems experienced in the audit life cycle, such as poor client relationships. But how? What would this look like? Would it look the same for every audit team? Can it work on every audit? What would we call it? The name *Agile auditing* felt right, and the rest of the story is provided for you in the pages of this book.

> Successful Agile projects are those that recognize failure quickly, through constant inspection, and rapidly adapt to identified failures.

In 2013, we began offering keynote addresses on Agile auditing concepts at conferences. As we continued developing our Agile audit framework, we also sought opportunities to put the framework into practice. Our first client was up for the challenge in 2014, and we knew we might not get it right the first time. In fact, failing, and failing fast, is a collective mindset in Agile disciplines. It is okay to fail. Failure is even expected! Successful Agile projects are those that recognize failure quickly, through constant inspection, and rapidly adapt to identified failures.

Our first full-day Agile auditing class was offered in Roseland, New Jersey, in September 2014. Back then, our Agile audit framework rigidly aligned the audit process and project management principles used in auditing to the Agile

Manifesto, Agile principles, and Scrum framework. Our first Agile audit methodology was too rigid and didn't incorporate our personal auditing experiences. With our second Agile auditing class in Albuquerque, New Mexico, in January 2015, we changed the methodology to reflect more of a framework and incorporated Participatory Auditing principles, more client collaboration, and professional standards for the audit profession. For private sector internal auditing, we turned to the Standards for the Professional Practice of Internal Auditing issued by The Institute of Internal Auditors (IIA). For public sector auditing, we reviewed the Generally Accepted Government Audit Standards (GAGAS), commonly referred to as the Yellow Book. For audits of external financial reporting, we researched the Generally Accepted Auditing Standards (GAAS).

As Steven Denning points out in his book *The Age of Agile*, Agile started as a movement that took off in 2001 as a set of values and principles articulated by the Agile Manifesto of 2001. The manifesto spawned various management methodologies including Scrum and many others (Denning 2018). Over time, it evolved into a movement of people with a specific mindset that focuses on delivering continuous value to customers. As we started our journey in Agile, we soon realized the importance of distinguishing a framework from a methodology to facilitate the Agile auditing movement.

So, what is the difference between a methodology and a framework? According to the Cambridge Dictionary, *methodology* is defined as "a system of ways of doing, teaching, or studying something" (Cambridge Dictionary 2020b). Basically, a methodology is a systematic way of doing or accomplishing something. If we apply an Agile methodology, we must have systematic procedures. Methodologies are prescriptive – they tell us how to do something in a step-by-step manner. On the other hand, the term *framework* is defined as "a supporting structure around which something can be built" or "a system of rules, ideas, or beliefs that is used to plan or decide something" (Cambridge Dictionary 2020a). Therefore, a framework provides guidelines or a structure that we can work under. A framework allows us to be flexible and adaptive. While a framework has a general structure, the user is not guided through specific steps or processes to get to results. A framework has flexibility within its structure, enabling the user to be supple and to adopt responses to change without having to follow specific steps. Therefore, Agile auditing is a framework that provides options to develop your approaches, methods, practices, and techniques to complete audits faster, with minimal waste, while emphasizing risks and delivery of value to customers. In other words, we are providing an Agile audit framework for you to create your Agile audit methodology. Nonetheless, our experiences have shown us that auditors need something more methodical to start implementing Agile auditing and to increase the success rate with the Agile approach. Thus, we found providing special "recipes" to implement Agile have been of great assistance to auditors in their Agile journey. You will find these recipes at the end of various chapter, as appropriate.

We have made every effort to provide as much useful information as possible to help you find your success on your Agile auditing journey. Thank you for choosing this book. Please enjoy!

Acknowledgments

When we set out to write this book, we soon realized the immensity of the challenges and opportunities we were facing. No matter how vast our knowledge and experience and how many books we read, we could not operate alone: we needed our Agile team!

This book would not have been possible without the help of all our former bosses and audit teams who taught us about auditing. We are very grateful to our fellow audit professionals as a whole. Without them, we would not have had great examples of lessons learned and ideas on improving audit processes. We acknowledge that Agile auditing would not have been possible if it were not for the authors and practitioners who pioneered Agile frameworks in system development and other organizational initiatives. Additionally, the Agile auditing framework wouldn't be where it is if it were not for our Agile auditing clients, conference participants, and classroom students who challenged our thinking and confirmed our approach. The bosses, fellow auditors, authors, practitioners, clients, conference participants, and students are too numerous to list, but we thank them all.

We especially want to express our gratitude to the magnificent and supportive staff of our publisher, John Wiley & Sons. They know their business and do things right. Sheck Cho, Elisha Benjamin, and Susan Cerra, you made this book happen. You unknowingly helped us confirm that using the Agile framework, anything can be done. We thank our many colleagues, friends, and family members who have played a pivotal role in completing this book or learning key concepts, or both.

Raven is especially thankful for the following:

- Ceciliana Watkins, friend and co-author, for stepping in to help me write the book, editing the book, and sharing her unique expertise and perspective as a government auditor.
- Carmen Catlin, sparkling daughter, for her beautiful smiles, warm hugs, encouraging words, and for being our delightful illustrator.

- Jean Louk, Mom, for her endless love and support.
- Christina Magargle, sister, for always knowing every one of my smallest thoughts and needs to finish the book even before I knew them.
- Vicki McIntyre, friend, for being a voice of reason and encouragement and for her endless hours editing the book.

Ceciliana is especially thankful for the following:

- Raven Catlin, friend and co-author, for her sharing audit knowledge, believing in me, and providing opportunities to expand my creativity and brain.
- Pheary Watkins, husband extraordinaire, for his never-ending support and for making my dreams come true.
- Helm Zinser-Watkins, my marvelous child, for editorial skills, support, and love and kindness in all my pursuits.
- Nancy Goldberg, friend and colleague with the biggest heart and support in all my pursuits, and through her deep thinking, logic, and thoughtful conversations throughout the years helped keep me focused on the right goals.
- Kathleen Webb, friend and colleague, for her support, insightful advice, fantastic brain, and adroit teachings and conversations in Agile and Lean practices, invaluable to my thinking process.
- Evelyn Calderon-Yee, friend and colleague, for her continuous support and belief in all of my innovative ideas, and her effective implementation of our Agile auditing framework.
- Judith W. Umlas, my kindred spirit, for her support and feedback and her unstoppable passion for helping the world become a better place by teaching how to be a grateful Agile leader and use the power of acknowledgment.

About the Authors

 RAVEN CATLIN

Raven is an expert in the auditing field and a globally recognized speaker and instructor in risk management and internal audit. Raven possesses over 23 years of diverse audit experience and 19 years of instructing and facilitating a variety of courses. She loves the sciences, especially chemistry and biology, and started her secondary education at 16 years old with dreams of becoming a neurosurgeon. In her freshman year at Virginia Commonwealth University in Richmond, Virginia, Raven realized that the medical field wasn't for her and changed her major to Accounting. She joined Beta Alpha Psi, took an overload of classes to catch up to the other accounting sophomores, and hasn't looked back. Like most accounting majors, she was groomed to sit for the Certified Public Accountant (CPA) exam and work for a big accounting firm. Unlike most, after graduating in 1997, she found her way into internal auditing after working as an accounting manager for a small manufacturing company whose number-one client was Philip Morris. The president of the manufacturing company helped Raven secure an interview with Philip Morris to launch a fantastic career in internal auditing.

Raven performed reviews and audits of not-for-profit entities, philanthropic organizations, mutual funds, general banking operations, trust operations, mortgages, real estate lending, construction activities, benefits, compensation, payroll, procurement activities, accounting operations, marketing, governance, information technology, treasury management, cash management, derivatives, secondary marketing, and debt issuance, to name a few. Her industry expertise and audit experience include mortgage operations, mortgage-backed securities, capital markets, human resources, and shared services.

She worked for NationsBank in Charlotte, North Carolina, and served as an audit consultant through the merger with Bank of America in Phoenix, Arizona. She served as an integral member of the financial restatement team for Freddie Mac in Fairfax, Virginia, where she currently resides. Additionally, she created project plans and coordinated over 150 individuals responsible for correcting security pricing as part of the Fannie Mae financial restatement. Raven performed a business process analysis and redesign (using Six Sigma and Lean) at the World Bank/International Finance Corporation and led an entity-wide Fraud Risk Assessment for a regional bank and trust company. She developed and redesigned the auditing infrastructure for internal audit functions, including developing internal audit policies and procedures, implementing audit software, designing reporting and time management templates, designing audit committee packages, and implementing databases to report and track the progress of audit concerns.

Raven embraces the definition of internal auditing as a value-added service and views all forms of auditing as being helpful to the success of an organization. Organizations in all industries have welcomed her fresh approach to auditing. The Agile audit approach explained in this book incorporates Raven's knowledge, experience, views, and people skills to form a fresh perspective to Agile auditing that auditors will find a great tool to add to their own audit toolbelt. In addition to maintaining her CPA license, she proudly displays her dedication to the audit profession by maintaining a Certified Internal Auditor (CIA), a Certified Financial Services Auditor (CFSA), and Certification in Risk Management Assurance (CRMA) designations.

Raven is the founder and CEO of Raven Global Training, LLC, a provider of in-house, virtual, and on-site audit, risk management, and interpersonal skills training to corporations, governments, not-for-profits, and associations. Raven began sharing her knowledge of and love for the audit profession in 2001 when The Institute of Internal Auditors selected her as a course facilitator. Moreover, Raven has been developing, instructing, and facilitating courses, including Agile auditing, worldwide since 2006 exclusively through Raven Global Training, LLC.

Raven is the proud mother of an 11-year-old aspiring actress, Carmen, two ferrets, two horses, one hedgehog, and an adorable Maltese, Pepper Sugar Spice. In her spare time, she enjoys cooking, island hopping, creating and tending a productive, though at times struggling, vegetable garden (a COVID-19 inspired hobby), rollerblading, bicycling, horseback riding, world-traveling, and tapping into her inner child at amusement parks (especially Walt Disney World). Her greatest joys are spending time with her family, making memories, and sharing knowledge with anyone who will listen.

CECILIANA WATKINS

Ceciliana (also known as Cecilia) has over 25 years of knowledge, leading multiple projects and performing a variety of audits from sales and use tax to internal audits including compliance, operational, and performance. Ceciliana's proficiency in internal audit and risk management involves directing, leading, and performing a wide range of audit, consulting, and advisory services. She helped her organization with governance, risk, and compliance by providing value-added solutions to complex business processes and systems. She retired from state service having last served as the manager for the internal audit division for a state government agency that employed over 4,800 staff. She incorporates her hands-on experience in risk management and government audit with her life experiences to help clients forge logical solutions to daily problems. She thrives on exploring opportunities to increase process efficiency and constantly looks for innovative and creative strategies to lead others in conducting effective audits better and faster. She is fully dedicated to the principle of continuous improvement, as shown through her obsession with nonfiction books, specifically on auditing and anything related to auditing including risk management and data analytics.

In addition to being the first facilitator to expand the Raven Global Training, LLC, instructor team in 2015, she has also been a faculty member in Boston University's Administrative Sciences department, where she has served as a course facilitator for the online Business Master's program, including the Business Analytics Foundation course.

As the project manager for her agency's enterprise risk management (ERM) initiative, she facilitated creation, development, and implementation of their risk assessment methodologies. Moreover, she successfully reengineered the internal audit program using the Agile auditing approach by identifying, evaluating, and implementing changes to each step in the audit life cycle, standardizing audit templates, and developing and documenting policies and procedures, which culminated in a comprehensive audit manual. The Agile audit reengineering project resulted in greater efficiencies in audit performance, increased productivity, and improved quality and timeliness of audits using a risk-focused Lean audit approach. This approach also provided the flexibility to adapt each audit as needed. Many mistakes were made through the project. However, the lessons learned have been invaluable to the development of the Agile audit framework.

Ceciliana graduated with her Master of Science in Business Continuity, Security, and Risk Management (receiving the "Excellence in Graduate Studies" honor) from Boston University in May 2016, and her BSBA in Accounting from California Polytechnic State University in 1992. She also holds a Graduate Certificate in Risk Management and Business Continuity from Boston University and a Master's Certificate in Applied Project Management from Villanova University. Ceciliana is a Certified Project Management Professional (PMP), a Certified Internal Auditor (CIA), a Certified Information Systems Auditor (CISA), a Certified Government Audit Professional (CGAP), a Certification in Risk Management Assurance (CRMA), and holds a Certificate as a Scrum Team Member (endorsed by Scrum Inc. and Dr. Jeff Sutherland, co-creator of Scrum).

Ceciliana is married to the love of her life, Pheary, and lives near Sacramento, California. She enjoys surfing, paddleboarding, reading, cooking, dancing, gardening, and landscaping. She is a salsa master and a Zumba dance aficionada. Ceciliana constantly applies her knowledge of project management, risk management, auditing, and Agile frameworks to her everyday life – take, for example, one of her largest landscaping projects, which was laying over 10,000 pounds of custom-built concrete pavers in preparation for her terrific child, Helm, and wonderful daughter-in-love, Nikkole (yes, "daughter-in-love," as their relationship is much more than what is required by law). This entire project was completed in just under two months using the Agile methodology. The Agile team was a crew of six family members – all part of the wedding party! They made use of a Scrum Board with the headings "Backlog," "To Do," "In Process," "Verified," and "Done." Each Team Member signed up for different user stories in the Backlog (tasks), and proceeded to go from To-Do to Done (Done = Ta-Dah!). Ceciliana's greatest joys are also spending time with her family, learning new concepts and skills, experimenting with new techniques (including raising chickens and worms), and sharing her newly attained knowledge with everyone she can.

Finally, Ceciliana is the founder and CEO of Team Oriented Solutions, an innovative organization of trained professionals with one dream: Make the world a better place by providing world-class education, training, facilitation, and coaching services to businesses around the globe.

List of Acronyms

ACL – Audit Command Language

AI – artificial intelligence

AICPA – American Institute of Certified Public Accountants

AP – accounts payable

CA – chartered accountant

CAE – chief audit executive

CAO – chief administrative officer

CEO – chief executive officer

CFSA – Certified Financial Services Auditor

CGAP – Certified Government Audit Professional

CIA – Certified Internal Auditor

CISA – Certified Information Systems Auditor

COSO – Committee of Sponsoring Organizations

COVID-19 – Coronavirus disease (formerly referred to as "2019 novel coronavirus" or "2019-nCoV")

CPA – Certified Public Accountant

CRMA – Certification in Risk Management Assurance

CSM – Certified Scrum Master

DA – data analytics

DSDM – dynamic systems development methodology

ELRA – engagement-level risk assessment

ERM – enterprise risk management

ERP – enterprise resource planning

FASB – Financial Accounting Standards Board

FDD – feature-driven development

GAAP – Generally Accepted Accounting Principles

GAAS – Generally Accepted Auditing Standards

GAGAS – Generally Accepted Government Audit Standards, commonly referred to as the Yellow Book

GAO – Government Accountability Office

GATAP – Generally Accepted Tax Accounting Principles
GRC – governance risk and compliance
GTAG – Global Technology Audit Guide
HIL – human interface layer
HR – human resources
IAASB – International Auditing and Assurance Standards Board
ICFG – Internal Control in the Federal Government, also referred to as the
Green Book
IEEE – Institute of Electrical and Electronics Engineers
IFRS – International Financial Reporting Standards
IIA – Institute of Internal Auditors
IPPF – International Professional Practices Framework
ISO – International Organization for Standardization
IT – information technology
KPI – key performance indicator
KRI – key risk indicator
ML – machine learning
MVGV – mission, vision, goals, and values
OCBOA – other comprehensive basis of accounting
PBC – prepared by client
PMBOK – Project Management Body of Knowledge
PMI – Project Management Institute
PMP – Project Management Professional
PARC – potential audit report comments
QA/QC – quality assurance/quality control
QAR – quality assessment review
QA&IP – quality assurance and improvement program
RCM – risks and controls matrix
RDA – robotic desktop automation
RPA – robotic process automation
RUP – Rational Unified Process
SEC – Securities and Exchange Commission
SOX – Sarbanes-Oxley
TAC^{4}O – timely, accurate, clear, complete, concise, constructive, and objective
TOD – test of design
TOE – test of effectiveness
XP – Extreme Programming

Introduction

Agile auditing is perfect for all types of audits across any industry. As Agile audit grows in popularity, different Agile audit methodologies develop. From our point of view, Agile auditing is a framework, not a methodology. The Agile audit framework presented in this book can be used to develop your Agile audit methodology (as indicated in the Preface). There are five critical differences in our Agile audit framework that are distinct from other Agile audit methodologies that we read, discussed, and studied.

1. *It is a framework, not a methodology.* It is intended to provide ideas and guidance for an audit team to quickly deliver value to audit clients and stakeholders. The framework allows audit teams to incorporate other practices and tools into an Agile audit methodology that they create.
2. *The framework requires and provides a structure and guidance for more collaboration with audit customers/clients.* Audit customers and auditees are Agile team members from day one of the Agile audit. Agile audits cannot move forward without audit customer engagement.
3. *The framework focuses on adding value from the audit client's perspective by centering the Agile audit on the value proposition.* The value proposition focuses on business objectives and business risks, not audit risks. More specifically, the Agile audit framework encourages adding value by helping audit clients evaluate whether they have put the right actions and controls to mitigate threats and risks to an acceptable level to help them achieve *their* objectives. This framework helps organizations increase resiliency; it

enables auditors to more quickly deliver insights on whether business and management controls are working as intended to reduce risks and help achieve objectives. It provides flexibility to help management and audit clients articulate their objectives and articulate how each process aligns with the organization's strategy. Similarly, if management hasn't determined the risks that may affect their ability to accomplish objectives, the Agile auditing framework helps management and auditors to collaborate in risk identification.

4. *The framework uses a risk universe, rather than an audit universe, to determine the upcoming priorities and an Agile audit plan.* We discuss the difference between the risk universe and audit universe in Chapter 8: Implementing Agile Auditing: The Audit Planning Process.

5. *Each Agile audit is completed in two weeks.* Audit planning, audit execution, and final result communications are finished in just two weeks. We recognize that a defined two-week project cycle deviates from Agile disciplines. We've discovered that this time constraint is the best way to get better at determining how much work each Agile audit team can complete. We also learned that to apply Agile auditing consistently, audit teams must think differently about traditional audit processes and deliverables. The two-week cycle forces the necessary thinking and related practices.

This Agile audit framework is a drastic, disruptive change for many audit teams. It is a change that the audit profession needs. We recognize unique challenges in adopting the framework. In the spirit of continuous improvement, we accept and consider all challenges presented by students and audit leaders. We love it when audit practices across the globe incorporate our Agile audit framework. We love it even more when others challenge the framework, thoughts, practices, and methodologies. For example, in a 2015 class of 30 students, when we suggested that an audit team, even a team of one auditor, could complete an entire audit in a two-week time frame one student called us "crazy." We deliberately decided on a two-week cycle to break the decades-long auditing practices that created many of the problems encountered in nearly every audit. Others also felt that Agile auditing was vastly different from traditional auditing and would be "impossible" to implement. Each challenge resulted in a reevaluation of the framework and the creation of more choices in it. It's comical that the same "crazy" and "impossible" comments were made when Agile entered other disciplines. However, it has been fully adopted in many disciplines!

A few weeks after the 2015 class, it concerned us that others couldn't see the value in this approach to Agile auditing. Once again, we were back learning, thinking, and analyzing the framework, and we realized there was a problem. The problem was not necessarily with the Agile audit framework, but with audit approaches, perceptions, and assumptions, specifically:

- Audits are supposed to be risk-based; we pioneered Agile auditing, thinking that all auditors used a risk-based approach. We were wrong.
- We pioneered Agile auditing believing that all auditors already collaborated with audit clients to complete audit work. Again, we were wrong.
- We assumed employees, auditors, and audit clients have a common goal: the organization's success. Unfortunately, there are many examples where the success of the organization is not a mutual goal.
- We thought all auditors wanted and needed to feel liked by their coworkers. As much as we don't like to admit it, some auditors enjoy being feared and disliked by their coworkers even today.
- We believed that if all employees understand the how and why of the audit process, audits can be improved.
- We pioneered Agile auditing, assuming that audit clients wanted to build relationships with auditors and vice versa. We also believed that audit clients wanted to learn more about the why and how of audit processes. Again, we were wrong; well, we already knew this was wrong, but it was wishful thinking!

Why would we develop a framework with these assumptions? Because, based on our audit experiences until that time, those assumptions reflected how each of the 15 organizations we had worked with approached auditing. Additionally, it is how countless training clients wanted to approach their audits. Auditing practices learned throughout our audit careers have heavily influenced our Agile audit framework, including an emphasis on risk-based auditing, Participatory Auditing, operational auditing, and relationship building. Our desire to overcome problems experienced in the audit process ultimately drives the Agile audit framework. We continue to adapt, champion, and encourage the implementation of an Agile auditing framework or methodology. Not every audit team may be able to implement a methodology exactly how a creator designed it. That is okay. We are giving you options for implementation in a framework, should you adopt Agile auditing. Using this framework and adapting it to fit your organization based on your cultures, experiences, governance practices, mindsets, client expectations, client interactions, and audit resources will lead to faster, better, and value-added auditing.

We implore you to identify your assumptions. If you share the assumptions, you are well on your way to making Agile work for you. Should you find any assumption that doesn't fit for your organization, adapt Agile auditing to work for you. Every audit team can implement some Agile audit framework elements and recognize significant benefits when transforming to an Agile mindset. The most common benefits realized include more value-add, more risk coverage, satisfied audit clients, increased confidence in audit results, streamlined audit practices, and happier auditors.

Adults learn through personal experience and the experiences and mistakes of others. We hope you learn from this book and the stories we share. As we've stated, our first several versions of our Agile audit framework weren't perfect. We made some mistakes, a concept accepted and promoted as a necessity to be Agile. We mentioned this earlier, but it needs emphasis: Agile is not about perfection. It is not about getting it right every time. Agile expects mistakes and errors, but you must identify and respond to the mistakes early and learn from them. We tried to help two organizations and a state government audit department implement Agile auditing without understanding what was necessary from an organizational and foundational standpoint. We learned about two essential fundamentals for Agile auditing success during those three attempts – the right culture and the proper communication. Chapter 17: Preparing Your Organization for Agile Auditing/Creating the Agile Culture is dedicated to these fundamental topics.

The ideas and stories presented in this book represent a collection of classroom, conference, and hands-on work experiences and client interactions that began in 2011. We thank our clients and students for helping us evolve our once-rigid Agile audit methodology into the flexible Agile auditing framework it is today. We continually adapt our Agile auditing journey and framework in response to new knowledge and an ever-changing environment. This adaptation follows a fundamental Agile principle's expectations: as your knowledge increases, your needs change.

There is still more to learn. We read books, blogs, and white papers on Agile for different disciplines, frameworks, and industries. Classroom interactions challenge us to examine, reevaluate, and improve the Agile audit framework. Nearly every class we teach creates a new idea for Agile auditing. We recognize that Agile auditing is not perfect for every organization or every audit. As you start your Agile auditing journey, remember:

■ Your organization's Agile audit methodology must reflect your environment, culture, and audit practices.

- Agile auditing is not a one-size-fits-all methodology.
- Even after your Agile auditing methodology and process is mature, look for continuous improvement opportunities, and adapt to your organization's constantly changing needs.
- Perfection is a myth. Agile allows for failures, mistakes, and errors.

The Agile audit framework described in this book incorporates project management practices, Agile practices, Participatory Auditing, and end-to-end risk-based auditing. Agile auditing begins with creating the audit plan by selecting audits of areas that pose the most significant risks to the organization and ends with communicating the results of an individual engagement based on which risks are not mitigated to an acceptable level; that is what we mean by "end-to-end risk-based auditing." We recommend using a holistic, risk-based view of the audit process, even though you may elect to start with one piece of the audit process as you roll out your Agile audit methodology.

In this book, you'll find information about various organizations' Agile audit methodologies, attempts, failures, and successes to help you implement Agile auditing. Most importantly, you will gain knowledge to help you determine the right Agile auditing approach for your organization.

At the end of each chapter, we share "nuggets," which are key takeaways, ideas, questions, suggestions, "aha moments" when the lightbulb comes on, and thoughts presented in the chapter. We want you to reflect on the content at the end of each chapter and encourage you to identify your nuggets.

Part I: Building an Understanding of Agile and Auditing acclimates the reader to Agile and auditing and consists of the following six chapters:

In *Chapter 1: What Is Agile?*, you will build an understanding of Agile and Agile project management so you are able to explain Agile to others. This chapter includes defining Agile and presenting the Agile Manifesto and its 12 principles. You will be introduced to the multiple frameworks under the Agile umbrella, including Scrum, the most popular framework, Scrum values, Scrum's three roles, three Artifacts, and five activities. You may even gain a thirst to obtain one of the Scrum certifications. You will also learn about using "recipes" for your Agile audit journey and explain how you can use the recipes provided in this book. You will find the Agile Manifesto, Agile frameworks, and recipe concepts to create your Agile methodology.

In *Chapter 2: What Is Audit?*, you will learn how to define an audit, describe the different types of audits, and list the professional standards for the different types of audits. This chapter clarifies the audit project life cycle activities and use of audit customers and audit stakeholders. You will obtain brief overviews of auditors' key knowledge areas, including governance, risk, control, finance/accounting, technology, and compliance and skills needed as a successful auditor. The brevity of the discussion of the knowledge and skills is necessary, as each can be a separate book. After reading this chapter, you will be able to explain auditing, audit customers, knowledge and skills needed to be an effective auditor, traditional audit project life cycle phases, and problems encountered in the audit process that contribute to delivery risks to interested parties. This chapter includes a recipe for building auditor knowledge and skills.

In *Chapter 3: Traditional Audit Engagement Process and Practices,* you will obtain information on tasks and activities in the traditional audit life cycle. Many of these activities were collected from work experiences and reviews of other audit methodologies and represent typical audit practices. Your specific traditional audit practices may vary, but you should see some similarities as well. This chapter helps you further understand the typical activities to complete audits in the traditional waterfall process and can be used to benchmark your current auditing practices. You will likely see the bottlenecks, redundancies, and inefficiencies created in the audit process and think of your Agile solutions as you read this chapter.

From *Chapter 4: What Is Agile Audit?* and *Chapter 5: Why Agile Audit?,* you will be able to describe what Agile auditing is and why it is beneficial to auditors and the organizations they serve. You will be introduced to the Agile audit framework and implementation options. You will discover some of the challenges encountered, the benefits of Agile, and how to get others to buy in to your Agile auditing methodology.

Chapter 6: Creating the Agile Mindset will help you develop a deeper understanding of Agile and the Agile mindset. You will also learn ways to assess if your auditors believe in your Agile Manifesto and discover ways to assess how strongly they feel about their ability to start an Agile process. This chapter also provides a recipe for how you can get your auditors to believe in your Agile Manifesto.

Part II: Implementing Agile Auditing provides ideas for and examples of techniques, methods, and practices for implementing Agile auditing and consists of the following five chapters:

In *Chapter 7: Implementing Agile Auditing: Deciding Your Approach and Your Agile Audit Project Roles,* you will learn about three different Agile strategies you can use for the implementation of Agile auditing, including full Agile, pilot Agile, and Agile lite. We will also cover Agile audit roles and responsibilities. In this chapter, you will discover challenges you can expect people to encounter as you implement your Agile audit methodology.

In *Chapter 8: Implementing Agile Auditing: The Audit Planning Process,* you will see a contrast of traditional annual audit planning using an audit universe and Agile audit planning using a risk universe. This chapter discusses three unconventional risk assessment methods: dynamic risk assessments, data-driven risk assessments, and risk universe prioritizations. In this chapter, you will also learn more technical Agile jargon in the audit context. This chapter includes two recipes for helping you prioritize and select your user stories, depending on your selected approach to implementing Agile auditing.

Chapter 9: Implementing Agile Auditing: Planning Agile Audit Engagements explains how to plan your Agile audit resources with self-managing teams. Further, you will review the Agile planning steps and discuss other Agile jargon specifically for planning activities. You will also learn how you can solve problems encountered during the engagement planning process with Agile auditing.

Chapter 10: Implementing Agile Auditing: Executing the Agile Audit includes discussing "testing with the audit client" during the execution phase. This chapter will explore workpaper documentation in an Agile audit environment and ideas on managing scope creep. Further, this chapter also discusses how audit findings are communicated in Agile auditing. You will explore and consider the different ways in which you can solve problems encountered during engagement execution or fieldwork process with Agile auditing.

In *Chapter 11: Implementing Agile Auditing: Communicating Agile Audit Results,* you will read of innovative means of communicating your audit results and will learn the different communicating activities that derive from Scrum, though applied to Agile auditing. You will have the opportunity to consider whether, with Agile auditing, you still need to write a formal report. You will review problems and explore the different ways you can solve problems encountered during the engagement communication process with Agile auditing.

Part III: Special Considerations provides valuable information regarding how new technologies are affecting the way we audit. You will explore using Learn and Kanban for Agile auditing. You will learn how to stop creating kitchen-sink audits, merging risk-based auditing and integrated auditing with Agile auditing. Part III consists of the following eight chapters:

Chapter 12: Agile Auditing in the "New Normal" Environment (Remote Auditing) presents in a thought-provoking fashion how Agile audit in the "new normal" must adopt and embrace disruptive technologies (robotics process automation, machine learning, and artificial intelligence) to be prepared to deal with global changes including the 2020–2021 COVID-19 global pandemic.

You will explore how existing technologies, such as videoconferencing and data analytics (DA), change the way we communicate and perform our audits. Also, you will examine techniques for effective virtual conferencing. This chapter provides an introduction to DA terminology and a synopsis of the DA process. You can consider using it as your recipe for starting your DA journey. This chapter examines some of the differences between these technologies and how they affect the way we work.

In *Chapter 13: Lean and Agile Auditing,* and *Chapter 14: Exploring Kanban Agile Auditing,* you will learn how to use these two frameworks with the Agile auditing framework. It is important to note that these are not mutually exclusive, and audit teams may find a merger of frameworks most beneficial.

In *Chapter 15: Merging Risk-Based Auditing and Integrated Auditing with Agile Auditing,* you will review different risk definitions. You will learn how to stop creating kitchen-sink audits. You will learn about risk-based auditing and will explore our extreme risk-based auditing approach. Further, you will realize that Agile auditing does not preclude one from completing integrated audits.

In *Chapter 16: Building the Auditor Toolbelt and Self-Managing Agile Audit Teams,* you will learn the importance of building an auditor toolbelt and filling it with the different skills to become an Agile audit. Also, you will see how using Scrum values can help create a self-managing Agile auditing team.

Chapter 17: Preparing Your Organization for Agile Auditing/Creating the Agile Culture explores how behaviors, norms, and perceptions can influence the organization, so it supports Agile auditing. You will learn about the influence a Grateful Agile Leader can have on the organization's culture and the Agile team. You will also learn what the ideal conditions for Agile auditing are.

Chapter 18: Passing Your Quality Assessment Review (QAR) in an Agile Audit Environment discusses the four areas of most concern regarding your QAR when implementing Agile auditing (independence and objectivity, planning, documentation, and supervision). It also provides an overview of the standards used for the three types of audits covered in this book.

In *Chapter 19: Nuggets for Agile Audit Success,* you are encouraged to summarize your new or refreshed knowledge from the book and identify your nuggets (which can be anything meaningful to you: an idea, a question, something to research later, something to tell someone else, an aha moment, or even a thought related to the content discussed). This chapter provides 10 nuggets for Agile auditing success.

Appendix A: Glossary of Terms, provides definitions of key words, concepts, and notes provided in this book.

Appendix B: Product Backlog Template, includes the business risks (with likelihood/impact assessments), value proposition, cross-functional dependencies and relationships to other risks, priority or projected date for the completed audit, resource requirement estimates, and an estimate of the effort to complete the Agile audit.

Appendix C: Agile Audit Example. This example consists of the Agile Audit time-lapse activities conducted during a one-week period for an Agile audit of remediation activities for a Security/Access Controls audit finding: *Deficiencies in the user provisioning process for terminations.*

Bibliography. Our journey as we wrote this book included reading over 100 books, reports, scholarly and trade journals, white papers, articles, interviews, and research papers on Agile, Agile frameworks, and Agile methodologies. The Bibliography includes references to many of the learning and discovery aids we have used in this book. We encourage our readers to seek these references, as well as many more.

Good luck, and let's start your Agile auditing journey.

PART ONE

Building an Understanding of Agile and Auditing

CHAPTER ONE

What Is Agile?

AGILE IS A FRAMEWORK

It felt like a no-brainer to answer this question, as we set our sights on publishing a book on Agile auditing. Through discovery, we found that Agile has different meanings depending on your view and approach. When you develop and work with Agile, it's vital that you describe what Agile is and what it means.

Authors of other Agile publications describe it as a mindset or a methodology. Agile, for example, in Rick Wright's *Agile Auditing: Transforming the Internal Audit Process* (Wright 2019), he uses big "A" and little "a" to distinguish between *doing* Agile and *being* agile. Used as a noun, Wright refers to the big "A" as doing Agile internal auditing using software development methodologies. Wright's little "a," used as a verb, describes, in general, process improvement efforts (exclusive of specific methodology) to achieve a nimbler, less wasteful process. Big "A" is essentially the technical aspect of completing an audit. Little "a" is the thinking behind being agile. Being agile is as unique to an organization as your DNA is to you. To *do* Agile well, you must *be* agile, so from here on we make no distinction between being Agile and doing Agile. Agile is both a mindset and a framework. We hope that your organization, including your audit team, will demonstrate business agility using Agile methods. Agile organizations identify changes and risks from internal and external sources, respond to those changes promptly and appropriately, deliver value to their customers, and remain sustainable. While this book is a framework providing options to implement Agile auditing, we've also provided various "recipes" with step-by-step examples of how to implement the framework. These recipes are as close as we get to prescribing a methodology. Remember, the recipes and the case studies provided in the text are just examples!

> *Agile* is not a methodology itself in any discipline. It is a philosophy, a mindset, or a way of thinking to get stuff done faster based on the interests of identified customers.

It is important to note that *Agile* is not a methodology itself in any discipline. It is a philosophy, a mindset, or a way of thinking to get stuff done faster based on the interests of identified customers. The roots of Agile as a philosophy originated in software development. It was software developers who combined existing frameworks to create the Agile movement to complete software development projects faster. You can think of Agile as an umbrella term for a set of different frameworks and practices all based on the original software development values and principles. These values are expressed in the "Manifesto for Agile Software Development," and the 12 principles as fashioned by the Agile Alliance are presented later in this chapter. Another key thought is that Agile methods are people-oriented rather than process-oriented. In Agile, people come first and people complete projects. Conversely, conventional project management and software development methods, such as waterfall, are process-oriented.

Before we continue describing Agile, we want to clarify that there is a time and place for traditional conventional project management methods, such as waterfall. For example, certain mandatory compliance audits with repeated processes year after year might benefit from a waterfall process-oriented approach. As a matter of fact, although there appears to be a mass adoption of various Agile methodologies in many organizations, there are still many that continue to use conventional methods successfully. We have also seen organizations transition into a hybrid Agile approach that combines aspects of both Agile and waterfall. Our Agile framework was developed specifically to help address common problems that arise when completing all audits using the traditional methodologies (i.e., waterfall).

DEFINITIONS OF AGILE

Agile is an approach to project management based on a set of values and principles. [The Agile approach] breaks projects into smaller, incremental deliverables that go through repeated iterations to focus on customers' needs and interests. It promotes adaptive planning, early delivery, frequent inspections, continuous improvement, and flexibility to respond to change (Catlin 2020).

Agile means quick, easy, and nimble. In business, it's a way of thinking, a way of working that is increasingly part of how many of the most successful companies work (Cazaly 2017).

Agile is the ability to move quickly and easily in response to your environment. To be Agile, you must be alert to your situations, and you must be flexible, nimble, and adaptable (Catlin 2014).

Agile is a lightweight software development method that aims to be more efficient than traditional, plan-driven development models. Agile seeks to do more with less:

- More team-level decision-making
- Faster development time
- Faster response to shifting customer demands
- Faster problem solving
- More customer satisfaction
- Smaller teams
- Less expense
- Less wasted effort
- Fewer features in the end product that either don't work or are never used (Mathis 2013)

As these definitions show, Agile is more than a project management tool, more than a mindset, more than an ability to be nimble and responsive, and more than a method to get things done. Table 1.1 contrasts three different views of Agile (LeMay 2018).

To understand Agile, it is helpful to examine the project life cycle and development life cycle. *A Guide to the Project Management Body of Knowledge* (*PMBOK® Guide* – Sixth Edition; Project Management Institute 2017) states that "Project life cycles can be predictive or adaptive. Within a project life cycle, there are generally one or more phases that are associated with the development of the product, service or result. These are called a development life cycle ... and can be predictive, iterative, incremental, adaptive, or hybrid models."

TABLE 1.1 Views of Agile

Agile as a Methodology	Agile as a Mindset	Agile as a Movement
Practices matter more than mindset.	Mindset matters more than practices.	Mindset and practices are inexorably connected.
The practices and methods of Agile were already determined by others.	The principles and values of Agile were already determined by others.	I have an active role to play in determining how Agile principles and practices are articulated and applied in my team or organization.
Individuals within teams must collaborate and interact in prescribed and predefined ways.	Individuals within teams must independently develop an Agile mindset.	Individuals within team must work together toward a shared set of goals and values.

The *PMBOK® Guide* goes on to explain that:

- The traditional model, otherwise called waterfall, is a predictive life cycle where the project scope, time, and cost are determined in the early phases of the cycle. Any changes to scope are carefully managed. However, Agile is an adaptive life cycle and it may be iterative and incremental.
- "In an iterative life cycle, the project scope is generally determined early in the project life cycle, but time and cost estimates are routinely modified as the project team's understanding of the product increases. Iterations develop the product through a series of repeated cycles, while increments successively add to the functionality of the product." Iterative means repetitious actions. In Agile, iterations of project designing, planning, executing, testing, inspecting, and improving are repeated until a project is complete. The iterations increase functionality during a project until it is complete. In comparison, the waterfall includes single stages for designing (requirements definition), planning (project planning), testing/execution, and inspecting. In waterfall, the project constraints of scope, time, and cost are estimated at the beginning of a project. Agile frameworks determine and allow for flexibility on scope, time, and cost during an iteration.
- "In an incremental life cycle, the deliverable is produced through a series of iterations that successively add functionality within a predetermined time frame. The deliverable contains the necessary and sufficient capability to be considered complete only after the final iteration.

- "Adaptive life cycles are Agile, iterative, or incremental. The detailed scope is defined and approved before the start of an iteration. Adaptive life cycles are also referred to as Agile or change-driven life cycles.
- "A hybrid life cycle is a combination of a predictive and an adaptive life cycle. Those elements of the project that are well known or have fixed requirements follow predictive development life cycle, and those elements that are still evolving follow an adaptive development life cycle."

Project managers must select the right approach, be it traditional, iterative, incremental, adaptive, or hybrid, to manage the project throughout the project's life cycle. The project manager, or the project team in some approaches, must balance the constraints of time, scope/quality, and cost. Constraints are anything that restricts the actions of the project team (Heldman 2005). In projects using some of the Agile frameworks, we restrict the time (i.e., Agile projects should be less than one month), and often restrict the cost, and estimate the scope. The scope is what will be covered or achieved, as agreed with the customer, in a particular project. The scope includes the functions, features, data, content, standards, and so forth that will be provided during the project. In some Agile frameworks, scope is adjusted frequently to fit in the fixed time and cost constraints and teams do not add more time to complete Agile projects. In Agile, all constraints are value-driven, meaning one starts with the value proposition for Agile projects. Therefore, Agile projects focus only on necessary and enough processes to create the product. Moreover, Agile encourages adapting the project as needed to accomplish desired and changing goals.

Agile is also a mindset reflected in your organization's culture. To do Agile project management, you must begin with the Agile mindset (see Chapter 6, Creating the Agile Mindset). Your culture must support your efforts to execute your projects in an Agile way. We've dedicated an entire chapter to creating the Agile culture (see Chapter 17, Preparing Your Organization for Agile Auditing/Creating the Agile Culture) because the right culture is essential to the success of being and doing Agile. As Denning once stated, the wrong culture can kill any Agile efforts (Denning 2018). Use the following guiding principles as a foundation for the Agile mindset, methodology, and movement:

- Agile means we start with our internal or external customers and continuously consider customer needs. Customer needs change. Sometimes customers don't know what they need until they see what they do not need. An Agile team's role in completing projects is just as crucial as determining customer needs and figuring out how to deliver value. Agile is customer-centric.

- Agile means we collaborate early and often. We start by identifying customer needs, write our requirements from the customer's view, and determine the work we can complete as a collaborative team. There is constant communication between team members. We do not wait until a specific meeting or time to communicate and collaborate. If you need to work with a Team Member, you let them know immediately. If you need something from a Team Member to complete your work, you tell them as soon as you know you need it, and preferably before you need it to complete your next task. Agile requires collaboration early in every project and frequently throughout the life of the project.

- Agile means we plan for uncertainty. We not only recognize uncertainty exists; we expect it and plan for it. We are equipped with the tools and knowledge needed to address ambiguity in processes and in customer needs. We are prepared for the unexpected because we planned for it. Agile is being prepared for change.

 ## THE AGILE MANIFESTO

Let's continue our understanding of Agile with a little history lesson. Agile was created for software development projects by 17 software practitioners. Collectively, these practitioners are referred to as the Agile Alliance. These 17 individuals met in Snowbird, Utah, in February 2001 to "uncover better ways of developing software." The 17 software practitioners created the Agile Manifesto, which states (Beck et al. 2001):

> We are uncovering better ways of developing software by doing it and helping others do it. Through this work we have come to value:
>
> **Individuals and interactions** over processes and tools
> **Working software** over comprehensive documentation
> **Customer collaboration** over contract negotiation
> **Responding to change** over following a plan
>
> That is, while there is value in the items on the right, we value the items on the left more.

The Agile Alliance, officially formed in late 2001, is a nonprofit organization that promotes, disseminates, and develops the use of Agile and supports people using Agile (Agile Alliance 2001). While the roots of Agile are in developing software, other industries, disciplines, functions, and professions use Agile, including marketing, sales, construction, event planning, and now auditing.

The four Agile Manifesto values set the basis for 12 principles as follows (Agile Alliance 2001):

1. Our highest priority is to satisfy the customer through early and continuous delivery of valuable software.
2. Welcome changing requirements, even late in development. Agile processes harness change for the customer's competitive advantage.
3. Deliver working software frequently, from a couple of weeks to a couple of months, with a preference for the shorter timescale.
4. Business people and developers must work together daily throughout the project.
5. Build projects around motivated individuals. Give them the environment and support they need and trust them to get the job done.
6. The most efficient and effective method of conveying information to and within a development team is face-to-face conversation.
7. Working software is the primary measure of progress.
8. Agile processes promote sustainable development. The sponsors, developers, and users should be able to maintain a constant pace indefinitely.
9. Continuous attention to technical excellence and good design enhances agility.
10. Simplicity – the art of maximizing the amount of work not done – is essential.
11. The best architectures, requirements, and designs emerge from self-managing teams.
12. At regular intervals, the team reflects on how to become more effective, then tunes and adjusts its behavior accordingly.

The values and principles discussed earlier in this chapter are essential ingredients of the Agile mindset and set the foundation of Agile frameworks.

 ## AGILE FRAMEWORKS

Many Agile enthusiasts consider Agile to be an umbrella for other types of rapid development and delivery options that foster collaboration among

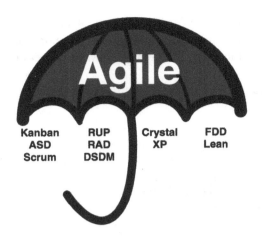

FIGURE 1.1 Agile Umbrella
Source: Illustration by Carmen Catlin.

cross-functional teams as depicted in Figure 1.1. Agile software development advocates adaptive planning, evolutionary development, early delivery, and continual improvement, and it encourages flexible responses to change (Agile Alliance 2001). When Agile was born in 2001, other methods to achieve faster development were already in existence, including the following (note, parenthesis in each bullet indicates the creation year and the creator's last name):

- Scrum (1986, Takeuchi and Nonaka [concept]; 1995, Schwaber and Sutherland)
- Extreme Programing (XP) (1996, Beck)
- Kanban (1953, Toyota)
- Rational Unified Process (RUP) (1987, Jacobson [concept]; 1996, Kruchten/IBM)
- Crystal (1996, Cockburn)
- Dynamic Systems Development Methodology (1995, DSDM Consortium)
- Feature Driven Development (FDD) (1997, De Luca)
- Rapid application development (1991, Martin)
- Adaptive software development (1974, Edmonds [concept]; 1995, Highsmith and Bayer)

After the 2001 Agile Manifesto, Lean software development was introduced in 2003 by Harry and Tom Poppendieck. We discuss Lean auditing principles in Chapter 13, Lean and Agile Auditing. There are several Agile certifications available to demonstrate your competency with the various frameworks. While each of these methods is distinct, they all require constant communication and team collaboration. The following is a brief, high-level description of some of these methods:

- Scrum is a timebound Agile method where each task or activity is limited by a specified duration. Scrum is the most popular framework; we discuss it in more detail later in this chapter.
- XP focuses on developing high-quality software in a short period of time based on customer participation, rapid feedback, and subsequent planning and testing. It leverages four values: courage, simplicity, feedback, and communication.
- Kanban focuses on productivity and flow when there are no "features" released to a customer. It works well for small teams and is typically used in manufacturing processes. Kanban is not time-sensitive.
- Crystal is a collection of Agile methodologies and recognizes that any project may need a unique set of practices. It focuses on early and regular product delivery by increasing user participation and eliminating bureaucracy, while reinforcing the need for communication, teamwork, and simplicity.
- DSDM emphasizes business needs, active user participants, team empowerment, and constant delivery. Requirements are determined early in the project and refined as the project progresses.

In many projects, including those using Agile methods, effective communication often determines the success of the project. Each Agile method reinforces the importance of communication and most include more frequent meetings, such as daily meetings for Agile teams to coordinate activities. The daily meeting is a unique element of Agile project management for delivering results faster, correcting errors sooner, inspecting the project often, and overcoming obstacles before the obstacles become bottlenecks.

Raven's first introduction to the daily meeting was during a financial restatement project led by the chief administrative officer (CAO). To make sure participants didn't "get comfortable and talk too much," the CAO literally removed all the chairs from the room. Each Team Member simply and quickly stated the completed activities from the previous day, the planned activities for that day, and identified any obstacles preventing moving forward with the project. We never skipped a daily meeting, someone was always present to discuss the work performed for each team, and it exceeded 15 minutes on only one occasion. In retrospect, the meeting was a Scrum of Scrums. A Scrum of Scrums is an Agile technique that integrates the work of multiple Scrum Teams. When there are many individuals in the team they are divided into smaller groups (usually five to nine members each), working on the same project. It allows the teams to communicate with each other to ensure that they are all working to accomplish the **Product Goal**. The output of each team is integrated with the output of all teams. This is vital in areas where there could be overlap or the sequencing of events is important. Ceciliana's first attempt to introduce the daily meetings and remove the chairs from the conference room during a project she was leading resulted in the participants becoming upset because they were going to have to limit the time they could speak and standing was not their preferred posture. After explaining that the reason for removing the chairs was to ensure a focused and speedy meeting, the team compromised, and the chairs were returned on a condition of brevity. This is a great "lessons learned" example regarding the importance of clear and timely communications. In this case, even after allowing chairs in the meeting, meeting time was reduced from approximately two hours to 30 minutes, on average, and communications were limited to actions needed to complete the project. In both examples, the daily meeting was essential in timely project completion and is thus one technique you can use today to be Agile.

There was one specific meeting that solidified the daily meeting's value for Raven, which is the main reason we adopted the daily meeting in our Agile framework. Something was said during one of the meetings that could have changed the successful outcome of the restatement project and would have undoubtedly led to bottlenecks to complete the restatement effort. A team leader presented the accounting manager's obstacle – the need to approve thousands of manual journal entries in a very short time frame. Another team lead suggested that the approval was "easy, just select all and click approve." Talk about correcting project errors sooner! Needless to say, the CAO took immediate notice of the obstacle and the potential risk and implemented corrective actions and safeguards against such behaviors and mindsets. One corrective action included adding additional journal entry approvers. As a result, accounting managers ceased the "select all and click approve" approach to approve manual journal entries. Additionally, the auditors monitored to ensure that this behavior did not recur by using the accounting system's embedded audit module. The auditors created a rule to alert them if one accounting manager, or any person with approval privileges, approved a certain number of manual journal entries within a limited time frame.

If it weren't for the daily meeting to identify obstacles, there is a high probability that the two team leaders may have had a hallway conversation about the obstacle that week and the solution would have been "select all and click approve." To a control fanatic, this is obviously the wrong solution. We found so much value in the daily meeting on that project that we started using it in other projects, not realizing at the time that it was an Agile technique.

SCRUM FRAMEWORK

Scrum is the most popular Agile framework. Scrum is actually a rugby term. It is not an acronym. Since we've never personally played rugby, please bear with us on the following layman's description of a Scrum. In a rugby Scrum, when the ball is put into play, the referee drops the ball in the middle of two teams whose arms are interlocked together. In the huddle, as each member is bound to another, the team communicates instructions so the team can work in unison to get possession of the ball quickly. Each team has the same goal: to quickly get possession of the ball and move the ball to the goal. To achieve this, the team passes the ball back to a Team Member at the back of the Scrum using only their feet, referred to as a hook, as their arms remain bound to others. The team must work together quickly and efficiently to move the ball to the back of their team before the other team takes the ball. Then, the team with possession tries to score as the team moves collectively downfield as they pass the ball back and forth numerous times as needed to take advantage of player expertise, skill, and position to score points. This collective, quick, and efficient movement is similar to an Agile Scrum Team working together quickly and efficiently to achieve a specific goal.

> A key concept under Scrum is that a project's time and cost are set early in the project and scope is modified as new information and client needs are determined.

A key concept under Scrum is that a project's time and cost are set early in the project and scope is modified as new information and client needs are determined. Applying this concept to the rugby Scrum, each game (or project) lasts 80 minutes – the time – and each half (or increment) is limited to

40 minutes – the time. [As a side note, there are even some who believe that the Scrum time itself should be limited, as long Scrums are a "waste of time and increase chances of player injuries." Luckily in Scrum project management, the Scrum time is already limited to one to four weeks. One could say that by limiting the Scrum time in Agile/Scrum project management, we are reducing waste and risk to the organization.] The number of players on the field – the cost – is limited. The scope, or how many points the rugby team will score, and how they will actually maneuver to score points/goals are fluid during the game. Depending on the other team and the environment – this is usually the customer's role in a Scrum – the team adapts its scope and method during play. Additionally, depending on the strengths, weaknesses, and availabilities of the team members, the project scope and methods evolve throughout the game. Usually, the team that adapts the best, wins!

Ken Schwaber and Jeff Sutherland, co-creators of *The Scrum Guide: The Definitive Guide to Scrum: The Rules of the Game*, updated the guide in November 2020. According to the co-creators, "The 2020 version aimed to bring Scrum back to being a minimally sufficient framework by removing or softening prescriptive language" (Schwaber and Sutherland 2020). While developing our Agile auditing framework and writing this book, we refer to the 2017 version. However, although we have endeavored to incorporate the changes as reflected in the November 2020 update, you will notice references to both versions. This has no substantive effect on our framework; the essence of Scrum has not changed; Scrum is still Scrum. The latest update nonetheless makes Scrum more adaptable to all disciplines, not only software development, and continues to become more streamlined, lighter, and easier to understand. It is one team approach working together towards one Product Goal. As Jeff Sutherland says, "Scrum works best when it is fast, easy, and fun." Following is a summary of the differences between the 2017 and 2020 versions (Scrum Guides.org 2020):

- The 2020 version aimed to bring Scrum back to being a minimally sufficient framework by removing or softening prescriptive language.
- One Team, focused on one Product. There is just one Scrum Team focused on the same objective, with three different roles or sets of accountabilities: Project Owner, Scrum Master, and Developers (i.e., individuals performing the audit work). You will note that in this book we use the word "Roles" to denote the different team functions. However, within the Scrum Team, there are no subteams or hierarchies. It is a cohesive unit of professionals

focused on one objective at a time, the Product Goal. The 2020 updated Scrum Guide no longer refers to roles but rather to "Team."

- A Product Goal. The 2020 Scrum Guide introduces the concept of a Product Goal to provide focus for the Scrum Team toward a larger valuable objective. A Product Goal provides focus for the Scrum Team toward a larger valuable objective. Each Sprint should bring the product closer to the overall Product Goal.
- Sprint Goal, Definition of Done, and Product Goal. Previous Scrum Guides described Sprint Goal and Definition of Done without really giving them an identity. They were not quite Artifacts but were somewhat attached to Artifacts. With the addition of Product Goal, the 2020 version provides more clarity around this. Each of the three Artifacts now contain "commitments" to them. For the Product Backlog the commitment is the Product Goal, the Sprint Backlog commitment is the Sprint Goal, and the Increment commitment is the Definition of Done. They exist to bring transparency and focus toward the progress of each artifact.
- Self-managing over self-organizing. The 2020 version emphasizes a self-managing Scrum Team, choosing who, how, and what to work on.
- Three Sprint Planning Topics. In addition to the Sprint Planning topics of "What" and "How," the 2020 Scrum Guide places emphasis on a third topic, "Why," referring to the Sprint Goal.
- Overall simplification of language for a wider audience. The 2020 Scrum Guide has placed an emphasis on eliminating redundant and complex statements as well as removing any remaining inference to IT work (e.g., testing, system, design, requirement, etc.).

For the most part, the concepts listed in the summary of differences between the 2020 and 2017 Scrum Guide versions were already embedded in our Agile auditing framework. When they were not, efforts have been made to include the most current updates. We appreciate these changes as they simplify the job of implementing an Agile auditing framework, especially focusing on one goal and the removal of inferences to IT work. As auditors we can and will continue to strive for better communications and greater efficiencies eliminating redundant and complex language and minimizing the use of audit jargon in all of our communications.

Ken Schwaber and Jeff Sutherland identify three pillars of the Scrum framework that facilitate collaborative work environments (Schwaber and Sutherland 2020):

- *Transparency.* When a Team Member says something is done, it is really done. Finished. No loose ends. Transparency enables inspection. Inspection without transparency is misleading and wasteful.
- *Inspection.* A check on progress. An opportunity to identify problems and potential problems. Inspection enables adaptation. Inspection without adaptation is considered pointless. Scrum events are designed to provoke change.
- *Adaptation.* Implementing changes based on inspection. A Scrum Team is expected to adapt the moment it learns anything new through inspection.

Additionally, there are five Scrum values (Scrum Alliance 2015). "These values give direction to the Scrum Team with regard to their work, actions, and behavior. The decisions that are made, the steps taken, and the way Scrum is used should reinforce these values, not diminish or undermine them. . . . When these values are embodied by the Scrum Team and the people they work with, the empirical Scrum pillars of transparency, inspection, and adaptation come to life building trust" (Schwaber and Sutherland 2020).

1. Commitment
2. Courage
3. Focus
4. Openness
5. Respect

> The three pillars of the Scrum framework (transparency, inspection, adaptation) facilitate collaborative work environments and the five values (commitment, courage, focus, openness, respect) give direction to the Scrum Team with regard to their work, actions, and behavior. When these five values are embodied by the Scrum Team and the people they work with, the Scrum pillars of transparency, inspection, and adaptation come to life building trust.
>
> (Schwaber and Sutherland 2020)

Each Team Member must demonstrate these pillars and values in the execution of their roles during the project.

Scrum/Agile Roles

In Scrum project management, there are only three recognized roles: one Scrum Master, one Product Owner, and various Developers. (The 2020 Scrum Guide explains that "Developer" does not mean software developers exclusively; it is intended to be an inclusive term. It refers to the members of the Scrum Team who are doing the work or developing the product. In this book we refer to a "Developer" as a "Delivery Team Member," which we have found more acceptable and more in alignment with audit terminology.) Collectively, those serving in these three roles create the Agile team (the equivalent to a Scrum Team). The Agile team members are self-organizing, to ensure the best complement of skills, knowledge, and capabilities, and self-managing, to increase accountability and workability of the team without the need for a manager, or, worse, a micromanager. There are no subteams or hierarchies. The team is a cohesive unit of professionals focused on one objective at a time, the Product Goal. The Agile team has total authority on the exact approach to get their work done, estimate how long work will take, create their schedule, and manage their own time. The Agile team is small enough to remain nimble and large enough to complete significant work within a Sprint. Most Agile teams have three to nine members. The Agile team is accountable for all aspects of the work (Rigby, Sutherland, and Takeuchi 2016). Following is a brief description of each role.

Product Owner

The **Product Owner** owns the "what" of the project. They create a prioritized list of all the things to need to get done (**Product Backlog**). The Product Owner maximizes the value of the product being delivered (the audit). The Product Owner determines the priorities for Agile teams and decides when a product is complete by assessing value from the customer's perspective. In some Agile variants, the Product Owner is referred to as the "initiative owner" (Rigby, Sutherland, and Takeuchi 2016). The Product Owner is not typically the customer, but someone who represents the customer's interest, voice, and mindset during the project. The Product Owner *must* have the Agile mindset; this is a critical role. Agile Teams cannot select just any manager to serve as the Product Owner in the same way managers are currently selected to manage traditional teams and projects. Even if one is a highly competent manager, that does not mean they have the right mindset and skills to be a successful Product Owner. Choosing the right Product Owner is as important as selecting an Agile framework. In the words of J.J. Sutherland, "if you keep doing things the way you have always done you will get the results you always got before. Good Product Owners are the key to winning with Scrum" (Sutherland 2019).

The Product Owner must understand the customer and the customer's needs. The Product Owner owns the Product Backlog (also known as a "portfolio backlog"), which is a list of requirements and deliverables for a project. The Product Owner works directly with the business community, stakeholders, customers, and users to obtain an understanding of the community and user needs. "For Product Owners to succeed, the entire organization must respect their decisions. These decisions are visible in the content and ordering of the Product Backlog, and through the inspectable Increment at the Sprint Review" (Schwaber and Sutherland 2020). The Product Owner prioritizes the Product Backlog list (see Chapter 8, Implementing Agile Auditing: The Audit Planning Process for more details on Product Backlogs).

Scrum Master

The **Scrum Master** owns the process and is held accountable for enhancing team performance. The 2020 update to the Scrum Guide elevates the role of the Scrum Master from a servant leader to that of a true leader who serves the Scrum Team and the larger organization (Schwaber and Sutherland 2020). In the 2020 Guide, the switching around of the words from a "servant leader" to "a leader who serves" is intended to recognize that the Scrum Master helps focus on the leadership role of the Scrum Master to help achieve the project goals. The Scrum Master is accountable for the Scrum Team's effectiveness by enabling the Scrum Team to improve its practices, within the Scrum framework. Nonetheless, the Scrum Master is not a boss, a project manager, or a decision-maker. The Scrum Master is a coach, facilitator, and an Agile champion. The Scrum Master is accountable for the Agile team happiness and why this is important. They remind the Agile team members of the benefits and value of the Agile approach whenever needed and encourage the right behaviors from the team members. For example, the Scrum Master may remind team members to be honest and transparent in their communications. The Scrum Master facilitates all meetings, including daily meetings. They coach the Agile team members in self-management and cross-functionality; help the team focus on creating high-value increments that meet the Definition of Done; and facilitate the removal of impediments or roadblocks and obstacles to help the team progress and remain efficient in completing Sprints, ensuring that all Scrum events take place and are positive, productive, and kept within the timebox. A **Sprint** is a short, timebound cycle within which team members complete an increment of work to deliver products the customer needs based on whatever is most important to the customer at the time.

Delivery Team (Developers)

The **Delivery Team** Members own the "how." They complete product tasks during Sprints. They are the individuals in the Agile team who are committed to creating any aspect of a usable Increment in each Sprint. They create a **Sprint Backlog**, a specific, focused list of tasks determined by the Delivery Team to complete an increment that guides their Sprint/increment work. An *increment* is a product deliverable, usually a small portion of the overall product. The Sprint Backlog is a specific, focused list of tasks determined by the Delivery Team Members to complete an increment. The team has total authority on the exact approach to get their work done, estimate how long work will take, create their schedule, and manage their own time. They are a cross-functional, self-managing group of autonomous individuals collectively possessing all the skills necessary to complete the Sprint backlog. In Scrum, Developers can be business developers, user experience researchers, customer experience specialists, mechanical engineers, lab technicians, doctors, nurses, carpenters, marketers, researchers, scientists, quality assurance specialists, and more.

We will review these roles, responsibilities, and options throughout the book. In Chapter 7, Implementing Agile Auditing: Deciding Your Approach and Your Agile Audit Project Roles, we will address the different roles of Product Backlog in an auditing context. In Chapter 9, Implementing Agile Auditing: Planning Agile Audit Engagements, we will apply Scrum concepts in an audit context, including the Product Owner, Scrum Master, Delivery Team, documents, and activities. Remember, Agile and Scrum are frameworks, and adaptations are expected; some Scrum implementations include additional roles.

Scrum Artifacts

Scrum Artifacts represent work value. Following are the three Artifacts, or documents, created in the Scrum framework (Sutherland and Sutherland 2014). Each of the three Scrum Artifacts has a corresponding commitment to drive focus and alignment. This commitment gives the teams a much better focus on the specific goals. The Artifacts are:

1. **Product Backlog** (see Chapter 8, Implementing Agile Auditing: The Audit Planning Process). The Product Backlog is a list of requirements and

features for a project that is managed by the Product Owner in order of business priority. Product Backlogs include estimates on business value and development efforts. The commitment for Product Backlog is Product Goal.

2. **Sprint Backlog** (see Chapter 9, Implementing Agile Auditing: Planning Agile Audit Engagements). The Sprint Backlog is a specific, focused list of tasks the Delivery Team believes it can complete in a Sprint. It is created by the team members, using a *pull* approach to complete an increment. Contrasted with a *push* approach, where an input is pushed into a cycle in hopes that it can be used as it is pushed, or can wait until it is needed, a pull approach pulls inputs into the process or production line on demand, as needed. The push approach may result in excessive production and unused work, while the pull approach is quick and efficient. The commitment for Spring Backlog is Sprint Goal.

3. **Increment.** An increment is production output at the end of a timeboxed Sprint. The commitment for increment is the Definition of Done.

We acknowledge that some Scrum adaptations include up to six Artifacts, or documents. However, creating more Artifacts that do not add value or that are otherwise created simply for the sake of creating more Artifacts does not align with the Agile Manifesto value of "more working software, less documentation."

Scrum Activities (Scrum Events)

The ideas presented in this section align with the typical projects that use the Scrum framework. The Scrum framework organizes work into one- to four-week increments called Sprints. The Sprint is a container for all other events. Each event in Scrum is a formal opportunity to examine and adapt Scrum Artifacts. These activities are specifically designed to enable the transparency required. Events are used in Scrum to create regularity and to minimize the need for meetings not defined in Scrum.

Optimally, all events should be held at the same time and place to reduce complexity and increase effectiveness of the team. Each Sprint should bring the product closer to the overall Product Goal and likely will evolve as the Scrum Team learns over time. All the work necessary to achieve the Product Goal, including Sprint Planning, Daily Scrums, Sprint Review, Sprint Retrospective, and Product Backlog refinement/grooming, happen within Sprints. The Product Owner is the only one who can abort the Sprint. There is a specific time frame for each Sprint and a time frame to complete each of the

Sprint activities described in the list that follows. The Sprint duration determines the time frame, or "timebox," for each Sprint activity as noted in the description for each activity. We define and relate each of the five following Scrum Activities to audit activities in Part II:

1. **Sprint Planning Meeting** (Chapter 9). The Sprint planning meeting is a timeboxed activity (two hours or less per week of Sprint length) held at the beginning of the Sprint to determine the features to be delivered in each Sprint. It is facilitated by the Scrum Master. The Product Owner is an active participant who provides clarity on the upcoming project and related customer stories. The team members collaborate to determine the Sprint tasks, a Definition of *Done*, and a Definition of *Ready*. For a two-week Sprint, the Sprint planning meeting would occur over a four-hour timebox. For a four-week Sprint, the Sprint planning meeting would occur over an eight-hour timebox.

2. **Daily Meeting** (Chapter 11). The daily meeting may also be called a Daily Sprint, Daily Scrum, or daily standup. For a two-week Sprint, the daily meeting lasts no more than 15 minutes; for a four-week Sprint, the daily meeting lasts no more than 30 minutes. The Scrum Master facilitates the meeting, which is held virtually or in a public location at the same time and place each day. Team members take part, provide updates, and give feedback during the meeting. The meeting helps increase transparency on the Sprint and increases communication among the team members. While only the development team provides updates, others may observe the meeting. The Scrum Master ensures meeting productivity and limits unnecessary contributions, updates, and questions.

3. **Sprint Review** (Chapter 11). The Sprint Review is the Scrum Delivery Team's presentation of their increment, or product, that will be provided to the customer. The development team also provides a summary of the increment and any incomplete tasks. The Product Owner has the authority to approve the increment during the Sprint Review. This review meeting occurs at the end of a Sprint. The Sprint Review is timeboxed to one hour or less for every week of Sprint length. For a two-week Sprint, the Sprint Review is limited to two hours.

4. **Sprint Retrospective** (Chapter 11). The Sprint Retrospective is a "lessons learned" and continuous improvement meeting that lasts one-hour for a two-week Sprint. Team members, Scrum Masters, and the Product Owner discuss what worked well and what can be improved on the next Sprint. This one-hour meeting is held immediately following the Sprint Review.

5. **Product Backlog Refinement/Grooming** (Chapter 8). The Product Backlog refinement meeting is led by the Product Owner, who engages the team members, Scrum Master, stakeholders, and others to determine the next highest priority item(s) on the Product Backlog for the next Sprint. Typically, this two-hour meeting occurs the morning after a Sprint Retrospective.

Nevertheless, while the durations provided in this list represent typical projects that use the Scrum framework, our Agile audit framework does not subscribe to doubling the time frame in the timeboxed activities unless there is a legitimate and valuable reason to do so. Additionally, we consistently use a two-week Sprint.

Figure 1.2 visually depicts how the Scrum roles, Artifacts, and activities fit together. In Chapter 4, What Is Agile Audit?, we alter this diagram for the Agile auditing framework.

There is plenty of evidence supporting Agile in any form. According to an article by Consultancy.eu (a European online platform for the advisory and consulting industry), a study by Organize Agile among professionals in 19 countries reported that 83% of respondents said "it is the ability to improve flexibility amid a rapidly changing environment" that makes Agile appealing. "Leveraging a quicker way of bringing incremental innovations and new products/services to the market, companies can timely cater to the changing needs of customers and try to stay ahead of their competition. Sticking to the traditional Waterfall approach in today's environment often means that organizations are left a step behind of their competition" (Consultancy.eu 2020). Auditing must adopt Agile practices to keep up with business needs and avoid being outsourced, or worse, eliminated tomorrow.

Even the Project Management Institute's flagship publication and fundamental resource for effective project management in any industry, the PMBOK (currently in its sixth edition), has been updated to include information on Agile practices alongside traditional approaches with its guidance. It states, "So why an Agile Practice Guide and why now? Project teams have used Agile techniques and approaches in various forms for at least several decades. The Agile Manifesto expressed definitive values and principles of Agile as the use of Agile gained substantial momentum. Today, project leaders and teams find themselves in an environment disrupted by exponential advances in technology and demands from customers for more immediate delivery of value. Agile techniques and approaches effectively manage disruptive technologies. In addition, the first principle of Agile places

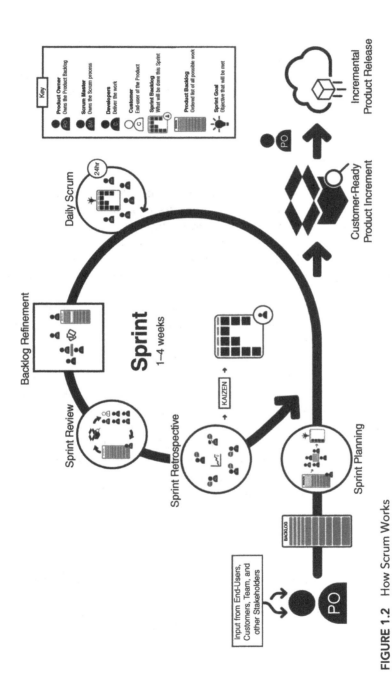

FIGURE 1.2 How Scrum Works

Source: "How Scrum Works: Scrum Framework," Scrum Inc., https://www.scruminc.com/scrum-framework/.

customer satisfaction as the highest priority and is key in delivering products and services that delight customers. Rapid and transparent customer feedback loops are readily available with the widespread use of social media. Therefore, in order to stay competitive and relevant, organizations can no longer be internally focused but rather need to focus outwardly to the customer experience" (Project Management Institute 2017).

 RECIPE: EXPLAINING THE CONCEPT

We are both cooks, or home chefs if you prefer. Sometimes we are bakers, when we attempt to re-create some of our favorite desserts from shows like *Nailed It*, *Sugar Rush*, or *Cake Boss*. As chefs and bakers, we start with a recipe. Usually, the first time we make a dish, it is "by the book" and we strictly follow the recipe . . . unless we lack an ingredient in our pantry. If this is the case, we are Agile and substitute another ingredient or simply make do without it. After the first or second time cooking the dish, we start to look for variations to improve the dish. Sometimes the variations are suggestions from others. Sometimes they are based on personal experience. Sometimes they are driven by food allergies, availability of pantry items, or other necessities.

This approach to using a recipe is analogous to your approach for your Agile audit recipe. Sometimes the recipe is perfectly designed, sometimes the variations make the product better, and sometimes the variations are a complete and utter disaster. Your experiments and learning experiences will drive continuous improvement and each successive dish you prepare will get better and better. Experiment and learn with Agile. This will make you a better Agile auditor and enable you to create better dishes to serve your customers. This is comparable to Scrum; rather than providing detailed instructions, the rules of Scrum guide people's relationships and interactions.

 NUGGETS

Agile is a project management approach to breaking down projects into smaller deliverables. It is a mindset of being able to move quickly in response to your environment. There are many frameworks and approaches to Agile project management, including Scrum, which is the most popular. The Agile Manifesto and Agile principles establish a foundation to build an Agile approach for your organization, regardless of which framework you select. Scrum includes a set of values and attempts to create value by collaborating with the customer, streamlining projects, and building efficiency using three roles, three Artifacts, and five activities in every Scrum project. Scrum projects include Sprints. Each Sprint lasts from one week to four weeks. Self-managing teams complete each Sprint. The team creates a Sprint Backlog to clarify the Sprint tasks the team intends to complete during the Sprint. The Sprint Backlog includes a series of iterations to design, plan, test, inspect, and improve the next iteration and Sprint. Once the Sprint Backlog tasks are complete, the Sprint is over, and a new Sprint begins. The Sprint iterations repeat until the team completes the Scrum project and provides an increment, or product, to the customer. An important aspect to remember is that while implementing only parts of Scrum is possible, the result is not Scrum. Scrum exists only in its entirety and functions well as a container for other techniques, methodologies, and practices. As you begin your transformation, take a look at the recipes to help you determine your methodology. Don't be afraid to adjust the recipes!

CHAPTER TWO

What Is Audit?

DEFINING AUDIT

Generically, an **audit** is an evaluation of something to reach a conclusion. In this book, we use audit and engagement interchangeably when referring to the service performed by auditors. **Auditing** is the process of identifying, gathering, examining, analyzing, evaluating, and concluding on information to form an opinion on a specific topic. Everybody audits something. You may audit the bill at the end of your meal, a chef's cooking abilities, your electric bill, your teenager's activities and whereabouts, your child's hygiene, your health, or your time management practices. As a professional auditor, once you get the audit bug, you will subconsciously audit anything and everything and speak about auditing without realizing it. And, once you get the Agile bug, you will find you can't turn it off and you will apply Agile to everything, including road trips, weight loss, and home projects. As an Agile professional and an audit professional, don't be surprised if you start critiquing the next summer block-buster to find errors and identify how the movie, and processes within it, could have been more Agile.

TYPES OF AUDITS

Auditors audit against an expectation or criterion and reach a conclusion based on evidence gathered and evaluated. The criteria used depend on the type and classification of the audit. There are three main types of audits in the professional audit world:

1. Internal audits, performed by individuals or consultants who work for the organization.
2. Government audits, including tax audits, performed by employees of country, federal, state, and local governments.
3. External audits, performed by professionals external to the organization such as financial auditors from accounting firms and regulators from regulatory bodies.

All audits are fundamentally the same, with the same project life cycle and deliverables. In this book we distinguish the main types of audits based on professional audit standards, including internal audits, government audits (which can be performed by auditors who may be either external or internal to the government agency), and external financial audits. We do not cover how regulatory auditors can use Agile, although we do hope that regulators will adopt Agile methods in their process, or at least consider that Agile auditing is a bona fide approach to conducting audits. Furthermore, we exclude tax audits from the scope of this book; as they are performed at such a meticulous level and require substantial amounts of testing, we feel this may be the last type of audit that will adopt Agile auditing. Having said that, all audit types can benefit from using an Agile framework.

Internal Audits

Internal audits evaluate the effectiveness of governance, risk management, and controls in accomplishing specific business objectives within a business unit, government department/agency, or association. Internal audits include compliance audits, financial assurance, controls assurance, information technology (IT) audits, operations audits, or integrated audits (Reding et al. 2009). Additionally, internal auditors may perform specific audits on environmental conformance, privacy, security, organizational performance, processes, IT general controls, and IT application controls. Our collective internal audit experience in manufacturing, financial services, higher education, not-for-profits, state government, and professional services firms are the basis of our understanding of audit practices and our primary application to Agile auditing.

Internal auditors often leverage the Committee of Sponsoring Organizations of the Treadway Commission (COSO) *Internal Control–Integrated Framework* in performing audits. The COSO internal control framework provides a structured approach to help management achieve compliance, reporting, and operational objectives (Committee of Sponsoring Organizations of the Treadway Commission (COSO) 2013). Considering the different classifications of internal audits, you may note a strong relationship between management's objectives and audit types. This relationship supports an Agile approach to auditing because Agile is customer-centric.

The Institute of Internal Auditors (IIA) is the globally recognized authority that sets expectations on the performance of internal audit activities. These expectations are codified in the IIA's International Professional Practices Framework (IPPF), commonly known as the Red Book. The IIA IPPF defines internal auditing as "an independent, objective assurance and consulting activity designed to add value and improve an organization's operations. It helps an organization accomplish its objectives by bringing a systematic, disciplined approach to evaluate and improve the effectiveness of risk management, control, and governance processes" (Institute of Internal Auditors 2017a). Can you imagine telling your parent or child that this is what you do for a living? Try it, just once, and remember the look on the person's face; it is a look you will not soon forget! Implementing Agile auditing, particularly preparing your organization and educating others on auditing, will definitely persuade you to develop your unique definition of internal audit that you can use to explain what you do to your audit customers, family, and friends.

Here are two example definitions/descriptions for internal auditing created by some of our class participants:

1. Internal auditing is a service for management and boards to understand the entity's objectives, assess threats that could affect the ability to accomplish their objectives, and evaluate the responses to reduce the likelihood of threats or reduce the consequences of threats.
2. Internal audit helps management by evaluating management's controls and providing assurance that controls are in place and operating effectively to mitigate threats and achieve objectives. Some internal auditors also perform consulting services and provide advice without stating an opinion.

[Note: While the IIA distinguishes between assurance and consulting engagements, we generically refer to all engagements as "audits" in this book. You will see the words "engagement" and "audit" used interchangeably throughout the book.]

For our fellow internal auditors, take a moment to think about and answer some of the following questions. Your answers will guide your journey to adding more value, hopefully through Agile auditing.

- What are your thoughts on the part of the internal auditing definition that states "to add value"?
- What exactly does adding value mean to you?
- What does adding value mean to your audit clients, customers, stakeholders, and auditees?
- Who determines if you add value?
- What do auditors do to add value?
- Do your audit clients think you add value?
- Do your stakeholders think you add value?
- How do you measure adding value?

Based on our combined 50-plus years of audit experience, audit adds value by focusing on the needs of our customers, boards, managers, process owners, and others responsible for carrying out work, creating value, and reducing risk to an acceptable level. Internal auditors focus on the organization as whole, starting with the vision, mission, values, and strategy to determine a work plan, or audit plan, for the entire audit activity over a given period of time before looking into the details and planning specific engagements. Auditors add value by offering solutions, collaborating with audit clients, and responding to the changing needs of the organization. As in any service process, the customer always determines value; if your answer to the prior question of "who determines if you add value?" was "audit," reframe your thinking. Customers determine value! It doesn't matter how good you think you are or how good you feel your product is – if the client doesn't think it is valuable, it isn't. How often do you ask your audit client if you are adding value? Have you asked them what you can do to add more value? If not, ask them now.

Government Audits

Government audits are performed by audit activities or Inspector Generals' offices of federal, state, country, and local jurisdiction government departments and agencies. Audit objectives focus on fraud, waste, and abuse as well as effectiveness and efficiency of risk management, control, and governance processes of programs, functions, departments, agencies, and operations. In the United States, government audits adhere to standards published by the Government Accountability Office (GAO). The Generally Accepted Government Audit Standards (GAGAS), commonly known as the Yellow Book; Standards for Internal Control in the Federal Government, also referred to as the Green Book; and the Financial Audit Manual, known as the Blue Book, are different standards for financial controls, operating controls, and enterprise risk management provided by the GAO. While many government audits are financial- or compliance-based and typically adhere to the Yellow Book, government auditors are increasing the numbers of internal controls, operational, performance, information technology (IT), fraud, and management audits.

Government auditors may be external to the entity, department, or agency they are auditing (known as external auditors in the government environment) or internal to the entity, department, or agency they are auditing (known as internal auditors in the government environment). For internal audits of government entities, auditors may use the GAO Yellow Book, the IIA Red Book, or both, depending on which standards they, or their stakeholders, elect for guidance and compliance. Generally, government auditors have been slower to adopt Agile auditing, but we will share a few examples of Agile audits in state government later in this book.

External Audits

External financial audits evaluate whether financial statements are fair, consistent, and accurate under specified standard accounting principles that are set by a given authority and adopted by a country. The most recognized accounting standards are the International Financial Reporting Standards (IFRS) and the Generally Accepted Accounting Principles (GAAP). External financial audits also include evaluations of internal controls over financial reporting, evaluations that began as a result of Sarbanes-Oxley (SOX) regulations in the United States and similar regulations in other countries. Financial auditors are typically Certified Public Accountants (CPA), Chartered Accountants (CA), or other employees in professional services firms who perform external financial audits. Several firms adopted Agile auditing approaches for attestations, external financial audits, and consulting services. External auditors in the United States follow Generally Accepted Auditing Standards (GAAS) and globally, the leading authority on auditing standards is the International Auditing and Assurance Standards Board (IAASB).

Another group of external audits include those performed by regulators and regulatory auditors. Each regulator has unique standards and audit requirements.

AUDIT CUSTOMERS

Agile requires continual focus on the customer. Throughout the book we use the term *audit customer* as a reminder that the customer is always number one. The term *auditee* is commonly used to identify the function or process and the individuals involved with or managing the process included in the scope of an audit. Years ago, there was a movement to shift the auditee's perspective of auditing, thus the terms *audit client* or *audit customer* are slowly replacing *auditee*. Customers are those desiring your service; they pay, or would be willing to pay, for your service directly or indirectly. Since most people don't like being audited, some argue that the proper term should be *audit constituent*, as they are a member of an organization and may not freely choose to be audited. It doesn't really matter what term you prefer; auditors provide a service to someone or some group – a customer.

To focus any audit in the right direction, audit teams must determine their customers. Moreover, audit teams should determine their primary customer and all services should aim to please that customer. There are many audit customers, or those we serve. Depending on your perspective and the audit type, the audit customer may be the process owner, process management, mid-level management, senior management, or a governing body, such as a board of directors. The process owners or governing bodies are the most common primary audit customers.

Customers are not the same as stakeholders, or those with an interest in the audit engagement results and outcomes. Examples of stakeholders include shareholders, investors, creditors, regulators, employees, vendors, citizens, and customers purchasing the goods and services produced by the organization. There may be other managers, leaders, and executives who are not part of the function being audited but who may receive information from, provide information to, or influence the operations of the function being audited who you consider a stakeholder. The governing body may also be a stakeholder in some types of audits.

When implementing Agile auditing, identifying your audit customer and understanding customer needs and priorities is essential to success. For the purpose of this book, we elected to focus on the process owner as the primary customer with the governing body a close second. For many of our clients in publicly held entities and highly regulated industries, the governing body is often the primary audit customer and the auditee is the group being audited. Your perspective on the customer will alter your approach to Agile auditing in a similar way that your audit function approaches the process and reporting for your current, traditional audits.

KNOWLEDGE AREAS FOR AUDITORS

With today's business environment, we face unprecedented change. During 2020, we dealt with a global pandemic while also experiencing continuous exponential growth in the volume of data we create, share, and store. We are witnessing the birth of multiple disruptive technologies, which have had and will continue to have a profound impact on every business and government, the way we work, and how we manage major aspects of our lives.

All auditors (internal auditors, government auditors, external auditors, and even tax auditors) must play a role in how an organization responds to disruption and transformations to be an Agile auditor. The "2019 North American Pulse of Internal Audit" study conducted by the IIA (Institute of Internal Auditors 2019a), notes that cybersecurity and IT issues have grown to represent nearly 20% of the average audit plan. This means that audit activities, and all auditors, must possess excellent technology capabilities to properly address risks and complete their audits. Moreover, digitization and expanding technology place a more significant burden on the knowledge expected from auditors. Increasing flexibility and leveraging existing technology within the audit departments also requires greater automation of some audit approaches and increasing the efficiency of audit operations. Auditors need to be open to explore and learn how to use new technologies. In Chapter 12, we share more on how you can perform audit services in an emerging technology world.

Auditors must become more customer service–oriented and increase their knowledge of the business. They must embrace the idea of change. Continuing professional development is a mandatory requirement for all professional auditors. As stated in the IIA IPPF Standard 1230, Continuing Professional Development, "Internal Auditors must enhance their knowledge, skills, and other competencies through continuing professional development" (Institute of Internal Auditors 2017a). We cannot underestimate the importance of continuous professional development of auditors' knowledge and skills. It is essential that auditors are familiar with fundamentals of strategic management, operational management, accounting, finance, marketing, economics, data analytics, robotics, personal communications, emotional intelligence, and negotiation strategies. Attending courses and seminars at universities, with professional training companies, by local chapters of professional associations, or through your own organization's delivery channels is a fantastic way to keep skills up to date and minds sharp. In addition to understanding how to audit and the methods applied in auditing, auditors must ensure that they possess knowledge and understanding of essentials including governance, risk, control, finance/accounting, technology, and compliance. Audit teams should strongly consider dedicating a physical area or creating a file-sharing structure to serve as a resource and training library and encourage all auditors to use the resources often and share their knowledge by sharing more resources. Through the collaborative efforts of one audit team, the auditors created a library room where the auditors would meet to expand their knowledge as well as to hold their daily Scrum meetings.

Governance

Governance means many things and is generally described as oversight of an organization's strategy and operations. Richard Steinberg, a nationally recognized expert on governance, risk management, and control, shares Canada's Dey Commission's definition of governance as "the allocation of power among the board, management, and shareholders" (Steinberg 2011). The IIA defines governance as "the combination of processes and structures implemented by the board to inform, direct, manage, and monitor the activities of the organization towards the achievement of its objectives" (Institute of Internal Auditors 2017a). Merriam-Webster defines governance as "the act or process of governing or overseeing the control and direction of something (such as a country or an organization)" (Merriam-Webster 2020). We describe governance as "noses in, fingers out" to distinguish between oversight of the organization and management's role of directing and managing the day-to-day activities of the organization.

On February 2, 2021, when we googled the word "governance," we found 262,000,000 results! An Agile auditor must understand their organization's governance definition, structure, roles, and responsibilities. Why is this a vital knowledge area for auditors? One reason is that auditors serve as one of the legs of governance, along with the board and management. Auditors aid in providing oversight and ensure that organizational structures are working as intended to help achieve organizational objectives. This naturally leads to the second reason – you must know how audit fits in the organization's governance model, what is expected of auditors, and where you are now to figure out how to go where you are going next. Or, as Sir Terry Pratchett once said, "If you do not know where you come from, then you don't know where you are, and if you don't know where you are, then you don't know where you're going. And if you don't know where you're going, you're probably going wrong" (Pratchett 2010).

Governance is concerned with the organization's structure, decision-making, accountability, control, culture, and behavior from the top through the bottom of the organization (see Chapter 17, Preparing Your Organization for Agile Auditing/Creating the Agile Culture). Governance influences how an organization sets its objectives and how it achieves them. Governance sets the risk appetite and the philosophy for how the risks are monitored and addressed. Governance is a system and process. It is not a single activity or action. Thus, a keen understanding of governance is essential, as it includes the organization's strategic planning process, risk management, and performance management. It is also essential, as governance contributes to audit philosophy and approach. For example, an entity with a low risk appetite often requires more assurance and meticulous testing with little to no room for error and misjudgment. This means that the auditors would engage in more thorough audits. This type of entity would adapt its implementation of Agile auditing to ensure that governance needs are met yet seek methods to turn around a completed audit faster.

How can auditors enhance their knowledge of governance? Specifically, how can you enhance your knowledge of governance at the organization you are auditing? Get involved; understand the organization's vision, mission, and values. Read the annual reports, look at the graphic representing the organization's structure, and understand the actual structure in practice, including reporting relationships and who makes the critical decisions. Monitor the organization's activities toward the achievement of its objectives by reviewing metrics and key performance indicators (KPIs). Have an open mind, listen, and remain objective. How often have you been in a crowded elevator, an organization's cafeteria, or even the bathroom and hear conversations about the company, the people, the culture, and the governance? Listen and learn. Seize every opportunity to understand your organization and its governance practices. Also, keep an eye on the news and current events. Is your organization making a positive impact celebrated in the media? Is it making waves? Don't just ride the waves; learn how to maneuver every wave just as a skilled surfer always looks ahead, ready for any change in any direction. Remember, auditors are part of governance and need to understand how it works and how to maneuver within, and sometimes influence, organizational governance.

Risk

Risk is often heard as a four-letter word, a very bad one at that. Simply stated, the International Organization for Standardization (ISO) defines risk in ISO 31000 as "the effect of uncertainty on objectives" (International Organization for Standardization 2018). This implies that risk is neither good or bad; it is just an unknown or uncertainty that could affect achieving objectives. For auditors, risk is generally negative, a threat, or something bad. Auditors struggle to see the positive, upside, or opportunities of risk. Even the IIA defines risk as neither good or bad: "Risk is the possibility of an event occurring that will have an impact on the achievement of objectives. Risk is measured in terms of impact and likelihood" (Institute of Internal Auditors 2017a). Why is this important? Auditors should view risk the same way that business managers, process owners, accountants, and boards view risk, as something that might get in the way of getting stuff done and objectives met. This business view on risk is even more important in Agile auditing. Yet, we still find that many auditors think of risk as a missing, lacking, or inoperable control.

One of the primary tools used in a traditional audit is a risk and control matrix (RCM). As we help prepare or review RCMs, we commonly see risks considered to be "lack of segregation of duties," "lack of review," "unauthorized access," or other controls that are missing or failing. The real risk, from the business perspective, is *why* we want the control in the first place. Why do you want segregation of duties? To reduce errors in the operational process and make sure one person does not have complete control over a process, as in the case where fraud risks are high.

While speaking at a conference in Des Moines, Iowa, we had the pleasure of hearing Dr. James Lam, a widely recognized pioneer in enterprise risk management, say "risk is not a product of likelihood and impact." Our brows furrowed, but we forced ourselves to open our ears and minds to hear what he meant, which was that risk is not *merely* a product of likelihood and impact. In his book *Enterprise Risk Management: From Incentives to Controls*, Lam recognizes seven major types of risk, including strategic risk, business risk, market risk, credit risk, liquidity risk, operational risk, and compliance risk (Lam 2014). There is so much more to the risk conversation than simply identifying risks to create risk awareness, measuring risks to aid in risk prioritization, and determining the right risk responses. Risk is part of life. We experience risk in everything we do. Our job as auditors is to understand risk well enough to create awareness and inspire the right actions to reduce risk to an acceptable level.

There are several keys to becoming more risk intelligent, recognizing negative risks, acknowledging positive risks, and using technology and data. As stated earlier, auditor focus is often on the negative risks that controls don't work as intended. However, we must also consider positive business risks to allow organizations to seize opportunities for new ventures, such as the acquisition of better technologies or better services. Today's technology is vastly improving organizations' ability to monitor and address significant risks. However, these tools are hampered by process owners', managers', and auditors' ability to use and understand the possibilities. Keeping up with technology is only one aspect of understanding what these tools are capable of helping us achieve from a risk management standpoint. Deciphering the information provided by the technology is another story and likely the more important aspect of understanding risk. The tools often only provide one-dimensional risk intelligence, which is of little value without the complete analysis and business acumen. Therefore, it is essential for organizations and auditors to adopt a risk-intelligent view to enable improving risk functions and quantify risks effectively with a robust, multirisk perspective. Auditors need to expand their knowledge on how to perform data analytics and interpret its results, including a good understanding of statistics, macroeconomics, microeconomics, and business acumen, to gain better perspectives on risk. Auditors must learn more about risk and be able to identify risks, measure risks more precisely (beyond mere qualitative assessments of likelihood and impact), and assess the design and effectiveness of controls to mitigate risk to acceptable risk appetites.

OnRisk 2020: A Guide Prepared by the IIA to Understanding, Aligning, and Optimizing Risk provides a robust and comprehensive view of the top risks for the coming year based on key players' perspectives in the risk management process (Institute of Internal Auditors 2019b). These high risks included: cybersecurity, data protection, regulatory change, business continuity, data, new technology, third parties, talent management, culture, board information, data ethics, sustainability, and environmental, social, and governance risks. As an auditor, are you prepared to help your organization address these risks? If not, you have an opportunity to learn – start today. Agile auditing works best when the team members are individually competent and collectively help overcome shortfalls in individual knowledge. In addition to identifying these as top risks in 2019–2020, *OnRisk 2020* found that perceptions between board members, executive leadership (the C-suite), and chief audit executives regarding these risks and their organization's capabilities to handle them were at times dramatically different. Nonetheless, all agreed that because of the ever-evolving nature of cybersecurity threats, knowledge of cybersecurity risk is low and is an area all parties can expand our capabilities.

As you probably noticed by looking from the beginning of 2020 until now, the list of risks noted in the preceding paragraph have changed and evolved. Less than a year after publishing the IIA's *OnRisk 2020*, a global pandemic rocked our world and gave all of us new perspectives on risk. Auditors and business professionals see new threats constantly, while the risks that have been around for a long time are evolving and some risks remain the same. The way you perceive your capabilities to manage risks, and your knowledge of the risks and how to mitigate them, may be different for each member of your organization. Having a strong foundation and understanding of risk and risk management from identification, assessment, analysis, evaluation, communication, and response is crucial for auditors.

Control

The response part of risk leads us to internal controls, also referred to as management controls, control activities, or simply *controls*. As Dr. Andrew D. Banasiewicz, in *Risk Profiling of Organizations*, points out, "There is a very thoughtful and systematic process of identifying and managing risk: some problems you have to ignore, some require you go buy insurance coverage, and some you may mitigate" (Banasiewicz 2009). Internal controls are "a process, effected by an entity's board of directors, management, and other personnel, designed to provide reasonable assurance regarding the achievement of objectives relating to operations, reporting, and compliance" (Committee of Sponsoring Organizations of the Treadway Commission (COSO) 2013). Governance, risk management, and controls are interrelated. Thus, having a clear understanding of the organization's governance is key to ensuring proper evaluation of controls. Controls have many classifications, the most popular being preventive, detective, and corrective. As auditors, we need to have a good grasp and understanding of these categories, and what types of controls could be used for each area of risk required to be addressed. Having this knowledge can mitigate or prevent risks ranging from innocent but costly errors to irregularities or fraudulent manipulations that could bear significant consequences to the organization, including damage to its reputation. Understanding the different types of controls and their applications and limitations is a knowledge area crucial for all auditors in performing ongoing reviews. This is foundational knowledge required to add value and assist management in improving the system of internal control and in monitoring the organization's operations and achievement of objectives.

So, what are preventive internal controls? These are the controls put in place to discourage or stop an adverse event from occurring. These are often automated within most applications, such as checks and balances built in to avoid entering incorrect information. Other examples would include physical or administrative preventive controls, such as key card access, dual access, and segregation of duties. What are detective internal controls? These are controls used after the fact of a discretionary event that identifies when errors occurred or attempts to piece together what happened. Detective controls lead to questions such as "What caused the event to occur?" "What process failed that allowed the event to occur?" and "What can we implement to keep the event from happening again in the future?" In addressing these questions, auditors need to have a good understanding of detective controls such as audits, reviews, reconciliations, transaction monitoring, and physical inventories. Finally, corrective controls are typically controls put in place after either the preventive or detective controls uncovered a problem and corrective controls are designed to fix the adverse activity. Examples can include disciplinary action for employees (including firing), installing software patches, and creating and implementing new policies prohibiting certain practices such as shadowing a person when entering a building.

Finance/Accounting

Ensuring that auditors can examine, identify, measure, classify, and evaluate an organization's operations and activities includes having essential knowledge of accounting, finance, and financial information. This knowledge enables auditors to speak to management in their language and substantiate their recommendations with factual, often quantitative, information. Internal audits' role is to assess the effectiveness of internal controls and governance processes. However, strong knowledge of the financial and accounting information can help auditors have a better view and understanding of the organization, provide assurance regarding the effectiveness and efficiency of internal controls, and better provide improvement solutions based on the financial and accounting information. Nevertheless, though finance and accounting knowledge are valuable, we acknowledge that as we continue to move into a new normal with new technologies, increasing complexity in financial reporting, and new services provided by audit organizations, new auditors attracted to the auditing profession are coming from different fields without an audit or accounting foundation or background. There is a growing demand for specialized professionals from operational experts, data specialists, mathematicians, economist, biologist, to environmentalists and everything in between. This diversity in audit professionals contributes to the success of Agile auditing, as Agile focuses on the collective abilities and knowledge of the Delivery Team.

Technology

Most business transactions and processes are supported by information systems and IT. Effective auditors must understand the opportunities and risks associated with legacy (i.e., old), current, and emerging (i.e., new) technology.

Technology allows us to go faster, do more, and improve effectiveness. However, with technology, new risks are introduced. As you audit business processes, seek an understanding of the relationships between the business objectives, risks, and controls and the technology used in the business process. Maintain an alertness to technology vulnerabilities, threats, threat actors, and risks. Even though technology introduces many risks, for example compromised data confidentiality and integrity through cybersecurity breaches, it provides solutions to those risks. Those solutions are the controls that technology provides to mitigate technology risks and mitigate business risks; for example, firewalls, encryption, and antimalware software. We discuss more about technology in Chapter 12, Agile Auditing in the "New Normal" Environment (Remote Auditing).

Compliance

Compliance means adherence to applicable laws and regulations (Steinberg 2011). Many include adherence to company policies and procedures (which include controls) in the definition of compliance. In all cases, compliance requirements must be current when used by auditors as the audit criteria. All laws, regulations, policies, and procedures serve a purpose and were imposed for a reason. The biggest reasons for nonconformance are lack of awareness or lack of understanding of the compliance requirements, and sometimes a lack of understanding the "why" behind the compliance requirement. Before your organization blindly adheres to a compliance requirement and before it is used as criteria in an audit, consider the legislative intent and the relevance to your organization. In risk-based auditing, auditors should also consider the risk appetite, especially if organizational management decides not to conform to a requirement.

> Why should auditors evaluate legal and regulatory requirements before using them as criteria or recommending conformance to the requirement? So we can make sure we are risk-focused and adding value to the audit customer.

Auditors will add more value by ensuring that compliance makes sense before testing for conformance to the law or regulation. We believe that sometimes auditors look for compliance or audit for a criterion that does not make sense. When organizations are forced to comply with requirements that don't make sense, it actually creates weaker controls or higher costs, exposing the organization to greater risks. Evaluate compliance using common sense and don't blindly follow the law. Consider that the reasons behind the requirement may no longer be valid or serve a purpose. Why should auditors evaluate the requirement before using it as criteria or recommending conformance to the requirement? So we can make sure we are risk-focused and adding value to the audit customer. For example, there was an old regulation that didn't make sense, but the auditors tested for conformance anyway. The regulation required providing a copy of an agreement in triplicate to a loan applicant. This regulation was written when carbon paper was used and the regulation was never updated. Auditors identified the violation and discussed it with management who said, "Why do I need to print it three times and provide it to the applicant when they don't even bother reading it once?" This was the auditor's nugget – stop testing for conformance with requirements that don't make sense or don't have any impact for nonconformance.

If you discover a law or regulation doesn't make sense or is antiquated, what can you do?

1. Don't use it as criteria.
2. Discuss the risks of noncompliance.
3. Document the organization's understanding of requirement and related acceptance of noncompliance risk.
4. Get the people in power to change the law or regulation!

Auditors should have early discussions with audit customers, management, and governance groups regarding important laws or regulations and any that the organization is knowingly not following or has chosen not to comply. If you discover a law or regulation doesn't make sense or is antiquated, what can you do? First, don't use it as criteria. Second, discuss the risks of noncompliance. Third, document the organization's understanding of the requirement and the related acceptance of the risk of noncompliance. Fourth, get the people in power to change the law or regulation!

Finally, with risk-based auditing, auditors must assess the risk of noncompliance and evaluate how much time they will dedicate to testing compliance. Even when a particular audit test is mandated by regulation, the risks of not performing the mandate should be evaluated and appropriate decisions should be made by audit leadership as to how much time the auditor will spend meeting the mandate.

SKILLS FOR AUDITORS

In evaluating important knowledge areas and skills for auditors, take a look at and evaluate available competency frameworks for your profession. A competency framework is a tool, such as the IIA's Global Internal Audit Competency Framework, that defines the competencies needed to meet the auditor's professional standards, such as the International Professional Practices Framework (IPPF) requirements for the internal audit profession. As you continue your Agile audit journey, you will find it even more helpful to create a specific competency framework based on audit plan requirements and the organization's needs. This competency framework provides a structured guide, enabling the identification, evaluation, and development of those competencies in individual internal auditors.

This IIA's Competency Framework outlines the 10 core competencies recommended for each job level, from audit staff to the chief audit executive. Knowledge and skills identified in the competency framework include professional ethics, audit management, knowledge and application of the International Professional Practices Framework (IPPF), governance, risk, and control, business acumen, communication, persuasion and collaboration, critical thinking, internal audit delivery, and improvement and innovation. Other skills needed to be an effective internal auditor include:

- Negotiation
- Time management
- Project management
- Listening
- Questioning
- Documenting

Teaching each of these skills would result in one very long book. Thus, we chose not to elaborate on each skill. Instead, we encourage you to identify the skills needed to perform your job well, identify your skills, assess your skills, and determine any competency gaps. Where you have gaps, improve your skills so you can effectively complete audits.

 AUDIT PROJECT LIFE CYCLE

The audit process and life cycle have changed little since the 1990s, when we first started our careers. Auditors often perform audits using an integrated approach that combines elements of compliance, operations, financial accounting, and IT. Regardless of the approach, traditional audits adhere to a structured, waterfall life cycle. PMBOK states "a project life cycle is the series of phases that a project passes through from its start to its completion. It provides the basic framework for managing the project. This basic framework applies regardless of the specific project work involved. The phases may be sequential, iterative, or overlapping" (Project Management Institute 2017).

The **waterfall life cycle** is a predictive succession-based process where one step or phase of a project is completed before moving to the next until the entire project is complete. Following are the Project Management Institute (PMI) project life cycle phases and deliverables (Blake 2004). We have also included the terminology used in the sixth-edition *Project Management Body of Knowledge* (PMBOK) as a cross reference, and we provide the corresponding audit life cycle phase in brackets next to the project management life cycle phase.

1. Project Initiation/Starting the Project [Strategic and Annual Audit planning]
2. Project Planning/Organizing and Preparing [Engagement planning]
3. Project Execution/Carrying Out the Work [Engagement fieldwork]
4. Project Closeout/Completing the Project [Engagement results/ communication]

As a project progresses through each phase, the project team produces various deliverables. We aligned the project deliverables with audit deliverables, where possible.

Phase 1: Initiation/Starting the Project

- Project charter [Audit charter]
- Initial scope
- Initial schedule [Annual audit plan]
- Budget estimates [Audit department budget]
- List of risks [ironically, auditors rarely identify risks that may affect their ability to deliver the project]
- Quality standards [auditors follow their professional or firm standards for quality]
- Communications plan
- Initial project plan [Annual audit plan]

Phase 2: Planning/Organizing and Preparing

- Project scope [Engagement/audit scope]
- Baseline schedule [Engagement/audit timeline]

- Project budget [Engagement/audit budget]
- Risk management plan [Audit delivery risk response plan, which rarely exists, since auditors rarely identify risks that may affect their ability to deliver the audit project. Coincidentally, we have been working with auditors for years to help them identify and assess risks to completing their project and create a response plan. Creating a risk response plan will be even more critical under Agile auditing to overcome obstacles in a timely manner.]
- Quality assurance/quality control (QA/QC) procedures [Audit quality assessment review (QAR)/quality assurance and improvement program (QA&IP) procedures are determined by audit executives and apply to all audits. Thus, QA/QC procedures are not determined at the engagement level.]
- Project plan [Engagement/audit program]

Phase 3: Execution/Carrying Out the Work

- Updated schedule [provided through ongoing communications with audit leadership and audit client]
- Actual budget [Engagement/audit budget versus actual comparison and justification]
- QC results [Engagement/audit supervision]
- Change control log [Engagement/audit program change review; a log is not typically maintained for audit projects]
- Issues log [In the technology world, this issues log would be a "bug" list of deficiencies in the coding process of a system development initiative. While auditors maintain an engagement/audit findings log, it excludes problems created or experienced in the project itself.]
- Status reports [Interim engagement communications, including audit status meetings, status reports, and dashboard reports]
- Acceptance forms [Engagement/audit report with management response. Management does not need to "accept" our audits in the traditional approach. However, with Agile auditing, this acceptance is desired, although audit results, conclusions, and opinions continue to be based on the objectivity of the auditor.]

Phase 4: Closeout/Completing the Project

- Project/product delivery [Engagement/audit report]
- Project assessment [Engagement client satisfaction survey and auditor performance assessments]

The audit life cycle closely aligns with the waterfall life cycle and deliverables at each phase, with few exceptions, as we previously indicated within each phase. The waterfall methodology is the foundation for adaptive models of project management, including Agile project management. In the preceding bulleted list, we pointed out the similarities between audits and the PMI life cycle. If you read the audit professional standards, you will see requirements in the standards that reinforce the traditional waterfall approach to managing audit projects. For example, in the IIA IPPF, IIA Standard 2240.A1 on Engagement Work Program requires the approval of a documented audit program prior to its "implementation," meaning prior to performing fieldwork. This approval requirement aligns with the waterfall process, where each phase of a project is completed before moving to the next.

The contrast of the audit life cycle to the project life cycle is not to say that the standard intends for all audits to follow the waterfall approach. Still, when professional bodies created the standards, the waterfall methodology was the leading approach to project management, and it may have influenced the standards related to audit processes. Don't wait for professional standards to start evolving and responding to the changing needs and demands of your organizations. If you wait for the standards to catch up, you may miss opportunities to respond to your environment and add value, and thus find yourself out of a job. The audit profession is adapting, but many audit professionals are laggards, or at least the late majority, as related to implementing something new. Applying Agile concepts in Agile auditing means we focus only on the desired change or provide the desired assurance, which presents some challenges when strict professional standards must be met. The good news is that the strict professional standards we think we have are usually someone's misinterpretation of the standard, which we will address in Chapter 18.

For all projects, there are three constraints: time, cost, and scope; each of these will impact quality, which should be determined at the beginning of a project with the constraints in mind. In project management, a project manager balances these constraints while emphasizing the need to produce a determined quality product. In the waterfall methodology, the project scope is supposed to be fixed when the manager determines the project plan. The manager has the flexibility to balance time and cost throughout the life of the project, as time and cost are flexible estimates. This project management approach is a stark contrast to Agile project management, where time and cost are fixed, but the Agile team determines project scope, and the scope is flexible and adaptable. It is important to note that in traditional products, significant efforts are taken to ensure that the product is error-free. However, in Agile, being error-free is not the goal. In Agile, being good enough, even if there are errors, is acceptable.

At a high level, here is the problem with the waterfall approach to audits: they take too long to finish to provide meaningful value to audit clients, boards, managers, and process owners. We will list the problems in Chapter 5, Why Agile Audit? Let's explore the traditional, waterfall audit process to discover why it takes too long to finish.

TRADITIONAL, WATERFALL AUDIT PROCESS: A REAL-LIFE VIEW OF THE PROBLEMS

The audit planning process (phase 1) takes a long time, sometimes months, to determine the audit priorities for the next audit cycle. Audit cycles range from one year to five years. We even saw a seven-year audit cycle once; could you imagine the effort to create an accurate seven-year plan? Worse, even though it takes a long time, the identified audit priorities are not descriptive enough to provide much value to the auditor completing the engagement planning (phase 2). It is almost as if engagement planning starts from scratch for every audit, even though audit cycles exist, and auditors repeat audits every one to five years. We do recognize that there are exceptions, where for some cyclical audits (often compliance-based audits) the audit plan may be dynamic and driven by risks and organization priorities.

Engagement planning ranges between 10% and 60% of the total audit time frame or budgeted hours. Auditors and audit leadership begin to feel like the audit is taking forever to start, and pressure is put on audit management to start testing something so we can feel like the audit started. As engagement planning progresses and approaches the engagement fieldwork start date, audit managers rush engagement planning to meet an arbitrary deadline. Some standards require audit management to document and approve the audit program before beginning fieldwork. Because of the pressure to approve the audit program and begin fieldwork, the engagement program may have broad, unclear test steps. These broad, unclear steps create problems when auditors begin the next audit phase, fieldwork.

Poorly written audit programs cause auditors to replan during the fieldwork phase (phase 3) because the auditors discover that some controls do not exist, which prevents performance of planned tests. Moreover, when auditors identify better controls during fieldwork, it creates rework if we previously completed the planned testing; we want to provide the best assurance possible by testing the newly identified control. Some audit activity policies require completion of all fieldwork before beginning to communicate audit results and drafting the final report.

The report-writing process tends to involve several internal reviews by various individuals. Sometimes one reviewer overrides what other reviewers wrote. One auditor, usually the audit manager, tracks the numerous revisions and makes all the changes. The auditor decides that she can't please everyone because everyone has their unique style and preferences and stops trying to better articulate the content; this mentality creates future problems on future audits, further delaying audit report issuance on every audit project. Finally, once the report is issued and distributed, workpapers are closed, and auditors receive individual feedback and move on to the next audit. At a future point in time, auditors may be temporarily pulled off an engagement to validate implemented corrective actions from a prior audit. This activity is also known as monitoring and audit follow-up. We exclude the engagement follow-up/monitoring process from this book, other than to say that corrective action follow-ups are a good pilot for testing your Agile framework and your Agile audit strategy.

Adopting an Agile approach to auditing requires flexible interpretations of applicable standards. External auditors employ Generally Accepted Auditing Standards (GAAS). Government auditors use Generally Accepted Government Audit Standards (GAGAS), or the Yellow Book. Internal auditors use The IIA Standards, or the Red Book. Agile may be easier to apply for principles-based standards than for rules-based standards; principles-based standards are subject to interpretation and negotiation and are not prescriptive, as rules-based standards are. Additionally, consider early communication with any group relying on or evaluating your team's audit to get feedback on your new approach and ensure that your work will meet stated standards. Refer to Chapter 18 for more information on how to communicate and gain agreement with other parties that your Agile audit approach conforms to professional standards.

IDENTIFYING, ASSESSING, AND RESPONDING TO DELIVERY RISKS

Delivery risks are the risks that may affect our ability to meet our objective of providing results by a specific time. One goal of every audit project is to deliver results to management within a planned time frame. Unexpected occurrences, such as unanticipated interruption of work, may affect our ability to achieve that objective. Delivery risks exist regardless of audit approach and have a greater impact when the framework requires faster audit results. Still, every audit team should have open and transparent discussions on delivery risk and create a risk response plan. We teach this in all our audit project management courses, including Agile auditing. For each audit methodology, develop a list of delivery risks, assess the risks based on likelihood and impact, and determine your risk response plan. If you do this well, you may only need to do it once and then reevaluate it periodically, particularly as the audit environment changes and audit processes mature.

Following are a few examples of universal delivery risks, regardless of the industry, audit type, or audit team size. There are also some risk responses for you to consider preparing for the identified delivery risks, should they occur. We took the liberty of providing our qualitative assessment of the impact and likelihood of these risks; we recognize that your experiences, bias, and judgment will likely result in a different assessment. These risks include:

1. Audit clients are engaged in performing day-to-day business activities and cannot participate in the audit, provide evidence, or meet to discuss the audit and their processes (likelihood = H; impact = M). Risk responses: communicate the importance of the audit; describe the benefits/value anticipated through the audit; inform audit clients of what is in it for them to prioritize audit requests; implement policies stating response time frames to audit requests; use a document request list as a team management tool to track requested items, data, evidence, and information; provide reminders on upcoming requested items due dates; escalate audit delay matters.
2. Auditors are not friendly and have a "gotcha" approach to auditing (likelihood = L; impact = M). Risk response: hire auditors with a shared philosophy (assuming you do not have the "gotcha" philosophy); provide emotional intelligence training; create self-awareness using communication/management style assessments; monitor customer satisfaction survey results; retrain auditors on the softer, gentler, "anti-gotcha" audit approach.
3. Being naturally curious creatures, auditors aren't satisfied with evidence gathered and "just want to make sure" by testing a few extra samples, talking to a few more employees, and looking at additional supporting evidence, thus creating scope creep (likelihood = H, impact = H). Risk response: develop and distribute audit methodology, including sampling policies; provide training on audit evidence attributes; implement

escalation procedures; hold status meetings; monitor work in progress; review completed work in a timely manner.

4. Audit management identifies another risk or another control that the audit team needs to evaluate before the audit is complete, thus creating scope creep (likelihood = H, impact = L). Obtain early approval on audit objectives and scope; agree on the audit budgets and resources; clarify the availability of additional resources if needed; use an Agile approach and put this item in the parking lot additional scope requests.

Having a ready-to-go risk response list from which you can choose the best risk response based on the available information will reduce your response time and have a smaller impact on any audit.

RECIPE: BUILDING AUDITOR KNOWLEDGE AND SKILLS

As noted earlier in the chapter, in today's business environment, we face unprecedented change. As we continue to deal with challenges and opportunities from a global pandemic to continuous disruptive technologies, our recipe for this chapter focuses on acquiring and keeping up with the skills to remain relevant as auditors. Not only do you need to be organized and have a plan, but you also need to embrace the proper mental attitude. The approach that has proven successful for our colleagues and us is as follows:

Create a proficiency gap (see Table 2.1 for a partial example):

1. Look ahead one year to 10 years and see what skills you identify as a need now and in the future, and write them down in a column.
2. List the specific processes and tasks needed for each skill in the next column. In the end, you will have a list of all skills required or desired (update it regularly as you become aware of different skills).
3. Assess your level of knowledge from zero to 100% for all processes and tasks.
4. From this list, select the skills you want to start improving. Remember, one step at a time: think useful and relevant. Also remember that there is a learning curve.
5. Make a plan of attack for each skill. Can you learn the skill on the job? Do you read a book? Do you practice the skill more? Can you attend a webinar? Should you attend a live or online course? Can you get certified in this

TABLE 2.1 Example of Proficiency Gap

Skill	Processes/ Tasks	Proficiency Score for Process or Task	Overall Skill Competence	Action Plan	Due Date
Data Analytics	Statistics	80%	78%	Review college course	12/31/2020
	Excel	80%		Take online class in Udemy	10/28/2020
	Basics of data analytics	95%			
	Visualization	85%			
	Different programs such as "R," Python, etc.	50%		Read articles on the topics	Continuous

Score: None or minimal (10% or less)

Limited experience (11–50%)

Medium exposure or experience (50–75%)

Good to excellent (75% or greater)

skill? Include in the plan: time, cost, and due date when you will complete the specific learning.

6. Continue adding actions you can take to improve each skill and add additional skills you become aware of that are valuable to your career.
7. Periodically reassess your level of the skills and remember, this can go up and down as you continue to test yourself on each skill.

You also have to remember that attitude is helpful, and here are some tips:

■ Embrace the **Kaizen** philosophy (*Kaizen* is a Japanese term meaning "change for the better" or "continuous improvement." To embrace it fully, you must also promote continuous change and improvement within your personal and professional circles. Individuals and organizations that are reluctant to change risk becoming obsolete. Successful individuals and organizations improvise, innovate, and learn how to be flexible and resilient.

▪ Reframe the way you think about knowledge, your abilities, and your skills. If you do not know something or are lacking the skills, don't say: "I don't know" or "I can't"; say instead: "I don't know *yet*" or "I can't *yet*." The point is, if you believe you can, you are more likely to achieve your goal.

▪ Be preemptive, not reactive. Don't wait until the change happens. Be the change!

▪ Challenge yourself! Don't be afraid to pursue multiple degrees and certifications.

▪ Be enthusiastic and work on having a contagious personality. If this is not your style, work on exuding a positive can-do attitude. Have you heard the English aphorism "Fake it until you make it"? It does work!

▪ Read. Get in the habit of always reading something, preferably for knowledge. Though we cannot read everything, start your "to read" list now. Don't make excuses, and find reading opportunities (while traveling, cooking, before bed, in the bathroom, you name it). There are many formats available, from hard copy to audiobooks, which means you can do anything from gardening to exercising while listening to a book.

▪ Reduce the time you spend feeding your brain unnecessary fluff. It is the zenith of television, the internet, and social media. However, be selective while still finding time to tune out.

▪ Surround yourself with like-minded people in search of greater knowledge. Find friends who encourage you to learn and question more. Include people different than you in other fields.

▪ Speak to people of all ages, including your elderly neighbor and your kids and those of others.

▪ Keep up with the news, and consider the source. Do not let it bring you down by listening to it 24/7 – enough to stay in touch and relevant. Stay informed without losing your mind.

▪ Expand auditors' image from service provider to leader and trusted advisor.

▪ Embrace technology in every aspect of your life.

To quote the marketing slogan of Nike, "Just Do It."

 **NUGGETS**

An audit is simply an evaluation of evidence to form a conclusion about a topic. Audit professionals perform four main types of audits; most auditors identify their profession by these audit types: external, government, internal, and tax audits. There is a unique set of standards determined by a standards-setting body for each professional group and type of audit. The intended scope and focus of the audit determine the audit classification. Examples of audit classifications include financial, compliance, information technology, operational, and integrated. Traditional audits use a waterfall approach to complete audits as follows:

- Audit planning, which takes months to complete, must be finalized and approved before any engagement can begin.
- Engagement planning must be complete before fieldwork begins. This requirement results in rushed, incomplete, and unclear engagement programs.
- Fieldwork must be complete before communicating results (though some auditors realize the value of delivering interim results and do so throughout the audit project).
- Communicating results signifies the end of the audit. The final report communication is completed only after all fieldwork is complete.

It is the waterfall approach and, to some extent, interpretations of auditing standards that create many of the problems experienced during audits. Nonetheless, as we stated in this chapter, there is a time and place for traditional conventional project management methods such as in certain mandatory compliance audits with repeated processes year after. Transitioning into a hybrid Agile approach that combines aspect of both Agile and waterfall might also work for these audits, especially in industries where compliance standards are fluid.

To complete any audit, auditors need a variety of general knowledge and specialized skills. You need not become an expert in everything. Seek opportunities to enhance your knowledge and skills and remember, in Agile auditing, you are not alone; you are part of a team, including your audit customer, with collective knowledge to complete an audit.

CHAPTER THREE

Traditional Audit Processes and Practices

 AUDIT JARGON

One thing we've discovered in our courses is that it is easy to confuse some of the audit jargon. For example, what is the difference between an annual audit plan and an audit program? We will clarify much of the audit jargon in this chapter and provide details on typical audit activities, which will help you understand more about the what and how of auditing.

If you have been auditing for several years, to understand how Agile auditing is different, we need to review current audit practices. Also, to determine which Agile method is best for your audit activity, you need to look at your current processes. Use this chapter to evaluate and benchmark your current practices. You may discover a practice that you can add to your current audit methodology. If you are a new auditor working in an Agile auditing environment, you may feel compelled to skip this chapter. Please don't.

TRADITIONAL ENTITY-LEVEL AUDIT PLANNING

To clarify, the audit plan is the entity-level audit plan, the organizational audit plan, or the annual audit plan. The audit plan is a list of the audits that will be completed over a certain timeline. The audit plan provides the upcoming audits. Each audit project, or engagement, has an audit program. The audit program includes the specific steps to complete the audit and achieve the audit objectives, or engagement objectives. Imagine you are going to the theater; think of the audit plan as the listing of all the Broadway plays, musicals, operas, and other shows that you can see – for example, *700 Sundays, Proof, The Play That Goes Wrong, It's Only a Play, To Kill a Mockingbird, Harry Potter and the Cursed Child, Cats,* and *Hamilton,* among many others. Thus, the audit program would be the specific acts, scenes, and songs that you would expect to see in a specific show. A program, which includes specific show details, is provided to you when you enter the theater. For example: *Hamilton,* Act 1 – Scene 1: "Alexander Hamilton"; Scene 2: "Aaron Burr, Sir"; Scene 3: "My Shot"; and so on.

The traditional approach to determine the audit plan begins with creating the **audit universe**, a list of all potential engagements, or auditable entities/units – the list of all Broadway options. The audit universe can be any topic, subject, department, process, or function within the organization or external to the organization. Auditors often use the following to create the audit universe: risk registers, regulations, business processes, organizational charts, financial statement line items, financial accounts, performance indicators, administrative processes, applications, committee activities, supply chain activities, vendors, projects, management requests, industry trends, emerging trends, and technology infrastructure. Creating the audit universe is an essential and customary step in traditional audit planning. The process of creating the audit universe aids in developing a thorough understanding of the organization to ensure that audit aligns its activities with the needs of the organization.

In accordance with the IIA Standards, the audit plan must be risk-based. External auditing standards also focus on risks. However, auditors may overemphasize audit cycle requirements determined by management, board members, regulators, and other auditors to complete specific engagements at specific intervals. Emphasizing audit cycle requirements deviates from a purely risk-based approach expected in professional auditing standards.

When using risk factors to establish an audit plan, the chief audit executive (CAE) selects the relevant risk factors (we recommend 8 to 12 risk factors). Some risk factors include:

- Change (in regulations, lines of business, management, key process owners, systems, etc.)
- Degree of automation
- Materiality
- Time since the last audit
- Transaction volume and complexity

Each risk factor in Table 3.1 is assigned a weight (e.g., materiality 30%, transaction complexity 15%) based on auditor judgment. Auditors then determine a score for each auditable entity for each risk factor and perform quick math to determine an overall score. Sorting the auditable entities from highest risk score to lowest score identifies candidates for engagements in the audit plan.

Because risks and business activities are continually changing, the CAE should perform periodic updates, and even reprioritize auditable entities throughout the year. This is particularly crucial for new regulations and unknown emerging risks not reflected in the audit plan. For example, think about the CAE's response to, and audit plan changes necessary to respond to, a black swan risk event like a global pandemic that caused countries to shut down, ban international travel, close borders, and halt logistics processes.

TABLE 3.1 Example Risk Scoring

Factors/ Weight	Materiality	Complexity	Transaction Volume	Regulatory Change	Time Since Last Audit	Risk Score*
	30%	15%	20%	25%	10%	
Accounts Payable	7	2	3	6	1	4.6
Derivatives	8	9	4	7	10	7.3
Marketing	1	6	3	5	8	3.85
Government Relations	1	10	6	2	7	4.2
Privacy	5	3	10	10	5	6.95
End-user Computing	3	8	10	1	4	4.75

* **Risk Score for Accounts Payable: 4.6** = (7 × 30%) + (2 × 15%) + (3 × 20%) + (6 × 25%) + (1 × 10%). Perform the same calculations for each auditable entity (Derivatives, Marketing, etc.).

These changes are Agile when executed properly. However, CAEs should exercise caution to ensure that the audit plan updates are indeed risk-based and not caused by recency syndrome.

Is your head spinning? This audit planning process sounds complicated, between selecting risk factors, weighting, scoring, and sorting, right? What's worse, with all this judgment, math, analysis, and reprioritization, we aren't focusing on the most significant risks to the organization. We are focusing on the individual areas that present the most prominent risks, or the riskiest processes. The audit plan should be based on a holistic risk approach, and include the areas most likely to impact the achievement of strategies and objectives. Many audit teams modify their planning process beyond risk scoring to include subjective assessments of strategic risks. These teams are demonstrating agility in their approach.

Most audits are defined in three stages: planning, fieldwork, and reporting. At the beginning of the audit, estimates are made as to when each stage will be completed. There are many factors affecting the completion of the audit, including accuracy of planning, number of individuals involved in the audit, number of auditors assigned to the engagement, cooperation of audit customers, number of discrepancies identified, and internal audit processes, checkpoints, and requirements. This unit describes typical experiences and is not intended to portray a single **audit activity**; each audit team determines its own process and requirements.

TRADITIONAL AUDIT ENGAGEMENT PLANNING

Starting any audit project begins with defining your project, your team, and your success. Audits are selected from the audit universe during the high-level audit planning process. Reviewing the risk details and audit profile, including preliminary audit objectives and scope, is the first step of traditional audit planning. Next, we gain an understanding of the business objectives, risks, and controls through our review of policies, procedures, and management reports. We have conversations and perform interviews and walkthroughs with process owners, management, and staff. These activities help auditors define projects, refine audit objectives, or purpose of the audit, and determine audit scope, or boundaries of the audit. Based on this understanding and the refined audit objectives and scope, the audit leader, auditor-in-charge, or audit project manager confirms planned audit deadlines, deliverables, quality expectations, and budgets. It is also helpful, but often overlooked, for the audit project management to identify and communicate the project's inputs, outputs, outcomes, assumptions, and delivery risks.

Defining the audit team is usually limited to focusing on the auditors who will perform the engagement. These auditors are often assigned based on availability, audit experience, and, to some extent, knowledge of the business process under review. The audit team typically includes the audit leadership, audit manager, and staff auditors. The business process owners and staff might also be considered members of the audit team. It is helpful for the audit team to coordinate with individuals who previously performed assessments and reviews of the business area, including those performed by the second line of defense. Second-line roles are part of management's responsibilities and not independent from management. The anticipated audit should be discussed with other assurance providers, including management control testers and external auditors. The stakeholders are not typically a member of the audit team, although understanding their needs and expectations will help ensure that the audit adds value and satisfies stakeholder needs.

Defining audit success includes identifying desirable direct and indirect outcomes, milestones, and deliverable deadlines. Also, there are performance metrics and key performance indicators (KPIs) established and monitored by audit leadership and stakeholders that audit project managers should consider and strive to achieve. Another measure of success may include audit clients' and stakeholders' perceptions of audit's value-added activities, gleaned through client satisfaction surveys.

Engagement planning may include any of the following activities and milestones. Many audit activities standardized some of these to gain efficiency and consistency in the audit process.

- Performing general research, including reading publications and white papers related to the business activity, function, or process under review.
- Reading related laws and regulations.
- Gathering general information from internal resources, including management reports and internal training.
- Creating audit templates, including templates for risk assessments, workpapers, checklists, potential audit report comments (PARCs), issues tracking, audit memos/emails, meeting agendas, and future audit recommendations.
- Identifying auditors and assessing auditor knowledge and competencies.
- Creating audit budgets for time/schedule and costs, including travel and training expenses.

- Conducting or obtaining needed training to develop knowledge of the business activity, function, or process under review.
- Preparing the announcement memo – a notification that the audit will begin on a certain date.
- Holding the entrance/kickoff meeting – the introductory meeting with audit customers and auditors to discuss the preliminary objectives and scope of the audit.
- Providing a document request list, also known as a "prepared by client" (PBC) list – a list of items auditors desire at the onset of an audit. Additional requests are added to the list and the list is updated, maintained, and communicated to the audit client periodically.
- Discussing fraud concerns and risks with other auditors and audit management.
- Holding high-level discussions with senior leadership and/or management regarding the process under review.
- Performing analytical reviews of data, including ratio, variance, and trend analysis to better understand the operations under review (e.g., employee turnover, employee tenure, transaction volume, transaction size).
- Preparing the internal audit planning memo or statement of work, which documents important information about the audit and business function. The planning memo may be shared with audit customers and stakeholders, but it is generally an internal planning document for other auditors to learn more about the audit.
- Drafting surveys and internal control questionnaires to distribute to audit customers, particularly in an audit with a large number of customers or spanning a large geographical area where individual interviews are not feasible.
- Conducting detailed interviews and walkthroughs with business process owners and staff.
- Documenting process flows and process maps based on policies, procedures, interviews, and walkthroughs.
- Performing an engagement-level risk assessment (ELRA) for the function under review. The ELRA begins with identifying the business process objectives and the risks that may affect achieving those objectives. Auditors, preferably with the help of the audit customer, prioritize the risks based on impact and likelihood assessments.
- Documenting the ELRA.
- Identifying control responses to identified risks.

- Documenting the risks and controls matrix (RCM). The RCM documents auditor understanding of the risks in scope during the engagement and the related controls in place to mitigate the risks. Many expand the RCM to include control classifications, such as preventive, detective, automated or manual, and related management assertions. These classifications aid in assessing the adequacy of the control design.
- Assessing adequacy of the design of controls, also known as test of design (TOD).
- Determining the criteria for the audit test step – essentially, the criteria is tied to a law, regulation, policy, procedure, or other standard of performance.
- Determining test steps and strategies for controls that passed the TOD. These test steps are known as test of control effectiveness (TOE).
- Documenting the TOE steps and strategies in an audit program.
- Obtaining approval of the audit program, which includes the audit objectives, scope, resources, and TOD and TOE steps.

Many audit activities consume 10–60% of budgeted audit time performing engagement-level planning. There are many documents, and sometimes redundancies, in the engagement planning process. With Agile auditing, this extensive planning process is more fluid, or incremental, instead of occurring all at once. Additionally, many of the tasks in the preceding bulleted list take less time to complete or are eliminated due, in part, to collaboration with the audit customers, cross-functional audit team membership, collective Agile audit Team Member knowledge, and shortened delivery time frames. Chapter 9, Implementing Agile Auditing: Planning Agile Audit Engagements, explains the streamlined audit planning process in an Agile environment.

 ## TRADITIONAL AUDIT ENGAGEMENT FIELDWORK

Once the audit program is approved and audit resources are assigned, each auditor completes their assigned audit program steps. The time to complete each step is rarely predetermined and varies drastically from step to step and auditor to auditor. The time to complete each step is heavily dependent on the audit customer's responsiveness, the auditor's ability to effectively communicate evidence needs and deadlines, and the auditor's motivation to complete each step. Many auditors elect to test samples of evidence, with the selection of samples performed on a judgmental basis. This means that audit tests are biased and that auditors cannot provide any estimates on the level of confidence that their conclusions are accurate. Moreover, little effort is made to verify the population of items prior to selecting the samples.

To complete the individual audit tests, auditors start by determining the evidence needed. While we prefer that auditors set up a meeting to discuss the audit test and request audit evidence, most auditors send an email requesting the evidence. Overreliance on email throughout the audit process contributes to delays in the audit process in the following ways:

- The emails often lack specificity on report names, file names, relevant dates, and delivery deadlines.
- Emails may include requests for documentation or other information that the auditor does not know exists or if it would even be useful (also known as kitchen sink audit requests, discussed more in Chapter 15, Merging Risk-Based Auditing and Integrated Auditing with Agile Auditing).
- Emails can be overlooked.
- Emails create opportunities for the receiver to read and respond at their leisure. Since the audit is rarely the audit customer's highest priority, the email could remain unread indefinitely. This situation is made worse when the auditor follows the first email with a second follow-up email and doesn't "call out" the recipient for not responding.
- Emails can be accidentally deleted.
- Emails, and other written forms of communication, are subject to the reader's interpretation. If a reader misinterprets a request for evidence, the auditor is more likely to receive the wrong evidence or only a portion of what's needed. On a side note, someone once told us "it is never the reader's fault." Should the recipient misinterpret the written words, the sender failed to communicate effectively and consider the reader's possible interpretations.

After receiving the evidence, auditors examine and analyze it by comparing it to expected criteria. The evidence evaluation determines whether the criteria were or were not met. If the criteria are satisfied, the test step is complete. If the criteria are not satisfied, auditors communicate the exceptions, generally via email, to the audit customer. Audit customers may provide additional evidence to clear potential exceptions. This back-and-forth process of requesting evidence, reviewing evidence, communicating possible exceptions, waiting for responses or additional evidence, and reviewing additional evidence, and again, communicating exceptions repeats for each audit test and possibly repeats multiple times for each audit test. Auditors evaluate additional evidence obtained, if any, then draw their conclusions to complete the test step.

Once the test step is completed, the auditor documents the work performed, evidence reviewed, exceptions noted, and related conclusions in the workpapers. Though workpapers are rarely provided to audit customers, they are used within the internal audit team as the essential support for the work performed and conclusions reached. Workpaper templates may require the following information: identifiers for the audit (a header), name of person completing the workpaper, workpaper completion dates, testing objectives, sources, populations, population verification steps, sampling methods, samples, tests performed, test summaries, and conclusions on testing objectives. It is important to note that while there are professional audit standards requiring auditors to document the work performed and conclusions reached, there are no specific workpaper requirements for the level of detail needed in each workpaper. Workpaper details and specific requirements are established by each audit activity. In our experience, most auditors overdocument just in case any questions arise in the future.

Finally, the auditor submits their workpapers for supervisory review. The audit supervisor, audit lead, auditor-in-charge, or audit manager reviews the workpapers for completeness and accuracy, making sure that workpapers are clear and understandable and support audit objectives and provides any review notes to the auditor. Review notes include any questions from the supervisor and developmental comments and suggestions.

Auditors clear the review notes and resubmit the workpaper for approval. In some audit teams, workpapers are subject to multiple levels of approval prior to finalization. Review notes provided by any reviewer would be cleared by the auditor prior to final workpaper approval.

For any criteria not satisfied, the auditor documents a related exception workpaper. The exception workpaper details the condition identified, the criteria expected, the cause of the exception or deviation from the criteria, the effect or consequence of the deviation, and initial recommendations. This exception workpaper may result in an audit report finding or issue. Exception workpapers are subject to the same supervisory review process described earlier.

The fieldwork, or execution phase, consumes around 50–60% of the budgeted time for an audit. Refer to Chapter 10 for testing in Agile auditing.

TRADITIONAL AUDIT ENGAGEMENT REPORTING

In a recent webinar on report writing, we posed an important question: Why do auditors write audit reports? The majority answered that audit reports are required by professional standards. While this may be true for external auditors and government auditors, it is not true for internal auditors.

The report writing process begins with determining which exceptions must be communicated to management in a formal manner. After identifying the exceptions, the auditors draft the audit issues, sometimes during testing and before determining the need for formal communication. Drafting issues too soon results in wasted time and effort if the issue will be eliminated, does not need formal communication, or is combined with a related issue. Each audit issue is subject to the same supervisory review process described in the previous section. Once the draft issue is approved by the audit team and leadership, usually after countless back-and-forth editing, it is provided to the audit customer for review and comment. If there are disagreements on word choices and other language in the audit issue, which is often the case, the auditors and audit supervisor determine how to reword the exception to clear the disagreement. Revisions to the initial issue draft require supervisory review and approval, particularly of audit management.

Once all issues are approved, the auditor in charge (audit lead) drafts the audit report executive summary from scratch or cuts and pastes content from the full report. The executive summary is designed for executives and governance groups. The summary provides a description of the process under review, audit objective, audit scope, audit methods, summary of issues, summary of satisfactory areas, and other useful information for high-level readers. The audit team typically determines a final opinion or rating for the process under review based on the audit issues and executive summary. The issues and executive summary are combined and submitted to audit leadership for review, similar to the workpaper review process. Audit leadership provides review notes and the auditors and the audit manager work together to adjust the report. There are multiple levels of review of the draft report and often multiple revisions of the draft report. This process may last several weeks, or months. Once the draft report is cleared internally to the audit team, it is provided to the audit customer(s).

Additional comments and suggestions are solicited from the audit customer(s), edits or updates may be made by the auditors and audit managers, and changes are reviewed by the audit leadership prior to being resubmitted to the audit customer. Some audit activities spend months finalizing audit reports prior to distribution to stakeholders, including executives and governing bodies.

At some point, the audit team holds an exit conference for customers and stakeholders. During the exit conference, the draft report is discussed, and the audit customer may learn the final rating of the process under review. Even though the report has undergone many revisions, it is common to have additional changes resulting from the formal discussion of the report draft. Any changes would be reviewed and approved by audit leadership. If the auditors collaborated throughout the audit, there are no revisions and the exit conference serves as final agreement on the report language. It is important that the final conclusion and related rating is the audit team's conclusion and it should not be open for debate; in reality, though, we've seen many debates and even late changes to audit reports to revise ratings.

After the final report is distributed, audit issues are documented in an issue tracking log for future follow-up and review by auditors. The reporting process is often designed to consume 10% of the budgeted time for an audit, but the duration of this phase may last months (but it probably feels like years to the auditors doing the writing and rewriting!). So, if you paid attention to the percentages, we could have a worst-case scenario of 130% . . . impossible, of course! The point we are trying to make is that audit durations are often over budget; even within budgeted timelines, we are not spending time efficiently.

Clearly, our traditional audit approach can use a freshening up! I hope you will give Agile auditing a fair chance as we share how to do Agile auditing in Part II, Implementing Agile Auditing.

NUGGETS

The traditional audit process begins with entity-level planning to select audits for completion over a specified period of time. Once the audits are selected, each audit includes three phases: planning, fieldwork, and reporting. The time and duration of each phase and the specific requirements and practices of each audit activity varies. There are numerous reviews and approvals built into the audit process that impact the timely completion of the audit, related delivery of final engagement communications, and audit efficiency. You've probably identified opportunities to improve your current processes and gain efficiencies even without implementing Agile auditing. Please remember to record your personal nuggets and share them with your team.

CHAPTER FOUR

What Is Agile Audit?

 THE JOURNEY OF AGILE AUDITING

In early 2013, when we first started speaking on Agile audit, it was so new that our conference and class participants thought we were talking about traditional auditing of Agile software system development projects. The auditors attending those early conferences were familiar with Agile projects and Agile software system development because those topics had been around since 2001, when Agile started. The participants were not familiar with applying Agile principles, frameworks, methodologies, approaches, and practices to audit projects. In the beginning, people referred to our Agile auditing proposals and talks as "alluring" and "thought-provoking" yet unreasonable and impossible.

Though a few auditors were catching on to the Agile auditing principles and methodologies and bringing these concepts to their audit practices, we started to see a big change around 2017, once people recognized Agile audit for what it is . . . a customer-centric, risk-based approach to managing audit projects to deliver faster results to audit clients and stakeholders (customer-centric is fundamental in Agile). By 2017, there were numerous blogs, seminars, and conference agendas that referenced Agile auditing. During these conferences and seminars, we learned of more audit teams applying some aspects and techniques used in Agile auditing. The recognition and application of Agile auditing was good news for our profession. One of the most prominent reports elevating the need for and status of Agile auditing was PricewaterhouseCoopers' 2017 State of the Internal Audit Profession Study, which stated that organizations and individuals that are prepared and adaptable are "Agile" (PricewaterhouseCoopers 2017).

Nonetheless, have you read this 2017 report, titled "Staying the Course toward True North: Navigating Disruption" (PricewaterhouseCoopers 2017)? Well, it isn't a very positive commentary on the state of the internal audit profession; in fact, it is quite gloomy. It implied that auditors aren't adding value, aren't trusted advisors, and don't respond well to disruption. The report was an eye opener to the internal audit profession's problems, perceptions, and possibilities. The report provided an introduction to Agile auditing for many of its readers. It presented seven keys to embrace Agile. One of the keys was related to flexible planning. The report stated, "73% of Agile internal audit functions change course and evaluate risk at the speed required by the business as compared to only 37% of non-Agile audit peers." Another key point in the report was "88% of stakeholders with Agile IA Functions report that Internal Audit is adding significant value to their organization today compared to 41% of stakeholders with less Agile internal audit functions."

Today, Agile auditing continues to grow in popularity. Now in our Agile auditing conferences we no longer have to explain that Agile auditing is about being Agile and Agile audit project management and not about auditing Agile software development and other projects. This is a good sign of progress.

As the internal audit manager for a government agency, Ceciliana and her staff implemented the Agile audit principles for various audits. Through collaboration with audit clients, audits using the Agile framework were not only completed faster but audit clients and stakeholders also accepted unfavorable results more easily. Nonetheless, there were multiple hurdles to overcome (Chapter 5 discusses some of these challenges).

WHAT IS AGILE AUDITING?

Agile auditing is the mindset and methods an audit function adopts to focus on customers' needs. It is a value-based, project management approach to provide quicker audit results and timely information on risk management practices and control effectiveness to audit clients and stakeholders. Agile auditing uses a risk-focused, collaborative, and waste-reduction mindset to help organizations achieve their objectives (Raven Global Training, LLC 2020).

Agile internal auditing is "the use of Agile software development values, principles, frameworks, methods, and/or practices in the execution of internal audit engagements" (Wright 2019).

From the start, Agile auditing challenges auditors and audit clients to determine the value to be delivered by the particular audit. Agile auditing prioritizes audits based on importance and urgency as well as readiness to perform the work. Agile auditing adds value by centering audit's value proposition on business objectives and business risks, not audit risks from the customer's perspective. The best value propositions are created only after observing what the audit customer wants and needs. Each Agile audit value proposition should:

- Relate to the organizational and business strategy (commonly referred to as critical linkage)
- Improve products or services
- Make customers/stakeholders happier
- Provide benefits
- Relieve pain points
- Help meet end-user or customer needs
- Create competitive advantages
- State the value offer
- Give a reason to believe it will provide the value declared
- Describe what the Agile audit does
- Identify how audit is uniquely qualified and positioned to provide the stated value.

Agile auditing is designed to be flexible and iterative. Rather than rigid audit plans, there are continuous updates to audits, projects, and tasks, prioritized based on the organization's risks and needs. Maybe you can relate to the following audit on information/data security. During a traditional audit, we spent nearly two months determining criteria and planning our audit test steps. When fieldwork finally began and auditors provided the initial documentation requests, the client's responses indicated that the organization had very poor security protocols, even beyond data security. But there was an expectation to assess against the determined criteria, complete the planned tests of controls, and document the results to the best of our ability. Response after response showed controls were so weak that the organization was at great risk, and we persisted with the audit. We had no option but to end the audit with untested controls and communicate the risks. An individual

Agile audit focuses only on necessary and enough processes to address the risks being evaluated, and it adapts to the entity's changing needs and new information. In contrast to the above scenario, in an Agile audit environment, we would have identified the key control, requested evidence for that control, realized the control was inadequate, communicated the problem, and likely made the decision to allow management to address the problems while moving on to the next highest risk audit area.

> Agile audit is not a rigid recipe that must be followed without adjustments. Rather, it is an approach based on values and principles established by the Agile Manifesto.
>
> Having said this, there are certain "steps" that can be used as guidance to provide direction in applying the Agile framework. . . . In this book, we refer to these steps as Agile audit recipes, which are included at the end of many chapters. These recipes will provide you with general direction in applying this Agile auditing framework.

As you will learn from this book, Agile audit is not a rigid recipe that must be followed without adjustments. Rather, it is an approach based on values and principles established by the Agile Manifesto that need to be observed in order to best succeed. Having said this, there are certain "steps" that can be used as guidance to provide direction in applying the Agile framework. Otherwise, how would we be able to complete each Agile audit in two weeks' time – from audit planning and execution, through communication of final results? In this book, we refer to these steps as Agile audit recipes, which are included at the end of many chapters. These recipes will provide you with general direction in applying this Agile auditing framework.

 ## OVERVIEW OF THE AGILE AUDIT PROCESS

Regardless of the best data analytics and the best risk assessments, organizations and audit functions can't predict market disruptions, last-minute regulatory changes, pandemics, or unexpected cybersecurity or data privacy threats. Therefore, to operate in today's dynamic business environments and continue to provide valuable insights and assurance, auditors must be Agile. We cannot continue to use traditional annual audit planning approaches. They simply do not provide the necessary flexibility to survive, thrive, and properly respond to emerging business needs in the new normal environment of continuous disruption.

The beauty of the Agile audit framework is that it's not rigid. It is based on a flexible, iterative plan performed on an ongoing basis in Sprints. Sprints are short spurts of planning, fieldwork, review, and reporting. (See Part II, Implementing Agile Auditing, for discussion of Sprint activities and processes.) Further, Agile audit focuses on collaboration and continuous communication with the audit team and the audit client. Communication is informal and more frequent, typically daily. Reporting is often through real-time dashboards and verbal updates rather than comprehensive, formal audit reports, which can absorb precious audit resources and take months to complete.

Agile auditing allows you to reassess and shift resources as priorities change. Every two weeks (or the Sprint length that is best for your organization), the Agile audit team reviews and adjusts upcoming priorities, tasks, and goals. This helps the Agile audit team identify major issues as they arise and allows audit customers to quickly respond to issues, instead of waiting until the completion of a lengthy audit.

Agile audit processes leverage characteristics of both iterative and incremental project management styles. Specifically:

- The requirements (also known as the scope) are dynamic.
- The activities, tasks, and steps are repeated until correct (remember, errors and mistakes are encouraged and will occur in Agile auditing).
- The delivery of results is frequent and bite-sized.
- The goal is bringing customer value via frequent deliveries and feedback.

Early feedback from the customer enables the Agile audit team to provide the customer with insights about business risks and controls, confidence that the Agile audit is focusing on the right values, and control of the results and output. Because the team can provide results earlier than using waterfall methodologies, the Agile audit will provide an earlier return on investment; the team delivers the highest-value work first. Delivering the highest-value work first using client collaboration increases clients' acceptance of the Agile audit results.

In an Agile environment, the team expects requirements to change. The iterative and incremental approaches provide feedback to better plan the next part of the Agile audit. Also, incremental delivery uncovers hidden or misunderstood requirements before too much time passes. For example, if the auditors planned to provide substantive or reperformance testing on a control that is poorly designed or known to be inadequate, early communication of the first discrepancy or inadequate design conclusion could eliminate the need for further testing. Early communication of a control design flaw changed the course of our first Agile audit of Accounts Payable, saving a substantial amount of time. We were testing automated approvals on invoices based on a three-way match or two-way match for service-type invoices. The procedures stated that these automated match controls were in place. The audit team's original expectation was that the automated control would require manual review if there were any matching process variances. We discussed the criteria and intended test during the Sprint Planning Meeting with the audit customer in attendance. We were also alerted that while the control was in place, the automated match control was set to allow a 20% dollar variance. We immediately wanted to review the original data and calculate the total variance. In our heads, we were already writing an audit issue. However, the audit customer shared their monthly controller report with their CFO, which already highlighted the variance. The report graph read "20% Automated Match Variance." Based on the documented procedures, the audit client's openness when discussing how the control actually worked, and the CFO report graph, the Agile audit team collectively concluded they would not test the control, citing management's risk appetite and monitoring of the automated control. This discussion in the Sprint Planning Meeting saved 40 planned hours, based on the prior audit of Accounts Payable, by eliminating walkthroughs, population validation, data analysis, sampling, obtaining supporting evidence, testing evidence, preparing workpapers, reviewing workpapers, and writing an audit finding. Remember, the Agile audit project aligns with customer needs and can be adapted as necessary, based on the Agile audit team and customer feedback.

The Agile audit process starts with the risk assessment in order to prioritize audits based on the organization's risk exposures. The risk exposure identification process creates a list of possible Agile audits. This may be referred to as the audit universe, Product Backlog, audit backlog, risk backlog, or risk universe (our preference). Unlike the traditional entity planning approach described in Chapter 3, Traditional Audit Processes and Practices, alternative planning approaches are used to determine the next Agile audit, including dynamic risk assessments, data-driven risk assessments, and risk universe prioritizations. In Chapter 8, Implementing Agile Auditing: The Audit Planning Process, you will learn more about how to complete planning using the alternative approaches. Many traditional audit activities refer to the list of upcoming audits as an audit plan. We do not use the term *audit plan* in Agile auditing because the audit team may not know what audit comes next due to the responsive and adaptable nature of Agile audits. We want to avoid the misconception that the audit plan is predetermined and cannot change; the Agile audit plan may change often, and drastically. Thus, we will refer to the audit plan as the *audit project backlog* for Agile auditing.

When a risk management office or similar function exists, the audit team can leverage the organization's up-to-date risk universe to select areas to review and develop the audit Product Backlogs, which will serve to track the anticipated, future Agile audits. Risks are stated as user stories and epics from the organization's perspective and describe the Agile audits in the audit Product Backlog. A user story risk description is very specific, whereas the risk description in an epic is more generally or broadly stated. User stories are desirable and help create the small, incremental areas to review in the next Agile audit. Most Agile audit teams leveraging the risk management office's risk universe discover very general, high-level risk statements, which are initially characterized as epics.

In addition, instead of setting and committing the audit activity to a predetermined rigid list of audits for the next year or more, Agile audit builds a much shorter plan, possibly as short as one month. These shorter Agile audit plans are determined by selecting the most critical, highest-risk areas, those that affect the achievement of the organization's objectives. Some Agile audit teams have monthly plans, while others use quarterly or semi-annual plans. Even with the shorter plans, remember the plan remains flexible depending on changes to the business environment and changes in risks.

Individual Agile audit engagements must be manageable and completed in a specified Sprint time frame. Therefore, if the risks are general and high-level epics, the Agile audit team will need to break up, refine, and restate the epics as user stories as auditors learn more about the risks. The idea is to have the risks selected for the next Agile audit broken down into specific, manageable user stories. To illustrate the difference between epics and user stories, it is akin to performing an audit of Accounts Payable, an epic, versus auditing the automated match process, aged invoices, or the delegation of authority, each being an individual user story.

Flexibility of the audit Product Backlog is important. As environments change, Agile audit teams must identify, add, and assess new risks and remove irrelevant risks in a timely manner. The ultimate goal with Agile audit is to collaborate and partner closely with management to ensure audits occur in the right place at the right time to achieve desired results. Periodically, preferably weekly, the audit team, including the audit client, will review the organization's risk universe and audit Product Backlog to identify the next critical risk facing the organization and thus the next Agile audit, or few Agile audits, depending on the organization's needed lead time to begin an Agile audit. This process continues until there are no more risks to evaluate, which never happens.

The individual Agile audit will accomplish everything from planning, testing, review, and communication of results within the two-week sprints. Each Sprint has an agreed list of tasks recorded in a Sprint Backlog. Some Agile audit teams design their Sprints to last up to four weeks. Creating Sprints longer than four weeks means you are not doing Agile and you will likely end up performing audits in the traditional sense.

In traditional audits, we typically view the audit as a fixed timeline with a flexible scope. Each traditional audit undergoes a series of stages in a life cycle of planning, testing, and reporting, as we described in Chapter 3, Traditional Audit Processes and Practices. We thoroughly plan the entire audit, and complete all testing before an audit lead reviews the testing and workpapers. Then the manager reviews the audit workpapers, draft findings, and draft audit report. Upon review, changes are made and agreed upon with the audit lead. Finally, auditors communicate the audit results to the audit client prior to distributing the final report. Depending on the type of audit, the final report may be distributed to senior management, executives, and governing bodies, including inspector generals, governors, and audit committees. Any errors or other issues found during the review process can create rework and extend the timeline past the arbitrary budgeted audit hours and due dates. Traditional audit timelines and due dates are determined based on a scope, which often expands during the course of the audit. Often, audit quality criteria are never established, or are misunderstood. In our traditional audits, we are often limited by the rigid structure of our audit process and the need to stick to the ill-defined quality, scope, and timeline.

In contrast, in the Agile audit life cycle, since the audits are very risk-focused with an agreed, predetermined audit scope, it is possible to structure the entire audit within a short time frame (e.g., two weeks). Each activity is planned, executed, reviewed, and reported to management with a short presentation, possibly in informal daily meetings or more formal Sprint Reviews that occur at the end of the two weeks. In this way, if we conduct the audit in shorter bursts of activity, we are better positioned to course-correct when we uncover something that needs exploring or abandoning. Agile auditing gives auditors the flexibility to explore, modify, adjust, and correct during the course of the audit without elaborate review processes. This is not to say that reviews are not allowed, but to point out that competent, trusted auditors are empowered to do what is right to provide assurance at the right level. Often, course corrections are discussed in daily meetings and implemented by the team unless there are objections.

The team works in iterations to deliver complete audit results. The Agile audit team works on the most important risks using agreed tasks or steps documented in the Sprint Backlog that is created by the Delivery Team. The team works collaboratively to finish the tasks. Then the team works on the next most important tasks and finishes those steps. These iterations continue until the Sprint Backlog is complete or the Sprint timeboxed duration elapses, whichever comes first. The team may decide to work on a few steps at a time, but the team does not address all of the work for the entire iteration at once. For example, the team would not complete all the testing steps, then perform all of the analyses, then document all the work performed, then review all the audit workpapers, and so on.

With an Agile audit approach, the team pulls items from the Sprint Backlog based on the team's capacity to start work, rather than on an iteration-based schedule. This results in faster completion of each task, as the team members can focus on the task at hand and overall rapid delivery of the project. The team defines its workflow, uses simple visuals such as columns on a taskboard, and manages the work in progress for each column. Each task may take a different amount of time to complete. Teams keep work-in-progress sizes small to better identify potential issues early and reduce the need for rework. The team carefully selects the items from the Sprint Backlog based on risk and value to the customer, being careful to not have too many in-process tasks at any one time. Without rigid iterations to define planning and review points, the team and all business stakeholders determine the most appropriate schedule for Sprint planning, Sprint Reviews, and Sprint Retrospectives. Customer satisfaction is essential; it increases with early and continuous delivery of valuable results. Further, an incremental deliverable that is functional and provides value to the client is the primary performance measure of success. Agile life cycles combine both iterative and incremental approaches in order to adapt to high degrees of change and deliver audit value more frequently. Figure 4.1 illustrates the Agile audit cycle. This figure was adapted from Scrum Alliance's *Scrum at a Glance*.

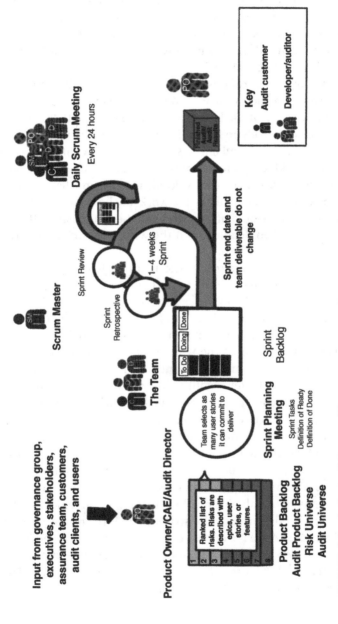

FIGURE 4.1   Agile Auditing at a Glance

Source: Illustrated by Carmen Catlin. Adapted from Scrum Alliance's *Scrum at a Glance (2020)*

SKILLS FOR AGILE AUDITORS

As we noted earlier, Agile is a mindset imbedded in your organization's culture. As such, there are core skills needed to successfully implement and perform Agile audits. While interrelated, the following skills are individually important to enable Agile audit success:

- *Communication:* As a member of the Agile team you will be communicating often with every stakeholder involved, including clients, sponsors, executives, management, developers, process owners, staff, and more. As such, you must consider everybody's needs and concerns. Your communication skills will be instrumental to ensure that everyone has a shared understanding of the goals of the project and the Definition of Done. By living the Agile Manifesto's "less documentation" motto, most project updates will be verbal, and great listening skills are essential. Epictetus (a Greek philosopher of first and early second centuries CE) said, "We have two ears and one mouth so that we can listen twice as much as we speak." Listen carefully to your Agile team members as they share their progress so you may identify themes, similarities, or opportunities to help overcome obstacles. Be careful not to interrupt your team members – manners matter!
- *Collaboration:* In Agile auditing we work collaboratively. Collaboration leverages on face-to-face communication and co-location. In Agile projects, co-location allows for face-to-face communication, but today's technology and our new normal work environment challenges original design Agile projects. Today, auditors should use collaboration tools and videoconferences to facilitate face-to-face collaborative environments.
- *Leadership:* Most auditors will be team members and not hold official "leadership" roles such as Product Owner or Scrum Master. As such, each Team Member will lead parts of each project. Agile audit leaders can effectively communicate the audit project value proposition to audit customers and stakeholders and inspire fellow team members to achieve it. As leaders, each Agile Team Member is accountable to all team members for their actions.
- *Build Trust:* Given the collaborative nature of Agile, trust between team members aids in honest and transparent communications. To build trust, each Team Member must honor commitments and communicate early when there are obstacles impacting work.

- *Time Management:* The very nature of Agile auditing aids in time management because team members are dedicated to the project, focused only on important tasks, and obligated to complete the actions committed to the prior day. This is great news! To help complete commitments on time, team members leverage the project taskboards and to-do lists. Also, remember that Agile is not about being perfect – mistakes and errors are expected. We find setting a time limit on a task, especially documentation tasks, is a great way to manage time and avoid perfection paralysis. Additionally, as team members meet their time commitments, trust increases.
- *Conflict Management:* The Agile audit team is a close group of individuals; conflicts will occur. If you are familiar with the conflict management model, you know that each conflict is evaluated based on concern for the problem and concern for the relationship within which the problem exists. Since you need to build trust and will complete the project with other individuals, conflicts cannot be avoided and ignored; competing is not an option. Thus, all team members must be prepared to accommodate, compromise, or collaborate to reach solutions.
- *Negotiation:* As you compromise and collaborate, you will negotiate at some point. Aim to seek consensus based on shared values, before negotiating specific solutions. For example, if you need your audit customer to review sample evidence, but they have a different pressing priority, start identifying and prioritizing the organization's needs. If the customer's priority is the one that adds the most value to the organization, maybe it makes the most sense to help them complete their priority so you can move forward together on the audit testing. Remember, you need to think Agile; maybe it makes sense for you to complete the audit test alone and review the results with the client the following day. Seek consensus on the right approach before proceeding.

NUGGETS

This chapter provided you an overview of the Agile auditing process. We will discuss how to complete Agile audit planning, execution, and communication in Part II, Implementing Agile Auditing. Also, as you review the core skills needed for Agile auditing, including communication, collaboration, leadership, building trust, time management, conflict management, and negotiation, you may want to identify skill gaps and resources to enhance your skills.

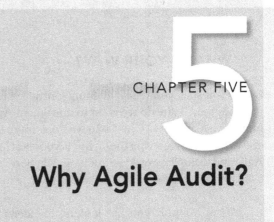

CHAPTER FIVE

Why Agile Audit?

 ## AVOID THE JURASSIC AUDITOR

If you want to be evolutionary, adaptive, and innovative, you are exploring the right tool. Agile auditing allows you to improve the value you provide to your audit customer, improve your audit approach, and evolve as an auditor. You must evolve so you don't become a "Jurassic auditor," a term used by Richard Chambers, president and CEO of the Institute of Internal Auditors (IIA), in a 2017 blog post (Chambers 2017a).

Agile auditing allows auditors to focus on stakeholder needs, accelerate audit cycles, and drive timely insights. It prompts auditors and stakeholders to determine the value expected from an audit before an audit begins. Because of its risk-based foundation, Agile auditing encourages auditors to choose the right level of assurance needed to protect the organization from the risks that may affect the sustainability and value of the organization. A Jurassic auditor approaches audits as if they need to provide the same level of assurance on each audit. The Agile auditor realizes that some risks may require an in-depth level of assurance that all controls are functioning as intended and other risks need high-level assurance that controls make sense.

WHAT'S YOUR WHY?

Before you start your Agile auditing journey, we implore you to ask and answer the question, "Why do we want to implement Agile auditing?" Every audit team may have a different "why," and we hope yours is better than "because everyone else is doing it"! Knowing the "why" is your best opportunity to inspire others to be Agile and to implement Agile auditing. Maybe one or more of the following reasons cited by other auditors are your reasons why you are exploring Agile auditing:

- As an auditor, you are looking for ideas to approach audits differently so you can complete audits efficiently and provide faster assurance on business processes.
- As an auditor, you want to improve audit client and stakeholder satisfaction so you can all see the value auditors provide to the organization.
- As an auditor, you want audit clients to see the relationship between their business goals, objectives, and risks and the audit process to the value of the assurance provided throughout the audit.
- As an auditor, you want to resolve problems experienced in the audit process so you can reduce auditor and client frustrations and improve auditor morale.
- As an auditor, you want to reduce rework and waste in the audit process to work smarter, not harder or longer.
- As an audit leader, you want to eliminate audit project delays so you can better estimate the completion time frame for your audits.
- As an audit leader, you recognize that audits take too long from start to finish and want to shorten the time to complete the audit so auditors and audit customers can see accomplishments, and improve business processes, sooner.
- As an audit leader, you believe that auditors consume the time budgeted to complete audits and may procrastinate in completing assignments, resulting in providing untimely insights.
- As an audit leader, you want auditors to stay focused and productive to increase auditor and client satisfaction and respond to new and changing risks sooner.
- As an audit client, you need faster feedback on processes and risk management assurance so you can fix problems and manage risks to achieve your objectives.
- As a board member, you need auditors to provide insights on more business functions, so you may exercise good governance.

Once you determine your "why," you can begin developing your Agile auditing strategy, including your plan to communicate and promote this drastic shift in your auditing approach. While there are other tools to help promote Agile auditing, you want to make sure that when someone asks you "Why are we doing this?," you have a great answer. Some examples of "Why are we doing this?" come from those who are in their Agile auditing journey.

One of our Agile auditing training clients provided training to all their auditors on the why and how of Agile auditing. They also prepared some promotional videos for auditors, audit clients, and audit stakeholders. Following is our favorite line from their materials that we feel summarizes their answer to "Why Agile Audit?":

"Our Agile transformation will help us achieve the following intended outcomes:

- Deliver deeper insights into strategic business objectives, risks, and issues.
- Respond rapidly to changing priorities and emerging issues.
- Become forward-looking in anticipating risks.
- Move to more risk-based audit planning and fieldwork.
- Streamline workpapers.
- Streamline and reduce "essential" audit-related meetings.
- Deliver impactful, relevant, and timely audit reports."

As we heard their why, we recalled an engagement performed in 2011. The engagement was not an Agile engagement by title; it was *Agile-ish*, as it was an engagement designed to streamline processes and documentation and reduce waste in the process. The objective focused on what the business needed to remain competitive by streamlining its lending activities. To get the process owners and staff on board with the Agile-ish engagement and streamlining initiative, the organization provided training to impacted parties. The training defined the value-added activities as tasks the lending customer would pay for or would need to perform themselves. The teacher also established a notion that there are non-value-added tasks in every process. Non-value-added tasks, by definition, are tasks that, if the organization attempted to invoice the client or charge a fee to perform, the client would laugh, dispute the charge, and refuse to pay for the cost. After the training, auditors and clients started identifying the value-added and non-value-added activities. We worked quickly to recommend eliminating the non-value-added tasks from their process as these were quick wins.

Before we eliminated their first non-value-added task, we realized the need to adapt the definitions and include a new classification, which was "non-value-added but necessary." This classification was essential, as the first non-value-added task identified was a regulatory requirement. We used this new classification to identify any task that the team felt the client wouldn't pay for, but knew they could not eliminate, in order to meet regulatory requirements. Because of our audit background, we knew that some non-value-added tasks were critical internal controls in the process. The business could not afford to stop the non-value-added but necessary tasks as part of the streamlining initiative, because removing the tasks would create operational and regulatory risks beyond the organization's risk appetite.

For the non-value-added but necessary tasks, we studied the tasks to determine if they met or exceeded the regulatory requirements. We estimated the time spent completing the tasks. For the tasks that exceeded the regulatory requirements, we worked with the client to determine if the excess work, documentation, and overprocessing were worth the costs. For some of the tasks, our client recognized that efforts applied to meet the regulatory expectations resulted in a mentality that the rules must be met with "perfection" to make sure there were no questions asked during regulatory reviews. When the excess costs exceeded the benefits, we eliminated some of the steps and decreased the time spent making the task "perfect." After all, they needed compliance, not perfection.

When implementing Agile auditing, you can use a similar approach and identify your value-added, non-value-added, and non-value-added but necessary audit tasks. Applying the Agile mindset that teams must adopt, encourage your fellow auditors to be mindful of these classifications. Tell your auditors to "raise the flag" should they encounter a job that may be non-value-added or recognize that they are spending too much time completing a step. When your team members escalate such tasks, you can reduce, streamline, and eliminate them to conduct audits more quickly and deliver more value.

The Agile auditing mindset allows for errors and never expects perfection. Use this mindset to reduce and eliminate excessive efforts to meet unreasonable expectations by audit supervisors, managers, and leaders masked as "necessary" to comply with professional standards or even meet regulator expectations.

Agile auditing can shift time and effort away from non-value-added tasks. The Agile auditing mindset allows for errors and never expects perfection. Use this mindset to reduce and eliminate excessive efforts to meet unreasonable expectations by audit supervisors, managers, and leaders masked as "necessary" to comply with professional standards or even meet regulator expectations. As we provide additional details in Part II: Implementing Agile Auditing, evaluate your audit processes carefully. Often, we see audit teams putting practices in place in their audit manuals and methodology because they believe the method is "required" by a standard. However, most of the time, the procedure is not required except in the minds of those who created the manuals and have not confirmed the professional standards.

Take a moment to think about your non-value-added tasks, including timekeeping, excessive workpaper documentation, perfecting workpapers, internal review processes, absurd (possibly rubber stamp) reviews, wordsmithing workpapers, findings, and reports, and addressing automated workpaper limitations. Can you think of tasks you can eliminate or reduce to create opportunities to focus on more value-added activities?

What are the value-added tasks you want to do more of? Maybe it is identifying risks, assessing risks, identifying better controls, or recommending improvements to current processes to reduce risks or achieve objectives. Perhaps you want to identify more issues or errors that significantly impact achieving goals. Or maybe you want to provide faster results with higher confidence using data analytics. This assessment of your audit process is a fantastic opportunity to begin socializing the shift to Agile auditing, get customer and stakeholder buy-in on Agile, and develop your Agile audit value proposition.

Did you ask and answer the questions on non-value-added and value-added tasks? If you did, congratulations! You are already thinking like an Agile individual. Auditors can also apply the Agile auditing mindset beyond just providing assurance. For example, use the Agile mindset to identify waste reduction and cost-saving opportunities anywhere in the organization. In short, Agile auditing will help auditors add more value to their organizations by focusing on what matters most to the organization's success.

 ## WHO IS USING AGILE AUDITING?

A quick internet search will identify the following organizations at various stages in their Agile auditing journey, each with their unique methodology, cautions, failures, and success stories. In addition to working directly with some of these organizations through audits, consultations, training, seminars, implementations, enhancements, and revisions to their Agile audit methodology, we've spoken with Agile auditing change transformation leaders (and similar titles) in a dozen of these organizations.

- Amazon
- Aviva
- Barclays
- BDO
- California State Auditors (select agencies and boards)
- Capital One
- Citi Group
- Deloitte
- Duke Energy
- George Mason University
- Hilton Worldwide
- KPMG
- MetLife
- Morgan Stanley
- Nike
- PricewaterhouseCoopers
- Prudential
- Raytheon
- Royal Bank of Canada
- Schlumberger Limited
- Siemens AG
- Suncorp.
- United Airlines
- Walmart Inc.
- YRC Worldwide

As Agile auditing grows in popularity, some organizations start where we did and are reading about Agile and retrofitting their audit process to be Agile. Use this book to shortcut the research process. Other organizations are leveraging the experience of Agile auditing pioneers to develop their Agile methodology. Each methodology we've read varies. The framework herein consolidates research, ideas, practices, and other Agile frameworks to help you create your Agile auditing style. Using this Agile audit framework, you get to decide your Agile audit methodology and approach. Keep an open mind and get the creative juices flowing to start making your Agile decisions.

STARTING YOUR AGILE AUDITING CHANGE TRANSFORMATION

Our discovery of Agile project management included reading over 100 books, reports, scholarly and trade journals, white papers, articles, interviews, and research papers on Agile, Agile frameworks, and Agile methodologies. We reference many of our learning and discovery aids in this book. Each source had a different approach to explain Agile and Agile project management. We used a technique called "mind mapping" to lay out all the ideas presented in the 100 publications. Mind maps are a tool to help you map out ideas, remember better, solve problems, and create plans (Davidson 2012). We've used mind mapping since 2006 for everything from business plans, risk identification, root cause analysis, website design, course design, audit project design, and assessing corporate culture to helping a 10-year-old remember content for a test on the colonization of America.

In Part III of the book, we address other Agile frameworks, namely Kanban and Lean, and their potential applications to auditing. We selected the Agile Scrum framework because our audits are distinct, temporary projects, with definitive start and end dates (Heldman 2005). Most of the books we read emphasized Scrum over the other methodologies, which likely influenced our decision to apply Scrum to auditing. **Scrum** is adaptive and flexible and is perfect for auditing, as each audit has its unique players, objectives, scope, and challenges.

For us, it made sense to start with a mind map to organize everything we were learning about Agile. Once we completed the Agile project management mind map, we referred to one of our older mind maps on audit project management to look for similarities and linkages. Based on the analysis of both mind maps, we decided to create a new mind map. The center of our map was labeled "Agile Auditing" and included a combination of audit ideas and Agile ideas. Eventually, two independent topics became one. It also became apparent that the Scrum framework for Agile projects would be the best fit for auditing. Perhaps this mind map approach would work well for you. Examine this framework, explore other Agile audit methodologies, learn more about Agile. Map your knowledge, map the options, then think about your culture and how you can make Agile work for you. If you are curious or want to create an Agile auditing mind map, search the internet and learn a little more about mind mapping, or contact us. We are always willing to help and learn even more about auditing and being Agile.

AGILE AUDIT FRAMEWORKS

One prescriptive Agile audit methodology by a leading professional services firm is more familiar to experienced auditors as it strongly resembles traditional audit processes and life cycles, which eases adoption. It recommends minor changes to the audit process and uses some Agile terminology. However, due to its familiarity, some of our clients who start with this approach are often confronted by auditors asking, "So what's different other than some changes to roles, meeting names, and documents?" We refer to the familiar Agile audit methodology as *Agilefall auditing,* since it layers the traditional audit methodology with Sprint concepts and Scrum timeboxing. There are three stages in Agilefall auditing: discovery, execution, and reporting Sprints. Stage one is the discovery, or information-gathering Sprint, which is timeboxed for one to four weeks. The activities completed in stage one and the resulting audit program is akin to the traditional engagement planning process. Stage two begins only after stage one is completed and the planning documents are approved – a waterfall mentality. Stage two is the execution Sprint, or fieldwork Sprint. There may be a series of execution Sprints that can be completed simultaneously or in succession until the audit test program is complete. Depending on the size of the audit, there may be a series of execution Sprints with varying durations. For example, there may be four execution Sprints of three weeks each, which means the execution stage may take 12 weeks. Stage three, the reporting Sprint, is timeboxed for two to four weeks and allows time for the auditors to document and present the final audit report. Agilefall is a modified approach to doing Agile using methods and tools found in original Agile frameworks and promoted by the Agile Alliance. Specifically, Agilefall requires daily meetings, audit finding discussions at the end of each Sprint, Sprint Reviews, and Sprint Retrospectives. The Agilefall auditing approach does require auditors to be Agile and to work quickly. It encourages collaboration and frequent communication. It is important to note that our clients who began their Agile audit journey using the Agilefall approach stated the reporting Sprint typically exceeds the planned timeboxed time frame of two to four weeks. We believe the missed deadline is due to the audit still *feeling* like a traditional, waterfall audit.

Our Agile audit framework applies the following:

- Customer collaboration throughout the audit
- Efficient planning based on the best available information
- Participatory auditing (Chapter 17)
- Risk-based auditing (Chapter 15)

- Quick engagements
- Scrum framework methods (Chapter 1)
- Self-managing teams (Chapter 16)
- Transparency

 ## WHAT ARE THE BENEFITS OF AGILE AUDITING?

One reason to implement Agile auditing is to harness the same benefits recognized by other early adopters of Agile auditing. Agile teaches auditors to think critically, give clients feedback and assurance quickly, educate audit stakeholders and clients on the audit process, improve transparency on the how and why of auditing, reduce bottlenecks in the audit process, and respond to risks faster.

Spiros Alexiou concisely stated, "an Agile audit gives auditors much more freedom during the engagement phase to come in contact with the system, settings, data, and the people and processes being audited. This enables a much better understanding of the issues and risks to be addressed as well as how to go about testing them in detail (e.g., what tests to devise)" (Alexiou 2017).

Next are 26 benefits our Agile auditing clients and students realized during their journey:

1. **The ability to rely more on other assurance providers in the Three Lines of Defense Model.** With the increased collaboration with other assurance providers in the second line of defense, auditors gain a higher understanding and better comfort level with the assurance work of the provider. Additionally, through increased collaboration with the business area management from the first line of defense, we develop a better sense of the control environment and risk management philosophies. Finally, since auditors may evaluate the same area multiple times each year, in Agile auditing they better understand the continuity of business practices in the first line of defense. Each of these points allows auditors to rely on the assurance work of others.

2. **A clear and direct link between audit work and business objectives.** Agile auditing's focus on the customer means we must first understand the customer and their business objectives. We must also review what matters most to the customer, which means identifying the risks they face that may affect their ability to accomplish business objectives. If there is

no direct linkage between the business objectives and risks and the audit work, do not perform the audit work and related tasks under the Agile auditing initiatives.

3. **Easy adaptations to remote auditing (tested and proven during a global pandemic).** Distant (remote) auditing is when auditors perform audits remotely from a location other than the physical location of the client. Although Agile auditing promotes co-location working collaboratively with face-to-face communications, today's technology and our new normal work environment challenges even traditional Agile projects. Today, auditors working on Agile projects are using collaboration tools and videoconferences to facilitate face-to-face collaborative environments. Technology, including data analytics, machine learning, robotics process automation, collaboration tools, and videoconferencing enables remote auditing. Technology also facilitates collaboration and reduces audit costs and waste. We discuss remote Agile auditing and the new normal in Chapter 12.

4. **Enhanced flexibility in identifying and assessing risks.** Agile auditing allows auditors to engage with audit clients early in the audit process to identify risks versus requiring auditors to preselect risks and controls before thoroughly understanding the business process. Furthermore, because of the constant collaboration, Agile auditing allows auditors and audit clients to discuss risks openly and, more importantly, assess risks with the audit client before deciding how to test the related controls in place to mitigate the risks.

5. **Fewer challenges from audit clients, especially late in the audit process.** Audit clients are involved in planning the Agile audit engagement, including stating objectives, identifying risks, assessing risks, and identifying controls. Audit clients may also help determine how to test controls. Thus, they better understand the relationship between audit tests, controls, risks, and objectives which, results in fewer "Why is that important?" challenges later in the audit process or upon receiving the audit results. Additionally, given that Agile auditing encourages testing with the audit client, the audit clients will see all the exceptions at the same time the auditor does, which reduces challenges on the factual accuracy of fieldwork testing and control evidence.

6. **Fewer missed deadlines.** Poor project management, procrastination, and failure to escalate problems early results in missed deadlines. Agile auditing directly addresses each one of these. First, there is no project manager, so the team is now solely accountable for establishing and

meeting their deadlines. There is no one to blame if budgets are not accurate because the team created the target. There is no excuse for scope creep because the team is accountable to each other to remain on task and remain focused. Second, the Agile team reports on their progress every day and other team members will notice if a team member's productivity is low. Team members will also notice procrastinators. Third, team members escalate problems in the daily standup meeting before they impact the project. Finally, in Agile auditing, the team sets and agrees on deadlines before the audit begins, and the deadlines are not flexible. When a Sprint expires, the team identifies, discusses, and backlogs any task that is not complete. The backlogged tasks may be part of a future Sprint. With experience, team members get better at determining what they can actually complete in a given time frame. The project will be completed on time regardless of outstanding tasks.

7. **Fewer redundancies in the audit process.** Agile auditors are in constant communication. They work closely together and it would be immediately apparent if two auditors are completing the same test. Through the daily Sprint, if two individuals notice a relationship in their work, they discuss the relationship and determine how to ensure no duplication of effort.

8. **Flexible processes and reporting mechanisms.** The Agile auditing framework embeds flexibility and fluidity. If something does not work for the team, the team is empowered to change it. The guidelines provided in the framework are just guidelines; the team decides how to operate with the guidelines in mind. This flexibility and adaptability are present in what the team decides to do, how the team decides to do the work, and how the team chooses to communicate the results of the engagement. Official, written audit reports may not be needed, and could possibly be redundant, in Agile auditing.

9. **Flexible talent models.** Agile audit teams are composed of cross-functional, multitalented individuals best suited to complete a specific audit. Because auditors may serve in different capacities and roles in an Agile audit, they have the opportunity to grow and learn skills that expand and complement their existing skills. Agile auditing should eliminate defining responsibilities as a function of a person's title in favor of assigning tasks based on the individual auditor's skillsets and developmental desires.

10. **Impactful, actionable audit reports.** If you chose to create an audit report, it would focus on the necessary actions to resolve identified problems. In Agile auditing, you can think of your final audit results as the

action plans or the activities needed to fix exceptions. You may consider replacing your entire audit report, including excessive language on process backgrounds, audit objectives, prior audit results, and similar report contents, with a simple list of action plans.

11. **Increased efficiency in the audit process.** A large part of Agile auditing is doing what is necessary to provide value to the customer. In other words, we execute the minimum viable product, nothing more; no extra work, no perfection. Some inefficiencies in the audit process occur because of the "we've always done it that way" mentality. Agile auditing encourages auditors to think differently about how things get done and improve how they are doing things continuously. If there is part of the audit process that doesn't make sense, team members present it as an obstacle in the daily meeting. One specific example of presenting an obstacle affecting audit efficiency occurred in the daily meeting on an audit of customer investment products. The auditors identified a required audit document that was not yet complete, an RCM summary. After the review of other documents, the auditors agreed that all the necessary elements were in other documents and it would be redundant to redocument in the RCM summary. Additionally, the tighter deadlines provided by the nature of a timebound Sprint provides the transparency needed to identify and eliminate barriers and inefficiencies.

12. **Less rework in the audit process.** Rework, particularly of audit tests, occurs long after the auditors submit test results for review. In Agile auditing, the audit clients or peer reviewers assess the documented work either as the work is performed (audit client reviewer) or shortly thereafter (peer reviewer). The reviewer must assess documented work shortly after the auditor submits the workpaper. Additionally, the work performed is discussed in the daily meeting, and Agile team members provide feedback as the auditor performs the steps to make sure the test is on task and in scope. Please note that, in Agile auditing, the review of the work does not need to occur subsequently; it is actually best to complete reviews in real time.

13. **More audits are completed in the same time frame.** One measure of an audit team's success is how many audits are "completed." Agile auditing breaks audits up into small increments. Agile auditing reduces rework and waste. These features of Agile auditing mean auditors complete more audits in the same time frame.

14. **More opportunities for data analytics in planning and performing engagements.** While auditors and audit clients work collaboratively on Agile audits, real business continues. Respecting that audit clients cannot be 100% dedicated to the Agile audit, dedicated audit clients would make

Agile auditing even more efficient. Auditors can perform some work independent of the audit client. Specifically, auditors can use data analytics techniques to understand the business, confirm business metrics and reports, identify risks, and identify exceptions that can be presented to the audit client in detail during the next collaboration meeting. Auditors work independent of the audit customer, extracting data, cleansing data, writing queries, testing queries, running queries, and identifying exceptions. It is helpful to discuss and show the processing performed by the auditor to the audit client before discussing the results and exceptions. As a bonus, once the audit client sees the benefits of the data analytics performed, they may even want to leverage the queries in their jobs after the audit. We discuss more on data analytics in Chapter 12.

15. **Less wasted effort/time.** There is a lot of waste in the audit process. Here are some examples of how Agile auditing reduces waste: As new auditors often discover, we waste a lot of time developing an understanding of a business process to identify risks. Agile auditing eliminates waste by letting the expert (the audit client) share their knowledge of the business and identify risks. Auditors use their risks and controls knowledge and the auditor's critical thinking skills to ensure the team considers all relevant risks. Auditors, particularly inexperienced auditors, waste time trying to interpret what an audit test means, especially when the test is written by someone other than the person executing the test. In Agile auditing, the team determines the audit test collaboratively and provides instant clarification when needed. Furthermore, auditors waste time attempting a test, however they interpret it, only to learn much later that they didn't perform the test correctly! Agile auditing's constant inspection would identify this error in almost real time. Moreover, we waste time writing audit findings and reports that will be edited by someone else later. The Agile team documents the results together, often in collaboration with the audit client, which means any finding is accurately written the first time without any need for back-and-forth editing. Additionally, if your Agile auditing methodology requires a report, it can be written in a collaborative environment.

16. **Shared ownership of audit completion by auditors and audit clients.** Auditors and audit clients determine what they will complete and how long it will take to complete. This approach creates ownership and accountability to finish the audit.

17. **Sharper risk focus.** By leveraging a risk universe as a Product Backlog, the Agile audit is already directed and focused on a specific risk. The Agile

team is accountable to stay within scope and avoid scope creep, even if the team identifies a shiny new control or control weakness for an unrelated risk. The Agile auditor would simply note the out-of-scope control or control weakness on the Product Backlog for consideration in a future audit.

18. **Shorter audit report delivery turnaround.** Some Agile audit teams deliver reports on the same day the Agile audit team met its Definition of Done. How did they deliver a report within hours? The Agile team, including the audit client and audit leadership, sit in a room for four hours to write the report and have simultaneous review and editing of the report.

19. **Shorter audit reports with data-based graphics and visuals.** You've heard it before – a picture is worth a thousand words. When auditors leverage data analytics in planning to understand the business, it is easy to create a graph to show the business details and metrics. When Agile auditors leverage data analytics to identify risks, they use distribution charts and parts-to-whole images to display risks. Furthermore, when Agile auditors use data to identify exceptions, outliers, and out of control situations, visual control charts, ranking charts, and deviation graphs summarize the exceptions. An excellent reference to enable you to shift from simply showing data to storytelling with data, is the book by Cole Nussbaumer Knaflic, *Storytelling with Data* (Nussbaumer Knaflic 2015).

20. **Support for transitioning to a dynamic risk assessment process.** Risks change constantly. Static, traditional annual audit plans do not allow auditors to respond to risks as quickly as they change. Instead, implementing flexible processes and leveraging data aids in performing dynamic risk assessments provides the flexibility to audit the most prominent risks.

21. **Ability to develop leadership skills.** Agile auditing empowers every auditor and provides opportunities to lead at any level.

22. **Knowledge growth for auditors.** Working closely with knowledge business experts allows auditors to learn more about the processes than simply reading about them or asking questions in a one- or two-hour walkthrough.

23. **More engaged auditors and audit clients.** Agile audits require auditor and audit customer engagement.

24. **Increased transparency in the audit process.** Close collaboration with the audit clients and including the audit clients in the behind-the-scenes communications provide insight into the how and why of auditing. Additionally, auditors should encourage and answer questions about the

audit process, including why the auditor is requesting some documentation (except for fraud investigations).

25. **Robust collaboration and teamwork with other auditors, audit clients, and assurance providers** (e.g., compliance functions, enterprise risk management, management control testers, or information security). Collaboration with others enables a more vigorous and effective control environment; it supports and collaborates the integrity of the information used for the audit as well as for internal decision-making by management. Collaboration creates a collective and more complete view of risks across the organization, which helps establish an enterprise-wide risk assessment approach to better manage risks across the organization as a whole. Face it, collaboration is about effectively coordinating all management including management and assurance providers up to top level executives in the organization; thus, in turn increasing collaboration, getting assurance in the right areas, and making sure resources are used effectively.

26. **Happy auditors.** Let's face it; most people do not like being audited. Unfortunately, sometimes there is no attempt to conceal one's dislike of being audited, even their dislike of auditors. Apparent or perceived dislike means auditors may feel unwanted. After years of being an auditor, feeling unwanted may influence how much you like your career choice or even how happy you are as an individual. A survey conducted by CareerExplorer, a comprehensive source of career data and information, asked individuals (over one million participants) how satisfied they were with their careers, revealed that "auditors rate their career happiness 2.5 out of 5 stars which puts them in the bottom 4% of careers" (CareerExplorer by Sokanu 2020). Have you ever felt like an outsider even though you were an employee-internal auditor for an organization? Has this affected your happiness score? The good news is, many of our auditor friends who complete Agile audits tell us they feel happy and like being an auditor in an Agile auditing environment. We can relate. Agile auditing creates a sense of belonging to a team or organization as a whole. Believe it or not, some of our auditors are regularly invited back to audit more processes because of prior value they have delivered to the business unit.

We hope you will find more benefits, though 26 from one approach is not a bad start.

CAN AGILE AUDITING HELP ME SOLVE PROBLEMS IN THE AUDIT PROCESS?

Another reason to implement Agile auditing is to help solve problems encountered in the traditional audit project. Remember, this is where our journey started on that warm evening in California (see the Preface). Agile auditing fixes 40 problems repeatedly experienced during traditional audits. The following list includes the 40 problems listed in order of the audit life cycle we collected through the years in our project management, Agile auditing, and root cause analysis courses. If Agile auditing does not directly fix the problem, it solves the root causes of the problems by building better relationships and changing the perceptions of auditors. The 40 problems include:

1. Low time budgets/estimates to complete audits
2. Unreasonable audit deadlines
3. Poorly defined supervisor expectations
4. Uncommunicated audit leadership expectations
5. Audit clients not attending entrance meetings
6. Not enough time to plan audits thoroughly
7. Too many assumptions based on procedures when determining test steps
8. Unclear audit test steps
9. Scope limitations by audit clients
10. Scope creep by auditors
11. Scope creep by audit leadership
12. Audit leadership changing audit direction in the middle of the audit
13. Scope creep by an audit client
14. Auditors getting placed on special projects during an audit
15. Data analytics failures
16. Analysis paralysis when using data analytics
17. Wasted time waiting for audit evidence that doesn't exist
18. Wasted time waiting for audit client responses to emails
19. Audit clients providing irrelevant evidence
20. Audit clients providing incomplete evidence
21. Incomplete workpapers
22. Irrelevant information in workpapers
23. Retaining too much information to "prove" work performed
24. Workpapers not supporting testing summary and conclusions
25. Perfecting workpapers
26. Unreasonable audit supervisor expectations

27. Nitpicky workpaper review notes
28. Too much time spent capturing hours worked on audits
29. Poorly written audit findings
30. Audit reports with too much "fluff"
31. Audit reports that don't state the right message
32. Audit reports that conceal what's really wrong
33. Audit reports that take months to write
34. Audit reports with a lot of internal back-and-forth between internal audit leadership
35. Audit reports with a lot of internal back-and-forth with audit clients
36. Audit reports that anger audit clients
37. Exit conferences with fiery discussions between auditors and audit clients/ executives
38. Low ratings on audit customer satisfaction surveys
39. Never receiving feedback on auditor performance
40. Failing an internal quality assessment review

This list of problems/issues is probably not complete. One noticeable shortcoming of the list is that all the problems are from the auditor's perspective and should likely include frustrations from the audit client perspective. You may not have experienced each of the issues listed – or maybe you have – and you are looking for solutions. As you look over the list, you may notice that many of the audit-related problems are people-related problems. Remember, Agile is people-oriented and while it is not a people management principle, you need the people skills, including interpersonal skills and emotional intelligence, to get the project done. For now, we'll leave this list right here and come back to the Agile auditing solutions for each problem as we discuss Agile auditing by the audit life cycle phase in Part II, Chapters 7 through 11 on implementing Agile auditing.

We don't know about your perspective, but if there were a tool that would add 26 benefits and solve 40 problems, it would be at the top of our list to start using. If you still aren't convinced that Agile auditing is a tool you need today, consider it as a tool that future generations of auditors will demand.

The auditing profession and practice needs to change to continue to attract future auditors, specifically those from the emerging generations. The mindset of emerging generations, including millennials, gen-Y, and gen-Z, is different from that of mature generations (i.e., baby boomers and gen-X) in today's workforce. Emerging generations have other work habits. Emerging generations are tech-savvy. Individuals in gen-Y and gen-Z are accustomed to changing a song they don't want to hear with the swipe of a finger or their voice. When they get bored, they select another app, a different game, or even a separate piece of technology. They demand constant stimulation and, in our experience, get bored quickly when not simulated.

Speaking as gen-Xers, we learned to just deal with boredom and moved forward and be persistent even when bored; boredom was typical. The following example reflects the life of a bored gen-Xer. Imagine sitting in the backseat of a blue 1976 Chevrolet Nova for five hours as your parent drove through the Appalachian Mountains in West Virginia towing a pop-up camper for a summer vacation. Imagine the long, slow ride where your only enjoyment was watching the trees go by, sliding around on the slick backseats that didn't have seatbelts, on a sharp switchback curve, experiencing the thrill of cresting a hill too quickly or riding a little too close to the cliff without a guardrail. There was nothing you could do about the long, boring journey that felt like it had no end in sight. There were no personal devices to play music, watch movies, or otherwise offer any entertainment. You were stuck on that long journey with only the trees, hills, cliffs, and family radio playing country music. Our traditional approach to auditing feels like this sometimes. Sometimes you may feel like you are on the audit that will never end. Will these new generation's auditors be patient enough to wait three months or more to finish a project, start something new, or learn a new skill? Probably not! Agile auditing will satisfy the emerging generation's need to be continuously challenged and stimulated.

 NUGGETS

Now that Agile auditing has been around for a while – it was 2011 when we started creating our framework and 2013 when we first started speaking on Agile auditing at conferences – we can confirm many benefits realized at 25 organizations or more. Agile auditing benefits include empowered, engaged, and happier auditors, reduced audit cycles, increased collaboration with audit customers and stakeholders, and increased transparency in the audit process. Agile auditing also solves problems encountered in the audit process, such as eliminating scope creep and time wasted waiting for responses to requests, testing low-priority risks and controls, and documenting "perfect" workpapers. Your organization can harness the benefits of Agile auditing by adding more value and providing timely information so your organization can achieve its goals. Start thinking about your strategy and getting auditor, audit client, and organizational buy-in on Agile auditing today.

CHAPTER SIX

Creating the Agile Mindset

 ## WHAT IS AN AGILE MINDSET?

An Agile mindset is about being nimble, adaptable, and able to adjust quickly to meet the shifting needs of the business environment driven by the customer. It's about responding to change in uncertain and unpredictable environments. An Agile mindset focuses on delivering value for customers, working in small teams with short cycles, and delivering products or results quickly. It's about thinking through, evaluating, and understanding what is happening in the environment, identifying potential uncertainties, and adapting as you proceed.

Create an Agile mindset, and everything else will follow. Remember that for Agile auditing to work, you and your team, including your audit client, must have both the Agile mindset and the ability to do Agile auditing. The mindset starts with the Agile Manifesto. Encourage your auditors to read the Agile Manifesto and provide their interpretations and thoughts on what each statement may mean when applied to auditing.

For example, what would life be like if auditors focused on "individuals and interactions over processes and tools"? Would auditors communicate with clients face-to-face or via videoconferencing, instead of relying on email tools to serve as our primary communication modality?

The next statement in the Agile Manifesto requires explanation, but ask your auditors anyway. What would life be like if we focused on "working

105

software over comprehensive documentation"? Sometimes, we feel like we can see the hope in auditors' eyes when they read this statement; maybe we've even seen a shimmer of a tear of joy. Why? Because somehow auditors misinterpret this as "no workpapers"! That isn't what the manifesto statement says. It implies that we can reduce our documentation, not that we will stop documenting work performed. To achieve this, we need to be deliberate about recording enough relevant information, and not spending excessive time creating perfect workpapers at the expense of providing timely insight and assurance on governance, risk management, and controls. We will explore how to document workpapers in an Agile audit in Chapter 10, Implementing Agile Audit: Executing the Agile Audit.

Additionally, auditors need to consider that we "produce" assurance that the right things are happening and inform management when we find control weaknesses concerning achieving organizational objectives. Sometimes auditors disregard this manifesto statement ("working software over comprehensive documentation") because we do not produce software. Ask your auditors to consider this statement. In audit terminology, this can read "Relevant and timely recommendations over comprehensive audit reports and workpapers." Now that we've clarified that point, let's move forward with the rest of the manifesto.

What would life be like if auditors "focused on customer collaboration over contract negotiation"? Contract negotiation can be haggling over how many items to test, when to test, or even whether something is in scope or not. Contract negotiation could also be internal negotiation on requirements to conform to professional standards. Could auditors work with the audit client to decide how to test controls? Could we test controls together with the audit client? Could we let the client help write audit findings, using their chosen words? And if the audit client did write the findings, could we review the results for accuracy and publish them in our report without further review and wordsmithing?

Finally, if auditors and audit plans "responded to change instead of following a plan," would that mean that our world would be chaotic? Would auditors feel out of control? Would auditors feel more empowered to change audit tests that don't make sense or replace manual tests with data analytics?

Getting auditors involved by analyzing the Agile framework is a precious exercise in our Agile auditing classes. We're willing to bet that you will find it a valuable training to educate your auditors on the Agile Manifesto. Moreover, we think you'll discover that this is a great technique to include auditors in the design and development of your Agile process, so they take ownership of and buy in to your Agile auditing methodology.

BUILD A PASSION FOR BEING AGILE

The Agile team must believe in the Agile Manifesto. When auditors analyze and interpret the manifesto, they develop an understanding of it, which is the first step in believing in it. Ask your auditors to examine the entire manifesto and interpret it into audit activities as we noted earlier. Some audit teams choose to create an Agile auditing manifesto to guide the team. Perhaps you could have a contest for auditors to write your Agile auditing manifesto to increase the team's buy-in on Agile auditing. Here are examples of two Agile auditing manifestos:

A financial services entity wrote:

By applying Agile project management principles, we are creating innovative ways of auditing.

▪ We value working with people over processes and tools.
▪ We value providing timely insights over comprehensive documentation.
▪ We value client collaboration and relationship building over objectivity concerns.
▪ We value doing what's right and adding value over following a static plan.

A manufacturing company provided this Agile auditing manifesto:

To be innovative and responsive, we have come to value the following:

▪ Being outcome- and value-driven.
▪ Doing the right projects with the correct depth and focus.
▪ Collaborating, co-locating, and working together daily.
▪ Challenging "that's the way we've always done it."
▪ Decisioning as we go with emphasis on transparency and organizational alignment.
▪ Continually communicating with Agile teams and stakeholders.

The manifesto cannot just be words on paper or hung on a wall. That isn't going to create Agile teams or make people believe in the Agile team any more than forcing Agile teams to recite the manifesto. Think about people who read lyrics or sing songs word for word; that doesn't mean they believe in or even understand the lyrics. It's apparent when someone believes in the music; they sing it with passion, often out of pitch and at the top of their lungs, their energy increases when they sing it, and they can explain it to others. What can you do to get your auditors to believe in your Agile Manifesto? How do you know if they even care?

START WITH AUDITOR SELF-ASSESSMENTS

We recommend that each auditor do a self-assessment to gauge how strongly they feel about their ability and interest to incorporate the following into their daily thinking, beliefs, attitudes, and behaviors. One approach we used was to have each auditor gauge their ability on a scale from "highly competent" to "require significant development" and rank their interest in each from most important to least important.

Action-Oriented

Agile project management is about completing actions, not talking about completing actions. We need to get work done. Additionally, for Agile auditing, we need to focus on the actions necessary to fix identified weaknesses.

Collaborate

To collaborate is to work jointly with another to produce or create something. Audits stall without audit clients providing information, evidence, and data in a timely manner. Auditors, audit teams, and audit clients must collaborate to complete the audit.

Co-locate

Agile teams need to reach each other, communicate often, share information, reduce wasted steps, and minimize delays. Whether you are in a remote setting, virtual environment, or physical location, teams should work together in the same "room" frequently. In a virtual environment, when the team's agreed workday begins, each Team Member should log in to the collaborative system, with their cameras on, as though they were sitting around a collaborate workspace (e.g., conference table) to complete the audit.

Innovate

Agile teams seek new methods, introduce new ideas, and work creatively to achieve outcomes. Auditing hasn't changed much in decades. Even though we talk about being innovative, we need to act on groundbreaking ideas. For example, auditors have talked about using data analytics throughout an audit for decades; however, few auditors use data analytics outside of a few select tests. Moreover, fewer auditors use data analytics in the planning and reporting activities of audits.

Iterate

Being iterative is achieving a result through a series of repeated iterations. In auditing, this means breaking up more extensive audits into smaller iterations and completing each iteration until the audit team provides assurance on the risk management, governance, or controls assessed. Performing iterative audits results in delivery of timely insight. Since iterations are quickly completed, the entire Agile team stays motivated. The Agile audit doesn't feel like the audit that just won't end!

Nimble

Auditors need to be quick to comprehend and take action.

Promote Efficacy

Efficacy is the ability to produce a desired or intended result (Oxford Dictionary 2020a). Think of efficacy as completing a task well to meet an expectation. For Agile auditors, our desired outcome is to provide value-added assurance services by helping the organization improve governance, risk management, and controls to achieve organizational objectives.

Quick

Agile audits are quick. They require constant, consistent energy.

Relevant

Agile auditors should consider how relevant they want to be to the organization by adding continuous value. Furthermore, Agile auditors need to be critical of their assessments to ensure they are looking at the right things. The right things are the things that matter most to the organization – achieving objectives.

Responsive

When an organization or client needs change, auditors must respond and adapt. As challenges arise, auditors need to find creative ways to resolve them.

Empowered

Agile teams have the authority and power to make decisions and do what they feel is right to achieve a goal. Auditors should be okay with making decisions and recognize if a decision is wrong. Auditors are also empowered to respond and change decisions.

Focused

In Agile auditing, we are specifically referring to being risk-focused and not easily distracted by trivial errors or weaknesses.

Informed

Being informed is having knowledge or understanding of a specific subject. Auditors don't need to be subject matter experts for every area of the organization, but they *do* need to have the desire to become informed on the audit areas assigned and the ability to know how to leverage subject matter experts to gain the knowledge required.

Self-Motivated

There is nothing worse than feeling like you need to push a Team Member to do something. It is frustrating for all parties if a Team Member isn't self-motivated to achieve a common goal.

Transparency

Shedding light on the how and why of auditing is a benefit to all parties. Get comfortable with discussing the details of the audit and the audit results without the need for preapproval. After all, if you are doing it right, the audit client is already on board.

Openness

Auditors must be willing to say what they mean and be honest and open. Openness includes auditors sharing workpapers before they are final, versus keeping them on their computer hard drives so others can't see their draft/ unfinished products.

Auditors who feel strongly in favor of these ideas will find early success with Agile. Others may need a little more persuasion to adopt Agile auditing, including seeing others applying Agile concepts, finding their success, and maybe even displaying their passion. One way to persuade others is to increase transparent communication. Let other auditors openly and transparently communicate their experiences with Agile audits. Additionally, perhaps you will evaluate the auditor self-assessments to determine which auditors are Agile-ready versus which auditors need more persuasion. You can also ask auditors if they believe they are Agile-ready or what they need to become Agile-ready.

You should also request auditors to self-assess their soft skills. Audits and projects happen with people, and collaboration intensifies during Agile audit projects. Being skilled in the following areas is critical to the success of Agile audit projects:

- Building emotional intelligence
- Building relationships
- Building trust
- Communicating with the right modality
- Communicating effectively, orally and in writing
- Displaying empathy
- Interviewing/asking questions
- Listening
- Managing change
- Managing conflict
- Motivating others
- Negotiating techniques
- Persuading others
- Presenting information
- Reading people
- Speaking publicly
- Thinking critically
- Using language skills and linguistics
- Valuing diversity, including generational diversity

Agile is not about processes, techniques, and tools. Agile *is* about how we can work together to achieve a common goal.

Agile is a journey for continuous improvement.

To create the right mindset, auditors and audit clients must recognize that Agile is not about processes, techniques, and tools. Agile *is* about how we can work together to achieve a common goal. Agile is a journey of continuous improvement. It is okay to try new approaches and make mistakes; we want to identify the mistakes early and make improvements to add value.

After auditor assessments with clients and through the life span of our training courses, we've realized there are some unyielding auditors who have a mantra of "that's the way we've always done it, and it's fine." For these auditors, consider whether or not you can ever bring them along on your Agile auditing journey. You may need creative solutions to deal with your stubborn auditors.

DO I NEED TO CALL IT AGILE AUDITING?

The short answer to "Do I need to call it Agile auditing?" is no. You can call this new approach to audit anything you want. However, before naming it, consider the following:

- Will the name reflect what the new approach is?
- Will the name be different enough to remind the stubborn human brain that we are auditing differently?
- What is the perception of auditing with our audit clients?
- If we pick a different name, perhaps one that doesn't include auditing, will audit clients still refer to it as an audit?
- Are other parts of the organization or other professionals within the organization familiar with Agile?
- Will others refer to it as Agile, even if we don't call it Agile?
- How often will we need to explain the new audit approach and how it has changed?

We pose these questions because of two specific experiences. The first experience was in 2012 when a chief audit executive wanted to change the name of its Internal Audit Division (IAD). The former name of this division was the Internal Security and Audit Division. We admit that the abbreviation of the previous name, iSAD, wasn't particularly appealing and perpetuated a negative perception of auditors. Temporarily, auditors from this division renamed it iHappy, though that didn't stick, and unfortunately, the negative perception of iSAD lingered even with the new name and abbreviation of

IAD. The proposed new name, the Change Agent Division, or Effectiveness Division, wasn't much more appealing because people don't like, and often resist, change.

Moreover, audit clients and stakeholders surveyed said the name didn't really matter, and, in the end, everyone would still know it was an audit function. So, why change the name at all? A light-hearted auditor is always desirable. We would probably even create a meme or department logo playing off the iSAD acronym . . . but that is just us!

The second experience was in 2019, when one of our clients who practiced Agile auditing prior to our involvement began to notice resentment toward anything "Agile-esque." We were even told not to mention our involvement with pioneering Agile auditing or even reference some of their current practices endorsed by Agile frameworks, such as daily check-ins (daily standup meetings) and lessons learned (retrospective meetings). As you can see, they already changed the traditional names of their Agile practices to start to disassociate with "Agile" methods. We asked, "Why is there such a stigma about Agile auditing?" Our question was never really answered, but we suspect it was because the change was only in language and not in the auditors' mindsets.

RECIPE: GETTING AUDITOR BUY-IN

It is best to have auditor buy-in early in your Agile journey. In our experience, several techniques work well to build auditor commitment:

1. Delegate the design and implementation to respected audit peers.
2. Hold workgroup sessions to educate on Agile principles and Agile auditing options and defer to a designated team of peers to decide how to implement Agile auditing.
3. Provide training and support for interested auditors to obtain Agile designations and certifications.
4. Select and handpick a group of change agents and thought leaders with open minds from existing audit resources to pilot your Agile audit.
5. Demonstrate how adopting an Agile audit environment will allow an audit activity to pass the Quality Assessment Review (QAR) (see Chapter 18).
6. Create a marketing or promotional video featuring audit peers who successfully completed Agile audits.
7. Ask for volunteers who want to adopt the new approach to auditing.

NUGGETS

Our first failure in implementing Agile auditing was due, in part, to our failure to recognize the importance of creating the right mindset before we implemented Agile auditing. Audit teams can help auditors build the right mindset. Use some of the techniques presented in this chapter, including auditor analysis of the Agile Manifesto and self-assessment of their beliefs, attitudes, behaviors, interests, and interpersonal skills, to build the Agile mindset. Also, recognize that you can't force someone to change their mind. You can present information, facts, and statistics, but developing the right mindset must come from within each audit professional.

PART TWO

2

Implementing Agile Auditing

7

Implementing Agile Auditing: Deciding Your Approach and Your Agile Audit Project Roles

 CHOOSING YOUR IMPLEMENTATION STRATEGY

Now that you know the benefits of Agile auditing and the problems that Agile auditing can help you resolve you can answer the following question: Does Agile auditing seem right for you? If so, you should start thinking about the right strategy to implement Agile auditing. We don't want you to get too far ahead of yourself, so don't pick your plan yet. We are introducing the three implementation options: full Agile, pilot Agile, and Agile lite. Your plan may be one of these options or a combination of possibilities.

You should evaluate which implementation technique works best for you, your audit team, and your organization. Our clients experienced successes and failures in each strategy. Agile is adaptive, and there is not a one-size-fits-all, right way of doing Agile. Agile auditing frameworks should not restrict adaptability. We provide helpful tips and ideas to increase your chances of Agile auditing success, so your organization can experience the full benefits of this approach to completing audit projects. Let's take a high-level look at the three strategies.

Full Agile Strategy

We fondly call the full Agile strategy the "all-in" approach. If you are a poker player, you already know the concept of all-in and when to use this strategy in a game. If you don't play poker, we call this the all-in approach because you are putting all of your money in, and you will either win the hand or lose it all and be out of the game; thus, you should be sure that you have the winning hand. We recommend going all-in if you have adequately assessed your culture, resources, methodology, and desire for change transformation. This assessment is akin to how you consider your fellow players, your hand, the cards on the table, and your appetite for risk in a poker hand. Full Agile auditing is a transformation, and the evolution may take years.

The full Agile strategy is the most aggressive of the three because it involves evolving existing audit systems and procedures to create efficient processes and add more value to the organization. Implementation of the full Agile strategy works well in the following situations:

- Audit leadership has socialized or plans to socialize Agile concepts before implementation.
- Your organization has implemented Agile project management approaches beyond IT system development, and the organization expects all aspects of the business to adopt Agile.
- Audit teams need a drastic change to become relevant, change perceptions, change audit processes, and add value. Auditors performing audits (bottom-up), audit clients, organization leaders, and governance groups, including boards, regulators, and other auditors (top-down), have communicated this need. They have a burning desire for change and are ready to be a part of it.

Management's interest in and commitment to collaborating with audit teams using Agile principles is essential to the success of a full Agile strategy. Audit teams need auditor, client, senior leadership, audit committee, and board buy-in for this approach to work effectively. Auditors should receive training on Agile concepts. Moreover, if organizational training is available, auditors should participate in the training with other employees, including audit customers. While it is preferred, it is not essential to have a defined Agile auditing methodology specific to your department. Many adopting the full Agile strategy create their Agile auditing methodology as they move through their evolution. We provided recipes to aid in transitioning the Agile auditing framework to a methodology. Also, remember that Agile means being adaptive. You will likely modify your methods as auditors complete a few Agile audits. There is a misconception that if we implement full Agile, we can't adapt. A principle of Agile is making mistakes and adapting quickly.

Pilot Agile Strategy

The pilot Agile adoption strategy is the strategy which we've seen have the most success. Pilot Agile auditing does not require substantial upfront socialization and communication outside of audit as the full Agile approach does. Audit leadership identifies select areas it believes would be open to collaborating more with the auditors to get the audits completed faster. We recommend selecting "easy" or common areas to audit to build confidence in the auditor's Agile abilities. Auditors still need to be trained on Agile, and some guidance is required to help the auditors perform the audit under Agile principles and professional standards. For the pilot Agile audit strategy, audit teams develop the audit methodology after the pilot audits. After soliciting auditor and audit client feedback on the techniques that worked best, the process adopts best practices from the "successful" Agile audits.

In the pilot adoption strategy, auditors may also pilot Agile auditing with the follow-up and monitoring of management's corrective actions that resulted from traditional audits. Beginning with the follow-up process is our preferred approach to initially exploring Agile auditing. The advantages of using the follow-ups include:

- The area's knowledge already exists.
- The scope is already focused.
- Remediation verification activities require less time to complete.

Additionally, formal reporting in the follow-up is not as robust, and it is a great way to explore creatively communicating results (see Chapter 11, Implementing Agile Auditing: Communicating Agile Audit Results).

Agile Lite Strategy

The Agile lite strategy selects specific Agile techniques and tools that are helpful to any audit team. Agile lite is a common strategy for audit teams working on being Agile and seeking to recognize the benefits of some Agile techniques. In this approach, auditors embed selected Agile practices into existing traditional, waterfall audits. Our favorite Agile techniques to include in every audit include:

1. **Break down audits and related audit tasks into manageable time-bound pieces.** On a few occasions, we carefully considered how long each audit task should take. Our approach was simple: ask the auditor how long each task usually takes or track the time to complete one example of the test. Then determine an average of the time to complete the step and multiply the time taken by the number of times they complete the action. For example, ask the auditors how long it takes them to complete a walk-through to understand a process fully. Remember, each auditor works at different speeds depending on skills and experience, so keep this in mind as you develop your timebound pieces. Another example is when you are testing 30 samples, ask the auditor to time how long it takes them to test three items, then multiply that time by 10. You can also time how long it takes to write a related workpaper and determine the ratio of the time it took to complete the work to the time it takes to document the workpaper. In several instances, we were surprised to discover that preparing supporting workpapers consistently took nearly double the amount of time required to perform the audit test. Twice the amount of time to write a workpaper to document for auditors, audit supervisors, and future auditors seems excessive and does not add value to the audit client. To be Agile, scrutinize current workpaper standards and decide on the essential workpaper elements in an Agile auditing environment (see Chapter 10, Implementing Agile Auditing: Executing the Agile Audit).

2. **Use consistent, short durations for your audits.** Consistent audit durations help auditors better estimate how much work they can complete in specific time frames. Quick audits allow auditors to stay focused on completing work and to limit procrastination. Creating this baseline also helps auditors become faster as they become more experienced and increases auditor accountability.

3. **Hold audit planning meetings with audit leadership, auditors, and audit clients.** Planning with the audit clients builds relationships with Agile team members, increases transparency in the auditing process, and shows audit clients that auditors are interested in what is best for them and the organization. To emphasize an auditor's interest in what matters most to the audit client and organization, use business objectives, risks, and controls to focus your audit planning meetings. These planning meetings may take four hours. Schedule breaks, provide coffee (we found adding

doughnuts increases attendance), and create a meeting agenda, so audit clients can determine when they are needed most if they can't attend the entire meeting. Chapter 9, Implementing Agile Auditing: Planning Agile Audit Engagements, provides an example of an audit planning meeting outside the Agile auditing context.

4. **Create project taskboards and make them visible to all interested parties.** In a physical environment, rolling whiteboards kept in an open, accessible area works well. In a remote/virtual environment, consider using one of the many technology-based solutions for Agile projects (e.g., collaboration tools, or Agile project-specific tools. Examples of these technologies include: Nrby, Monday.com, Bloomfire, Trello, ClickUp, Smartsheet, Asana, Aprio, Beekeeper, Forecast, Asana, Hygger, Jira, Proggio, Agile Taskboard, Backlog, and Wrik, just to mention a few).

5. **Hold a meeting every day at the same time for no more than 15 minutes.** Be consistent and devoted to holding this daily meeting; no exceptions. In a physical environment, organize and conduct the meeting around the project taskboard, which allows for real-time changes to the taskboard. In a remote setting, use videoconferencing technology and screen sharing to display the project taskboard. This daily meeting is in place of, not in addition to, weekly status update meetings.

6. **Hold a review meeting periodically, typically every other week.** Review meetings are held to discuss complete and incomplete tasks and decide whether unfinished tasks are still necessary to complete or if an activity can be scoped out of the audit.

7. **Hold a "lessons learned" meeting at the end of each audit.** This will help audit leaders, auditors, and audit clients determine what can be improved on the next increment or audit.

> Whether you choose the full, pilot, or lite Agile strategies using our framework or other methodologies, you can't go wrong when adding Agile auditing to your toolbelt.

Regardless of your implementation strategy, you must carefully consider delivery risks (see Chapter 2, What Is Audit?, for more information on delivery risks). Because you are timebound to complete a Sprint in less than one month, and preferably two weeks, failing to identify any delivery risk event and make quick decisions on how to respond will jeopardize your Agile audit completion date, which cannot be extended. If the delivery risk does not affect your completion date, it will increase the number of incomplete tasks at the end of the Sprint, which is equally undesirable.

 DEALING WITH TITLES

Some challenges will be faced when you're implementing Agile auditing. One of those challenges is breaking the mindset of having a "boss" or "manager" during the Agile audit. This mindset is ingrained in our concept of professional work: we work to get ahead. Getting ahead is often defined as getting a promotion and a more senior title.

Once, a friend was handpicked by a CEO for a lateral move because of his phenomenal efforts in establishing better governance, including developing internal audit policies and procedures, establishing a risk management program, implementing a governance, risk, and control (GRC) system, and managing a crisis response team for a global pandemic. He was excited about the transition to a more significant governance role, which did not exist previously; excited, that is, until he learned his title changed from "Internal Audit Manager" to "Governance Consultant." He felt like it was a demotion; it broke his heart. Why? Because we tend to tie ourselves and our success to a job title.

On the other end of the job title spectrum, some see additional responsibilities as an opportunity to prove their readiness for the next promotion to senior, lead, supervisor, manager, director, and are excited to show their advancement with a new job title. Do you recall the first time you had supervisory responsibilities? Maybe your boss asked you to review someone else's workpapers? Were you excited? Did it feel like the opportunity took an eternity to arrive? Even if it wasn't officially a lead title, did you jump at the chance? Were you confident that you would get promoted to an audit lead or manager if you did the job well? Were you devastated when you got all the extra work, but not a title? We've been in similar situations many times. If only professional life wasn't tied to titles. Well, good news, in Agile, it isn't.

For Agile auditing to be successful, we need to forget about titles. In Agile, we don't have a manager. If we rigidly adhere to the Agile principles, there's not one person who's leading the project. The lack of a project leader or manager in Agile auditing means a supervisor is not reviewing workpapers and making sure the audit achieves the engagement objectives. A lead auditor or audit manager does not ensure the quality of work per internal policies, procedures, and professional standards. A manager is not present to determine the project tasks, create the project plan or audit program, or determine if the audit added value. If there is no manager, no identified leader, who selects audit tasks? Who approves an audit program? Who makes sure the audit project is complete? Who moves the audit along to meet deadlines? Who verifies the accuracy of workpapers? Who ensures the achievement of audit objectives?

"Who" isn't *a person* in Agile; it is the self-managing Agile team. The Agile team is left to its own devices to complete an audit on time, adhere to quality expectations, and add value to the customer. In Agile, everyone is a Team Member. You hold yourself and each other accountable to get the job done the right way. In Chapter 16, Building the Auditor Toolbelt and Self-Managing Agile Audit Teams, we discuss what your organization needs to do to build self-managing audit teams and what to avoid if you want to have effective self-managing teams.

Before introducing and discussing Scrum roles, let's briefly mention a new radical alternative to command-and-control-style management where using titles are the norm. "'Grateful Leadership' is a style of leadership that is somewhat newer than other styles of leadership" (Parente 2019). Each of the three roles in Scrum can adopt this style, as titles are not necessary. "It speaks to the fundamentals of providing acknowledgment for people on your team, what they do, and how they contribute." Further, Parente makes a connection between this style of leadership and Agile project management. This management style is vital in influencing a culture that supports Agile and successful self-managing Agile teams (see Chapter 17 for additional discussion on how "Grateful Leadership" influences the organization's culture). Parente recognizes that "it's difficult to do work when you don't feel appreciated. Have you ever felt that way? Both Servant Leadership, as well as Grateful Leadership, allow one to influence without authority." These leadership styles are critical for Agile projects where you may be a Team Member, Product Owner, or even a project manager (Parente 2019).

As previously discussed in Chapter 1, the only three recognized roles in Scrum are:

1. Product Owner
2. Scrum Master
3. Delivery Team (Developers)

Following is a discussion of the Scrum roles and skills needed to be effective in these roles. We also provide examples of teams using Agile principles.

Product Owner

Officially, the Product Owner is ultimately responsible for defining the work that needs to be completed and prioritizing it. The Product Owner is also responsible for approving the completion and delivery of the product and sets the vision for the audit, prioritizes upcoming audits, assesses the value proposition, and manages stakeholders. The Product Owner works closely with the team during the planning phase of an Agile audit and less during audit fieldwork, although they remain actively involved throughout the audit. The Product Owner will stay informed of the audit's progress by attending the daily meetings. As a supplement to the daily meetings, the Product Owner may meet with the Scrum Master.

In forming our first Agile audit methodology, the process owner or executive management and the chief audit executive (CAE) shared the Product Owner role. This shared role, or "co–Product Owners," seemed natural since someone must represent the customer's voice in Scrum. It was apparent to us that a member of the audit team needed to be the Product Owner given the nature of auditing and the independent assurance auditors provide. We also felt that collaborating with the process owner was the right approach because of the values-based view of Agile projects and emphasis on serving our clients. After all, who would be better at representing the customer's voice and determining if the audit provided value than the process owner?

However, for regulators and other stakeholders relying on audit's independent and objective assurance, having process owners or company executives as the Product Owner, making the final determination of whether the audit was complete, was problematic. It was also challenging because the co–Product Owner role was not clear. If you've ever tried to "co" anything, you probably know that well-defined roles and responsibilities are critical for success. Ill-defined roles and responsibilities result in duplicating meetings, conflicting directions, frustrating communications, and missed deadlines, particularly when you believe the other person is doing something they're not. Failing to clarify the roles and responsibilities of the co–Product Owner roles was a great lesson to learn, twice.

As regulators and external auditors challenged our first methodology, a few great questions arose. What if we didn't focus on the right customer? Do we want the customer heavily involved in the audit results? Is the customer too involved in the audit? What if we focused on the end user? What if we focused on other stakeholders?

In the second version of the methodology, which we now offer as a framework, we insisted that the head of the audit team serve as the Product Owner.

The head auditor, as the Product Owner, is aligned with professional standards for assurance and attestation engagements. As required by professional standards, the auditor must determine the scope of engagements, and the conclusion is the auditor's opinion. A sole Product Owner is more natural for smaller audit shops, which perform fewer audits, and is very challenging for large and extra-large audit teams. For large and extra-large audit teams, relying on one Product Owner for all audit projects is not manageable. Currently, we are more flexible with who serves as the Product Owner. For most of our Agile auditing clients, the Product Owner is a leader in the audit team who reports to the CAE. However, we have seen audit managers serve as Product Owners with great success, due, in part, to having the right skills.

Skills for Product Owners

The following skills are essential for Product Owners to have, to increase their effectiveness and the project's success:

- **Provide leadership:** While not the "leader" of the team, Product Owners, like all team members, need leadership skills. Leaders build trust, inspire and encourage others, and reward achievements. Additionally, a leader promotes integrity. These "lead from the top" behaviors encourage the team to demonstrate the same actions as they work together to achieve a common goal. A Product Owner must have empowerment and decisiveness.
- **Allow flexibility:** The Product Owner provides guidance and may provide suggestions. However, the Product Owner needs flexibility with setting expectations, especially with how the team decides to deliver the product.
- **Listen attentively:** The Product Owner listens to the customer to understand their needs and listens to the team to verify the team is delivering the right product. Being incredibly attentive to feedback and questions submitted by the Scrum Master and team ensures that the product satisfies the customer's needs.
- **Present articulately:** The Product Owner's articulate presentation of the product's vision, goal, and expectations serves to inform the team and provide direction. Additionally, the Product Owner contributes to the demonstration of the iteration and delivery of product results to the customer.
- **Communicate effectively:** A Product Owner must be skilled at communicating the customer's needs to the team. The Product Owner is the customer's representative. If the group is deciding on a course of action that does not align with the customer's interests, the Product Owner must communicate the discrepancy.

- **Influence positively:** Product Owners influence customers and Agile teams to deliver the products needed for the organization's benefit. The Product Owner does not manage the team.

- **Negotiate for a win-win outcome:** Skilled negotiators recognize when negotiation is needed by assessing the situation based on the people's interests and the problem. Based on the assessment, negotiators seek a collaborative agreement or compromise to reach an agreeable solution for all parties. To get the agreement, the negotiator understands both the science and the art of negotiating.

- **Demonstrate empathy:** Agile teams work very hard to deliver a quality product on time. If the team cannot provide all the product elements at the end of the Sprint, the Product Owner needs to be empathetic. Remaining engaged and informed during the project gives the Product Owner the ability to demonstrate empathy. Seeing the team's effort reduces any doubt on the team's commitment to the project. It also provides perspective on the team's performance. Product Owners need to respect that one can only work so hard for so long, and criticizing a team or pushing a team beyond their capacity usually backfires and harms relationships and future product deliveries.

Scrum Master

The Scrum Master is not your boss and can be a peer to the team members. They are a facilitator and a coach. They help remove obstacles, resolve conflict, coach the team on Agile and Scrum processes, measure velocity, and track the Sprint's completed and remaining effort. The Scrum Master is a true leader who serves the Scrum Team and the larger organization of the Scrum Team, but is not a project manager or supervisor. The Scrum Master helps boost productivity of the entire team by identifying things that are slowing it down or getting in the way. The Scrum Master also serves the organization by leading, training, and coaching it in its Scrum adoption, as well as helping in the planning and advising Scrum implementations within the organization, and helping employees and stakeholders understand and enact Scrum as well as removing barriers between stakeholders and Scrum Teams.

Where is the audit manager role? Most Agile audit shops appoint the lead auditor, senior auditor, auditor-in-charge, or audit manager to serve as the Scrum Master. Selecting these traditional titled roles makes sense, and these individuals are a natural choice. On the other hand, some of these appointed Scrum Masters simply can't let go of controlling the audit in such a way that contradicts the Agile principle of empowered, self-managing teams. We recommend that anyone appointed to the Scrum Master role for Agile auditing receive Scrum Master training, possibly obtaining the Certified ScrumMaster (CSM) designation (Scrum Alliance 2020).

Additionally, the Scrum Master must carefully self-monitor to make sure they don't slip into old habits, such as managing the project, dictating how the team completes the project, or micromanaging. Generally, the Scrum Master should encourage the Delivery Team to speak up if the team feels like the Scrum Master is "managing" the project or the team. For example, audit leads serving as Scrum Masters tend to review workpapers, complete checklists, and edit audit findings and reports; these are team responsibilities – not the Scrum Master's responsibilities. We also exercise caution when assigning an audit manager to be the Scrum Master. There is a tendency for the team members to look to this person as an audit manager and not as a Scrum Master or Scrum facilitator, a scenario we've witnessed on numerous occasions.

The Scrum Master needs to monitor the Delivery Team to ensure that it doesn't start treating the Scrum Master as the project manager or decision-maker. Agile auditors must overcome mental blocks or barriers to break down traditional and existing work structures. The key to overcoming existing mindsets is to set expectations up front and commit to meeting them as a team. If ever in doubt when serving as the Scrum Master, use this approach: any time the Delivery Team asks for your opinion, your first answer is, "What do you think you should do? Remember, you are empowered to make this decision."

Skills for Scrum Masters

We recommend selecting a Scrum Master based on competencies, not job titles or roles in the traditional audit staffing model. Following is a list of skills and abilities a Scrum Master should possess:

- **Facilitating meetings:** The Scrum Master facilitates all the team meetings, including the Sprint planning meeting, daily meetings, Sprint Review, and Sprint Retrospective. As facilitators, their role is not to tell or inform, but to encourage and engage others. They need to know how to get people to talk, answer questions directly, and provide truthful information.
- **Communicating effectively:** This skill is not unique to the Scrum Master. All team members must communicate effectively, honestly, and in

a timely manner. Waiting for the perfect moment to share a critical piece of information is disastrous. Additionally, using the wrong communication modality or medium distorts communications.

■ **Enforcing rules:** We choose to state "enforcing rules" as tactful ways of saying that the Scrum Master must be willing to cut people off and say no. Specifically, the Scrum Master needs to cut off someone who is not on the Delivery Team, even the president of the organization, if they ask questions or speak during daily meetings. And if the Product Owner or Delivery Team tries to creep on the defined scope, they need to courageously remind them of the selected scope and encourage them to put the scope creep item on the Product Backlog.

■ **Estimating time and budget requirements:** The Scrum Master does not create budgets but should know what can be reasonably completed within a specific time frame and be comfortable challenging the team on their estimates of the level of effort to complete an in-progress job. The Scrum Master facilitates initial planning meetings to estimate the level of effort and may adopt various tools to create better estimates.

■ **Managing time:** Any Agile audit team member's poorly managed time will impact the agreed deliverables. The Scrum Master respects the time-boxed nature of Agile auditing and manages the time spent in each meeting precisely. A meeting must start and end on time, and the Scrum Master is accountable for managing the meeting time.

■ **Motivating individuals:** Inevitably, all team members will need to stay focused, stay on track, deal with ambiguity, and get work done. Motivation is specific to an individual and applies to teams as well. A skilled Scrum Master understands how to motivate individuals and groups, even without leveraging extrinsic rewards individuals and teams may desire.

■ **Planning projects:** The Scrum Master must understand how to plan Agile projects, even though they do not create the plan. Remember, the team members plan Agile projects. The Scrum Master should know what is needed during planning and help the team reach consensus on the intended scope, tasks, activities, priorities, and due dates.

■ **Removing obstacles:** The Scrum Master helps boost productivity of the entire team by identifying things that are slowing it down or getting in the way (impediments). The first step in removing barriers is identifying they exist. The Scrum Master leverages their communication and facilitation skills to encourage team members to identify and share obstacles as soon as they arise. The Scrum Master discusses the obstacles, possible solutions, and planned approach with the team members experiencing or impacted by the barrier. The Scrum Master then works to resolve the hindrance while allowing the team members to continue productive Sprint activities.

■ **Resolving conflicts:** People perform all projects. As such, the Scrum Master needs to identify when a conflict exists, assess the conflict, and leverage conflict resolution tools to manage the conflict. The Scrum Master must avoid dictating or demanding a specific solution as this undermines the team's autonomy to complete the project.

■ **Selling, championing, and cheering for Scrum practices:** Does a Scrum Master need to be a former cheerleader? No! However, the Scrum Master is the cheerleader for Agile and for the Agile team.

■ **Writing a user story:** While the Product Owner is responsible for eliciting user stories from the customer, the Scrum Master helps write the user story to provide the team members enough information to understand the Agile project's ultimate purpose and outcome.

Delivery Team Members (Developers)

Any other person involved in delivering the product who is not the Product Owner or Scrum Master is a Delivery Team Member. Delivery Team Members are the people in the Agile team who are committed to creating any aspect of a usable Increment of each Sprint. They are those individuals essential to getting the audit completed. To complete the Agile audit, Delivery Team Members include all auditors and audit customers. Auditors cannot conduct the audit without audit customers, process owners and employees who provide information, explain their process, retrieve evidence, explain the evidence, review workpapers, provide input on potential audit report comments, and implement corrective actions. The Delivery Team is a dedicated, multi-functional team with varied expertise focused on production and collaboration. They are empowered to make decisions and work autonomously. There is no micromanaging allowed, and Delivery Team Members are accountable to themselves and each other for completing work as promised. Delivery Team Members "are always accountable for: Creating the Sprint Backlog: a plan for the Sprint; aligning on the Sprint Goal: The single objective for the Sprint; instilling quality: by adhering to a Definition of Done; adapting their plan each day: toward the Sprint Goal; holding each other accountable: as professionals" (Schwaber and Sutherland 2020).

When managers are working on the audit and are not the Product Owner or Scrum Master, they are simply another Delivery Team Member. This realization is hard to grasp, and it is harder to overcome decades of associating titles with roles and responsibilities. There are several organizations that, in their Agile journey, eliminated all job titles. Through our research, we have found that removing titles works, but it takes time to change the culture and mentality. You're trying to change a culture to get people to treat each other as equals, challenge each other regardless of seniority, speak up when a Team Member is going out of scope, teach each other, and work together as one team. Chapter 17, Preparing Your Organization for Agile Auditing/ Creating the Agile Culture discusses culture, as we recognize the potential for an agile approach to create confusion, doubt, or fear which must be dealt with through culture shifts.

Skills for Delivery Team Members

- **Estimating individual productivity:** Every individual knows what they can do when they are passionate and fully committed to a single effort. Each person has different levels of energy and productivity. Delivery Team Members should be encouraged to be honest about their productivity estimates and when productivity is less than expected. For example, in writing this book, daily standups with the editor and authors included updates stating, "I had a horrible productivity day," or "Other priorities came up yesterday. I'll do better today." Even in planning, we challenged each other on how much we were committing to complete, and we adjusted accordingly, especially when one person said, "It is aggressive but doable." Maybe it was, but listen when someone says something is aggressive. That can be your first clue they are overextending themselves and will likely miss the target.

- **Estimating time to complete tasks:** This is a skill that takes a lifetime to master. Learning by doing is not only the best way to become better at estimating, it is the primary way to estimate how long it takes one person to complete something. For example, a skilled auditor conducting the same audit for the fifth year in a row precisely knows how long it takes to finish a specific test, if they do it and if there are no hiccups in the process. Assign another person to the task, and the previous time requirement is helpful, but likely not accurate. Agile iterations allow Team Members to learn how long it takes one individual to complete their assigned tasks. As Delivery Team Members perform repetitive tasks, the time to complete the task decreases. The learning curve theory describes this decrease in time. Learning curve theory states that you will save time as productivity doubles the more you perform repetitive tasks. Each Delivery Team

Member can estimate the time to complete their task depending on actually performing the task or similar tasks. You and your team members will make mistakes estimating times required to complete tasks; it is okay to make mistakes. Someone will make an error in estimating time. Encourage your team members to learn from their mistakes and adjust future time estimates accordingly.

■ **Working independently:** There will be times that each Delivery Team Member needs to work independently on assignments and sometimes figure out how to do something without assistance. Even as audit supervisors, we encouraged our team members to apply reasonable effort to complete a task before asking for help, but to not wait too long, as we don't want to waste time. We know it is a delicate balance. Team members need to be willing to try to figure out how to complete something independently, including researching to get questions answered, or allowing other team members to complete their work. To aid in working independently, we aim to have three tasks assigned to each person at a time, so that when they encounter problems, they can move on to another task without disrupting other Delivery Team Members' workflow.

■ **Working collaboratively:** It may sound contradictory to say that team members need to work independently and collaboratively at the same time. However, to get things done, both independent work and collaborative work are required. Collaborating is a critical principle in Agile. We designed Agile auditing around this principle. You must work together with your team to reduce the time spent or wasted going down the wrong path. We collaborate on what work to complete, provide general guidance on how to do the work, and, at times, work together to do the job. One example of where collaboration is essential is completing a test with your audit customer by pulling evidence, reviewing evidence, and concluding on evidence together. This collaborative work avoids drawing incorrect conclusions, which creates rework and increases the time spent explaining the results or persuading the audit customer to accept the outcomes.

■ **Managing time:** Time management is a skill needed by all but mastered by few. A technique that works for one person, such as a to-do list, may not work for another. Experiment and find a method that works best for you. The following are a few techniques our students identified through the years. If you struggle with time management, experiment with these. Give each technique one week before moving to another.

■ *Daily to-do list:* A list of all tasks you need to complete each day. Pick the five top-priority tasks for any one day and roll the remaining items to the next day.

■ *Online taskboard:* A taskboard is a card-based system with specific tasks needed to complete each card. Usually, there is a deadline for the tasks and the cards.

■ *Time blocking:* A daily schedule of time blocks to dedicate time to complete tasks. For example, 9:00 to 10:00 in the morning to research, 1:00 to 2:00 in the afternoon for returning phone calls and emails, 3:00 to 3:30 in the afternoon to meet with your team, and so on.

■ *Time/energy management:* This technique requires you to know your moods and energy highs and lows. If you are a morning person, spend your mornings doing items that require brainpower or more stamina and not checking emails or planning your day's activities.

■ **Staying focused:** One fact of life is that we all get distracted. A Delivery Team Member must do what they need to do to stay focused, and this varies from person to person. Some people need complete silence; others require many activities happening around them. One technique to stay focused for visual individuals is a visual taskboard; it must be kept in sight. Before Agile auditing, we provided all auditors a laminated "in scope/out of scope" card to help auditors stay focused. We also used frequent check-ins and the automated workpaper tool to stay abreast of each auditor's progress and scope. If we noticed auditors moving toward an out-of-scope area, we would talk about their approach as soon as possible. For example, using an extreme risk-based approach to auditing, we agreed to do only stop-and-go testing with a target sample of five items. Stop-and-go means that if the target sample had no exceptions, we would stop testing and move on to the next audit step. One auditor was on their seventh test, and all sampled items were clean. We asked the auditor the reason for testing more items than required. The auditor simply said that concluding on only five items didn't feel right. We immediately informed and educated on extreme risk-based auditing and successfully prevented such scope creep on the remaining tests performed by that auditor. The auditor wrote an encouraging sticky note, "5 is fine!" to keep himself focused.

■ **Avoiding procrastination:** Procrastination means you avoid, delay, or postpone something to do something more appealing. For example, in the remote work environment, many people procrastinate doing "real" work because doing the dishes or dirty laundry is more attractive than the actual work at hand. How do you avoid procrastination? Organization of your workspace, including your home if that is where you work, and prioritization of tasks are good starters. Two other techniques are to set time limits for tasks and create a personal reward system for when you remain focused and meet a time requirement.

In Agile auditing, you need the right people who possess the skills identified to fill the Agile roles. You may have noticed that the skills overlap, and the reality is you want to create a good team. Actually, the team members compile the team, as they are self-managing teams. What happens if you have a Team Member frequently left out of the self-management teams? Look at the skills, identify any deficient skill, and develop that skill. The deficiency may go beyond those skills needed to serve in the Agile team roles. Chapter 3 provides a recipe for building auditor knowledge and skills and explaining how to create a proficiency gap analysis. Consider adding Scrum roles and the Agile framework to the skills column in the analysis.

DEALING WITH PEOPLE CHALLENGES

In addition to overcoming the challenge that people depend on titles for clarity on roles, responsibilities, decision-making, and authority, you should consider a few other challenges. Before you finalize your approach and start your Agile auditing journey, let's discuss some of the people challenges you can expect to encounter based on the experiences of other entities during their Agile auditing journey. Those with a plan to address the following challenges have more success implementing Agile auditing:

1. **Auditors are skeptical; it's in our nature, and it is part of what makes great auditors.** Convincing auditors that Agile auditing is the right approach or that the audit approach's changes are positive requires careful planning and communication. Just saying something doesn't make it so; auditors need convincing evidence. One marketing company, which has since abandoned all Agile auditing efforts, tried to prove the value of Agile to auditors, senior management, the board, and audit clients. Following a few pilot Agile audits, management requested that the Agile benefits be monetized. In response, the auditors performed an Agile audit of an area that underwent a traditional audit two years prior. Using the prior audit's time capture and the average hourly rate per auditor, auditors monetized the previous audit's cost. When performing the new

Agile audit, the auditors captured their time and estimated the client's time based on collaborative interactions. It was an encouraging discovery. Overall, the audit saved just under 10% total combined hours of audit and audit clients' time than the previous audit's reported auditor hours. But because the auditors' average hourly rate was higher than the average hourly rate of the audit customer, it saved 22% in payroll costs. Applying learning curve theory, which recognizes increased efficiencies over time, we expect the company would have experienced considerably higher long-term cost savings if they had elected to continue with Agile auditing. Additionally, based on other experiences, audit quality would have improved, and the company would have noticed additional cost reductions because of Agile auditing's focus on risks.

2. **Auditors like consistency and, like most people, resist change.** Agile auditing is a significant change in the audit process and mindset. Some auditors will continuously point to their profession's standards to identify why they shouldn't do Agile audits. Other auditors will complain about some changes in the demands on their schedule created by Agile auditing. There will always be a tendency to go back to the "way we've always done it." Changing our habits and behaviors is not an easy task. An excellent source to understand why habits exist and how to change them is the book by Charles Duhigg, *The Power of Habit* (Duhigg 2014). Many auditors have found this a great source to help them embrace the Agile mindset and help others embrace it. Think about the last time you started a healthy lifestyle plan. Did you find yourself resuming old habits? How did you get yourself back on track? You'll need to find ways to help your auditors stay focused, so the Agile auditing approach becomes the norm and is the established, consistent process for your audits that provides the necessary flexibility to remain nimble.

3. **Auditors like predictability.** When applying Agile auditing to annual audit planning (see Chapter 8, Implementing Agile Auditing: The Audit Planning Process), auditors may learn of their next audit a mere two weeks before starting. By identifying the next audit so close to its start date, the predictable schedule we've come to expect at the start of the audit year will not exist. Some Agile audit shops attempt to overcome this challenge by creating a three-month/nine-month plan, which establishes some audit effort predictability. Under this audit plan, the upcoming three-month audit schedule is approved and does not change. The following nine-month audit plan is tentatively designed to allow auditors to respond to their organization's needs and risks. This workaround contradicts one

of the best benefits of Agile project management, being responsive to the organization's most crucial need.

For example, in January 2020, one large national bank's internal audit team presented an audit plan for audit committee approval that consisted of a set three-month schedule of audits that were "guaranteed" and a nine-month estimate of audits on the coming horizon (referred to as a three-nine plan). Less than two months later, a global pandemic hit the world, businesses shut down, office buildings closed, and employees began mandatory work-from-home. There was a short downtime on in-process audits because of the chaos, but the auditors continued with their approved three-month audit plan. After the three months, auditors completed scheduled audits, with most audits delivered after the anticipated deadline. It took three months for audit efforts to focus on the areas where risk increased, including pandemic response, information security, and business continuity.

4. **Auditors like to plan and don't enjoy "replanning."** To plan well, auditors expect to know their upcoming engagements and related travel requirements months in advance. When audit executives develop the audit plan, many auditors expect little change and plan professional and personal schedules around that plan. To be Agile, auditors must identify and respond to changing business needs, changing business requirements, changing risks, changing risk priorities, and even changing the organization's appetite to accept risks. To be Agile, you must be flexible. You must adapt to not knowing the upcoming audits for the coming quarter or even the following month. In Agile auditing, you will need to address the shorter planning time frame and get comfortable not knowing assigned engagements or travel requirements until two to three weeks before the Agile audit begins. Luckily, the concept of self-managing teams helps alleviate any concerns auditors have on travel requirements. Additionally, Agile audits are flexible to accommodate work-from-home and remote auditing, situations we will address in Chapter 10, Implementing Agile Auditing: Executing the Agile Audit.

5. **Auditors think in terms of risks and controls.** In Agile auditing, you must consider adding value and helping an organization accomplish its objectives as your first thought instead of what the auditors think is risky. In Agile auditing, we are not as concerned about audit objectives or what audit thinks is essential. Some Agile audit shops eliminated "audit objectives" from their Agile auditing methodology and everyday vocabulary; others substituted "audit objectives" with "value add" or

"value proposition." Additionally, risk and control matrices were updated (finally!) to precisely identify the business objectives.

NUGGETS

Whether you choose the full Agile, pilot Agile, or Agile lite strategies using our framework or other methodologies, you can't go wrong when adding Agile auditing to your toolbelt. One of the challenges affecting the success of Agile initiatives, including Agile auditing, deals with the importance professionals place on job titles. In Agile, there are only three titles: Product Owner, Scrum Master, Team Member. In Agile auditing, auditors at any level, and regardless of job title, can be the Product Owner, Scrum Master, or Team Member on any project. Auditors should have the right competencies to serve in these roles and be prepared to move between roles in Agile auditing. As you analyze your Agile strategy, consider your current positions and staff to determine who may be ready to serve in the new Agile audit roles.

Implementing Agile Auditing: The Audit Planning Process

NONTRADITIONAL AUDIT PLANNING (AGILE AUDIT PLANNING)

In Chapter 3 we discussed traditional entity-level audit planning. We discussed how rating based on how risky a process is is not the same as rating the risks that create the most significant exposures to the achievement of the organiza- tion's objectives. Let's look at some audit planning alternatives that are more Agile and closely align with the risks that may prevent the organization from achieving its objectives.

Recall that this planning process culminates in a work plan for the entire audit team for a period of time. Frequently, many refer to this plan as the annual audit plan. It is less common to refer to this type of planning as entity- level planning. However, organizations with enterprise risk management (ERM) activities create entity risk assessments, and some audit functions adopted this language in the audit process. For example, the audit function may indicate that they leveraged the ERM entity risk assessment to determine the entity audit plan. Audit teams applying nontraditional audit planning approaches constantly reevaluate the entity's needs. They may project a work schedule for only a handful of audits for a couple of weeks at a time. Thus, the audit team must deal with ambiguity and remain flexible in responding to the organization's changing needs.

On a side note, Agile auditing requires collaboration at many levels. If your organization has an enterprise risk function, leverage existing methods and results while determining your audit plan for a specific period of time.

The following approaches are not commonly used, even for organizations using a more mature Agile audit methodology. But consider one of these three alternatives, or nontraditional audit planning methods, as you are developing or enhancing your Agile auditing methodology: dynamic risk assessments, data-driven risk assessments, and risk universe prioritizations.

Dynamic Risk Assessments and Audit Planning

Agile auditing adopters are moving to dynamic risk assessments and audit planning. Using this alternative, auditors regularly reassess and reprioritize risks based on the best available information currently available. The audit plan is not set at the beginning of the year, and, for some Agile audit teams, the audits are determined every one to four weeks. Waiting to respond to the risks and decide on your next audit a week or so before the audit begins presents some logistic challenges. Dynamic risk assessment requires:

■ Greater collaboration with audit committee, senior leadership, and process owners
■ Iterative planning with focus on emerging risks
■ Increased use of technology tools such as data analytics, robotics process automation, machine learning, and artificial intelligence (see Chapter 12)

For internal audit teams, IIA Standards require the audit committee's approval of the audit plan and any significant changes (Institute of Internal Auditors 2017a). If the chief audit executive (CAE) meets with the audit committee quarterly, how would they approve the audit plan and changes before auditors start a newly identified audit the next month? Suppose you want to use dynamic risk assessments for audit planning. A process change may be necessary to align with the professional standards or reimagine the professional standard intent. To adopt the dynamic risk assessment and audit planning approach, get creative with how the board or audit committee receives and approves audit plans.

Data-Driven Risk Assessments and Audit Planning

This data-driven risk assessment alternative is an objective, quantitative approach to risk assessments used in audit planning. Yet, applying data-driven risk assessment is not utilized frequently, though more audit teams are exploring this option. If you are changing to an Agile approach, you might consider evolving to data-driven risk assessments simultaneously. We don't necessarily believe that the quantitative data-driven risk assessment approach is better than other qualitative methods, based on years of business experience, business acumen, and knowledge of risks and controls. We do believe that living the Agile life means trying new things. Data-driven risk assessments can reduce risk assessment errors caused by bias and estimation errors.

To perform a data-driven risk assessment, you need data, and you need to understand your risks. You likely appreciate risk and already have a risk inventory; if not, you need to create one that is specific and unique to your organization. You can also leverage existing key performance indicators (KPIs) and key risk indicators (KRIs), which are data-driven, to help you identify and understand organizational risks. Next, you need to identify your data, extract the data from data sources, and start combining data to identify trends, relationships, patterns, and variances. With the right software, you can make your data-driven risk assessment easier by creating dashboards to monitor risks based on the data. Using the dashboard, you can continuously update your audit plan. Remember, being Agile means being transparent, so we encourage you to make your risk information, KRIs, and dashboards available to any interested party. Remember that although we rely primarily on the data, we don't ignore feedback and qualitative insights from stakeholders and subject matter experts.

Risk Universe Prioritizations and Audit Planning

Risk universe prioritizations directly align the audit plan to the strategic objectives and significant risks that affect the achievement of entity goals. If you are lucky and your organization has an effective ERM process, using the risk universe approach just got easier. The ERM activity may have an existing risk universe, also called a risk register or risk inventory. If ERM has a risk inventory, you can use it to create the audit team's risk universe. However, as noted in the IIA Standard 2050, *Coordinating and Reliance,* when coordinating activities, the CAE should ensure there is an established and consistent process for the basis of reliance. You need to start your risk universe by reviewing the organization's strategic plan if an enterprise risk assessment or risk inventory is not available or is not reliable. Once you determine the organization's risks, then you assess the risks using qualitative, quantitative, or a combination of qualitative and quantitative techniques. You can map the identified risks to business units or business operations responsible for managing the risks related to achievement of objectives. It is important to note that in some instances (i.e., public sector orgs, highly regulated such as financial services), depending on the IA Charter,

IA might begin building the risk universe from the regulations impacting the organization. Also, there may be instances where the charter says IA's primary responsibility is compliance audits; in this case the strategic plan may not be the best tool to begin this exercise.

> In Agile auditing, you assess the controls for the highest-rated risks.

In Agile auditing, you assess the controls for the highest-rated risks, provided you can complete the review within the Sprint duration (we will discuss this more in Chapter 9, Implementing Agile Auditing: Planning Agile Audit Engagements). If a map of the risks to business units exists, it aids in selecting the Agile teams with germane business acumen. This approach is the closest to being genuinely risk-based. The attention is on the risks that impact the achievement of objectives and not which process or line of business is the riskiest to the organization. Several audit thought leaders support the risk universe approach instead of the audit universe approach, even in traditional auditing absent of any Agile influence.

To further explain this approach, here is an example. Suppose you have 50 risks identified in the risk universe. The highest-rated risk is a disruption in the supply chain caused by a politically imposed tariff on imports from the country providing critical supplies, as was the case for a domestic car manufacturer. The following business units contribute to managing this risk: legal (lobby group), procurement/sourcing, treasury/budgeting, and supply management. These business units would be in the scope of the audit. However, you would only assess how these groups manage the risk of disruption in the supply chain caused by politically imposed tariffs on imports. You would not evaluate every part of each business unit's process. You would not examine activities unrelated to tariffs. For example, you would not look at competitive bidding processes. You would only determine if the procurement department identified qualified sourcing providers from various countries, including options from domestic providers.

This is a good time to review and explain some technical "Agile" jargon in the audit context. One of the errors we made in rolling out our initial Agile audit methodology was using technical Agile jargon too early in the process. Another error was providing training on the new terminology only one time. Don't worry, we learned from that mistake. This book will help move you forward in your Agile journey by relating the Agile jargon to auditing.

In our transformations, we let audit teams determine if they want to use Agile vocabulary or not. We encourage you to use the Agile jargon, or some version of it, to reinforce the Agile mindset and acknowledge the different approach you are taking by doing Agile auditing. Your organization might already be familiar with and even be using Agile practices in other business areas such as IT or HR. You need to determine if Agile jargon is right for your teams.

 ## PRODUCT BACKLOG

In Agile, the **Product Backlog** is the list of requirements and deliverables for upcoming projects, features, changes, and fixes a team might deliver broken into "epics," "themes," and "user stories" (see "User Story" and "Epic" sections as follows). Because Product Backlogs are revisited, refined, and reprioritized periodically to ensure the team is working on the next most crucial deliverable, some Product Backlog items may remain forever as "not started." The **Product Owner**, a Scrum concept, is the guardian of the Product Backlog and is responsible for ensuring that the team delivers the desired outcomes or items from the Product Backlog. The Product Owner may decide to delete items from the backlog based on customer needs or requests. Some Product Owners maintain a separate "parking lot" for deleted Product Backlog items for tracking purposes.

> For Agile auditing, your risk universe or audit universe would be your Product Backlog.

For Agile auditing, your risk universe or audit universe would be your Product Backlog. The Product Backlog is groomed or refined by the Product Owner and Delivery Team every two weeks to determine the next iteration or the next most crucial deliverable. In Agile auditing, you select your next Agile audit or several Agile audits every two weeks.

We practice Product Backlog refinement regardless of the audit planning process used at the audit planning level. At the organizational level, auditors may opt to plan using a traditional, risk-factored audit universe, dynamic risk assessment, data-driven risk assessment, or risk universe prioritization process. The backlog would be reviewed at the refinement meeting when the Product Owner and Delivery Team select their next Agile project. It is important to note that most of our clients apply Agile auditing at the engagement level before applying it to the audit plan level. They use a traditional approach to audit planning and select all the audits the entire team will complete during a time period, usually one year. While there may be some adjustments to the audit plan, there is no product refinement meeting with the team to determine the adjustments.

Our clients adopting a full Agile strategy hold refinement meetings at the end of the determined Sprint duration. For example, for two-week sprints, the Product Backlog refinement meeting would occur at the end of the two weeks after completion of the Sprint. We recommend starting the subsequent week with the Product Backlog refinement meeting to allow the Delivery Team some downtime where they do not think about the upcoming Sprint. Weeks can start or stop on any day, depending on the organizational environment. For example, if most of your organization's workforce works a flexible workweek (e.g., four days a week for 10 hours each day), schedule the refinement meeting for when most Agile team members can attend. Therefore, they would also be available for the Sprint planning meeting that follows the refinement meeting.

In Agile auditing, auditable entities from the audit universe or risks from the risk universe make up the Product Backlog. An Agile audit team may have several Product Backlogs, typically delegated to deputy chief auditors or other audit leaders. You may have one Product Backlog for each line of business or risk theme or category. For example, an audit activity in the banking industry had one Product Backlog for each of the following lines of business: accounting, commercial lending, compliance, consumer lending, deposits, high-net-worth customers, human resources, information technology, mortgage, online banking, teller machines, and treasury management. Alternatively, using the risk universe approach, you may have one Product Backlog for regulatory risks, one for security risks, one for customer risks, one for strategic risks, and so on. There would be one Product Owner for each Product Backlog. It is possible to have one Product Owner own several Product Backlogs, but we discourage having more than one Product Owner for each backlog.

User Story

Product Backlogs include a combination of user stories and epics. Because of the complexity of writing and ranking user stories, described as follows, many audit teams opt for alternatives, such as risk statements. Try several techniques to compile your product backlog and select the one best for you.

A **user story** is a statement that defines the needs of a product from a user's perspective. User story templates document what is needed from a user's perspective using this structure: "As a [type of user], I want [some goal] so that [some reason]." A user story should include the minimum amount of detail, including key elements of "who," "what," and "why," needed to fully capture the value that the product or feature is meant to deliver to facilitate making planning decisions. For complex Agile projects, user stories are ranked according to difficulty to complete, by the Delivery Team, based on expert voting and **Delphi-method** qualitative analysis. If you've never heard of Delphi qualitative analysis, know that it can take a long time to reach a consensus. This estimate of the difficulty of completing a story is called a **story point** (Mathis 2013). In *Scrum: The Art of Doing Twice the Work in Half the Time*, the authors introduce "planning poker" to shortcut determining the level of effort by averaging team members' selected Fibonacci cards (i.e., cards with numbers 1, 3, 5, 8, 13, and 21) (Sutherland and Sutherland 2014). By using planning poker, the influence between the participants in ranking of the user stories importance is minimized, and therefore produces a more accurate estimation result. Ranking user stories helps determine resource requirements, level of effort to complete, level of effort remaining, and velocity. **Velocity** is a measure of the rate of progress, or units of work completed in a specific timeframe, during an Agile project. Agile teams determine velocity by measuring the number of user stories or story points completed per iteration or Sprint. The Scrum Master monitors velocity. Velocity is a tool the team can use to determine how long a project will take (Agile Alliance 2001). Velocity, or momentum, is also a measure of an Agile team's success.

Since auditors serve the organization in our Agile auditing framework, our users or customers are process owners, managers, audit committees, and board members. For a branch or banking center audit, the user story may say, "as a branch manager, I want to know if tellers are processing customer transactions completely, timely, and accurately so that we retain our customers and conform to required banking regulations." Another user story example may be "as an accounts payable manager, I want to pay invoices by the due date and take advantage of available discounts so that I save the company money and reduce vendor complaints." As you can see, creating user stories from the organization's perspective helps to see the audit from the client's point of view. This view can generate clients' acceptance of the findings during the Agile audit. (Note: In Chapter 11, Implementing Agile Auditing: Communicating Agile Audit Results, we will discuss writing findings, sharing results, gaining acceptance on conclusions, and getting agreement on corrective action plans.) These user stories help auditors identify why they perform the audit, state the value proposition or audit objective, and determine the audit scope.

In other Agile audit methodologies we've studied, auditors write user stories from the auditor perspective rather than the customer perspective. In these methodologies, an example user story may be "As an auditor, I want to determine that our organization pays invoices accurately and by the due date so that we can ensure the organization is conforming to contract stipulations, maximizing discounts, and minimizing late fees." This approach is audit-driven and not customer-driven; you need to decide your approach to user stories.

User stories are detailed and defined well enough to create a single iteration or Sprint. An iteration or Sprint in Agile auditing is a focused audit completed within one to four weeks. Depending on defined iteration duration, resource requirements, and level of effort to complete, Agile teams may select more than one user story per Agile audit. We'll discuss sprints in more detail in Chapter 9, Implementing Agile Auditing: Planning Agile Audit Engagements and Chapter 10, Implementing Agile Auditing: Executing the Agile Audit.

User stories are a big part of Agile project management, but not one of our Agile auditing clients currently practices user stories at the time of this writing. Instead, our clients use narrow titles for their Agile audits, such as "Accounting: Accounts Payable – Invoice Payments" and "Accounting: Accounts Payable – Vendor Master List." We asked many of our clients why they prefer titles over user stories. Here are the reasons:

- Auditors perform audits because the auditor believes there are risks to achieving organizational objectives, not because the issues are vital to the audit client. Therefore, writing a story from the audit client's perspective is not needed and is not helpful to the auditor.
- Auditors struggle with writing and applying user stories.
- There was too much debate on user story language when writing user stories with audit clients.
- Titles make more sense to auditors and audit clients. We are accustomed to seeing titles and don't want to change.

Maybe our clients will revisit this valuable part of Agile auditing in the future. We do know that Walmart and YRC Worldwide Agile audit teams apply user stories. We encourage the use of user stories because they help determine the level of effort and how much we can fit into an Agile audit that lasts two weeks (or whatever you decide for your Agile audit duration). In this book, as in our Agile audit framework, we assume the use of user stories in Agile auditing. Truly Agile auditing is analogous to a disruptive technology. We challenge you to break the barriers and completely redefine how you audit.

Epic

Epics are loosely defined ideas or large user stories. Epics exist because we don't have enough information or understanding of the requirements to be more specific and describe a user story. As the Agile team learns more about the epic, the epics are refined and split into smaller user stories. For our full Agile clients, epics were the auditable entities in the audit universe. When the Agile team completed the risk assessment for an auditable entity, they created user stories. The user stories replaced the epics in the Product Backlog. The user stories were prioritized based on perceived value to provide risk-based assurance. They were either selected for the next Sprint or remained on the backlog for reevaluation during the Product Backlog refinement process.

 ## RECIPE: PRIORITIZE AND SELECT YOUR USER STORIES

Our Agile audit framework uses the risk universe approach. Appendix B shows our Product Backlog template. The template includes the business risks (with likelihood/impact assessments), value proposition, cross-functional dependencies and relationships to other risks, priority or projected date for the completed audit, resource requirement estimates, and an estimate of the effort to complete the Agile audit. The Agile team estimates the resource requirements and effort to achieve by user story (see as follows) at the product refinement meetings. Following are two recipes to prioritize and select your user stories depending on your approach to implementing Agile auditing.

Recipe 1: Use Your Current Audit Universe
1. Split your audit universe entities into smaller topics (e.g., "accounts payable (AP)" splits into "AP – Vendor Master List," "AP – Invoice processing," "AP – Aging," "AP – Financial Statement Liabilities").
2. Create user stories for each split entity.

3. Determine which user stories provide the most value to the organization (keep risk in mind, as it could be that the user story that provides the most value to the organization might be well controlled and not worth audit effort/resources).
4. Select user stories for the upcoming period.

Recipe 2: Create a New Risk Universe with Refinement Meetings
1. Obtain the ERM risk inventory.
2. Make sure the risk inventory is complete.
3. State each risk in relation to an objective as a user story.
4. Assess the likelihood and impact of each risk or user story.
5. Identify the value proposition for each user story.
6. Prioritize the user stories.
7. Identify the business units responsible for managing each risk or satisfying each user story.
8. Determine the resource requirements and story points for each user story.
9. Note any dependencies with other user stories/risks.
10. Select the user story for the next iteration.
11. Evaluate the time needed to complete the user story. If the user story does not fill the selected Sprint duration, add a related and dependent user story. Note: The Agile team is essential in determining how many user stories it can complete in a given Sprint/iteration.

Key points to remember with either of these two recipes when estimating the time to complete the user stories:

- Agile team members, as a group, estimate how much effort individual user stories will take to complete.
- The Agile team members' estimates are averaged to arrive at the final estimation, and if there is a large gap between the lowest and highest estimates, the members with those estimates get an opportunity to explain their reasons and then the entire team gets to reestimate the time.

A great tip for writing user stories comes from Agile Alliance (2001). Use the acronym INVEST. This acronym helps the team remember a widely accepted set of criteria, or checklist, to assess the quality of a user story. If the story fails to meet one of these criteria, the team may want to reword it. A good user story should be:

- **Independent** (of all others)
- **Negotiable** (not a specific contract for features)

- Valuable (or vertical). The team should know why they are doing what they are doing.
- Estimable (to a good approximation)
- Small (so as to fit within an iteration)
- Testable (in principle, even if there isn't a test for it yet)

 ## NUGGETS

Periodically, audit leadership creates a plan of audit activities based on risk for a specified time. Traditionally, the audit leader uses an audit universe and a set of risk factors to prioritize and identify audits. In Agile auditing, the traditional planning approach may not work. Audit leaders are starting to implement alternative planning approaches to create the audit plan, including dynamic risk assessments, data-driven risk assessments, and risk universe prioritizations. A Product Backlog serves as the document to track the anticipated Agile audits. User stories and epics describe the Agile audits in the Product Backlog. Assess your current planning process and determine if any alternative approaches may help you align your Agile audits to organizational risks more effectively so you can add value to your organization.

Implementing Agile Auditing: Planning Agile Audit Engagements

 PLANNING AGILE AUDIT RESOURCES

Now, the Agile team takes over to plan the Agile audit.

Let's start by talking about your audit resources. IIA Standards require auditors to identify resources for each audit. Before you begin planning your Agile audit, you must have the right team with the proper knowledge; Agile assumes knowledge exists, and auditors don't have the time to build the knowledge during a two-week Sprint. This lack of expertise is why your audit client, the knowledge expert, is critical as part of your Agile audit Delivery Team. Let's contrast Agile audit planning to traditional audit planning and resource assignments.

In traditional audit planning, audit management assigns auditors to projects based on auditor availability and technical competencies. In an Agile audit, team members form the self-managing teams based on each individual's knowledge and expertise. Provided that all Sprints are the same duration, resource scheduling hassles are not an issue. For example, many audit teams have multiple audits with varying start dates in progress during a given time period. Audit management schedules resources based on planned start and end dates. It is common to experience delays in the audit, which affects an individual auditor's ability to complete their assigned tasks when expected. Most audit teams accept these delays and allow auditors affected by the delays to complete their work before beginning the next audit on their schedule. When an auditor completes their tasks and moves on to the next audit, or "rolls off" one audit to another, the auditor begins assigned tasks on the audit. If the auditor does not "roll off" when expected, it impacts the audit deliverables on the following audit. The Agile alternative is to stop on the scheduled end date and reassess, reassign, or eliminate any incomplete items. Agile teams are supposed to be self-managing. To create the best self-managing Agile team, you need to understand the knowledge, skills, and competency requirements of each audit project and each auditor's competencies.

SELF-MANAGING TEAMS

Cluster or virtual organizational structures, rather than departmental or centralized organizational systems, offer the best environment for highly functional, self-managing teams. A matrix structure also facilitates self-managing teams. Many Agile organizations adapt the traditional command organizational structure to find a path to creating self-managing teams and implementing Agile successfully. These command-type organizational structures start by breaking down the notion that centralized, top-down decision-making is the best approach to getting stuff done. Disrupting this notion does not require dismantling the departmental or centralized structures, at least not in every case. However, it does require Agile teams to have:

- Alignment to the organization's goals
- Minimum rules for teams to adhere to
- Autonomy
- Empowered decision-making

You may want to use an approach used by a large privately owned financial services firm audit department who implemented two practices that supported their Agile auditing journey. The first practice was moving to a pool of auditors with known competencies, where the auditors could select and prioritize the audits they felt they could add the most value. The second practice was that every auditor was assigned a specific time limit for their audit assignments and was dedicated to the Agile audit. Each auditor had a deadline to complete all work, including clearing workpaper review notes. Once the deadline date arrived, the auditor rolled off the audit and couldn't complete any additional work on the recent audit. This practice resolved the problem of auditors getting placed on special projects during an Agile audit. It also eliminated delays in reviewing workpapers and decreased the number of nitpicky workpaper review notes. Think of this deadline-driven work protocol as if the auditor had completely changed jobs or companies. The roll-off deadline practice changed how auditors completed their work, how the Scrum Master monitored the engagement milestones and effort to finish the audit, and how reviewers completed reviews. These two practices aren't technically Agile, but they are a good starting point for those looking for ideas on managing resources and facilitating self-managing teams.

The pooling concept is unnecessary for smaller audit teams as resources are already scarce, and rigidly aligning audit work based on an organization chart is uncommon. Small audit teams work well in the Agile auditing environment because they are likely already collaborating closely with subject matter experts, business areas, and audit clients to quickly expand their knowledge. One of our Agile audit clients found success on an audit with one auditor, one Product Owner, and one audit client contact. There was no Scrum Master; however, the auditor was familiar with Scrum Master roles and responsibilities.

Our preference for essential attributes of self-managing teams includes:

1. Designated auditors with specialized expertise in operations, accounting, compliance, and information technology.
2. Designated auditors who collectively have interpersonal skills, including communication, emotional intelligence, negotiation, and project management skills.
3. Designated audit customers/process owner resources, preferably the employees who are performing the day-to-day work. They are the knowledge experts who have the answers to all the questions.

Once a self-managing team forms, it is helpful for the Agile team to move together, as a whole, from audit to audit as team members with few replacements and substitutions. Keeping an Agile team together creates efficiencies. As Stephen Denning asserted, keeping as many members of an Agile team together creates team continuity. Denning describes Microsoft's approach of "keeping the members of the teams together, with the same people working on the same team as long as possible" as a "champion sports team" (Denning 2018).

Lebron James, the U.S. basketball superstar, comes to mind as each of the three professional basketball teams he played on found varying success. Success on these professional teams usually came after the team learned each other's strengths and weaknesses. The group became a real team and was not dependent on one person's, namely Lebron's, abilities. The Agile audit team that moves together can estimate how much work the team can complete in a specified time frame on a given Agile project with greater precision. The team learns how to work together effectively. There are other benefits to having an Agile team move together, including increased awareness of work habits, increased comfort, trust, and better team communication.

An understanding of Bruce Tuckman's four stages of group development aids in explaining why teams who stay together work better (Tuckman 1965). Tuckman identified the following four stages:

1. Forming
2. Storming
3. Norming
4. Performing

The forming stage occurs when a team is established, and the members are introduced. In this stage the members might feel enthusiastic about the work ahead. Since the team is new and just starting to learn about the work ahead, they might not know how to collaborate. During the storming stage employees start to learn more about each Team Member and start to see potential disagreements on how to best perform the project or other challenges. Personality and work styles emerge. The team members can become frustrated with one another and might squabble. At this point team members are learning about each other's abilities and learning to trust each other. The norming stage happens when team members begin recognizing each other's assets and get more comfortable working together. The team will also start socializing more and collaborating freely. In the performing stage employees are happy working together and often have developed strong relationships and streamlined their processes. At this stage the team reaches their peak productivity.

A fifth stage, adjourning, is commonly identified with the previous four since most teams will not stay together forever. This stage occurs once the team has completed the audit and the team members move on to other projects. However, the adjourning phase is not always applicable as some teams will stay together in all projects. Tuckman's study implies that each group moves through the four stages at varying paces. The more change a team experiences, the more a team may recycle through the stages. It takes pushing through the first three stages before a team begins to perform. A performing team is one that has group norms and established roles. The performing team has a shared goal, collective focus, and knowledge. It is the performing team that can operate autonomously and can make decisions without supervision. This autonomous, performing team is the team we want in Agile auditing.

> The auditors must be dedicated to complete one audit when assigned to an Agile audit.

We need to address dedicated auditor resources. For many audit teams, we don't have, or can't have, dedicated auditors assigned to only one audit project. Because of the audit plan schedule, delays on individual audits, and auditor availability, the auditors roll on and off projects at varying times throughout the traditional audit project life cycle. The auditors may never work on the same project again or with the same team members. For one financial services organization, auditors were completing both traditional audits and their pilot Agile audits. The auditors had multiple priorities or other audits to complete. The Agile audits suffered and the Delivery Team extended their deadlines several times. Their most important lesson learned was that the auditors must be dedicated to complete one audit when assigned to an Agile audit. The frequency of communication and encouraged free-flow thoughts and collaboration encouraged in Agile means auditors will be interrupted by their Agile team members. Peers will want to bounce ideas around, test theories, and experiment. Imagine working on another audit and getting interrupted by thoughts unrelated to the Agile project. After nearly a year of identifying the need to have dedicated auditors, the client has yet to achieve this. Still, they are aware of the requirement and continue their endeavor to have dedicated auditors. To increase success with Agile audits, try to dedicate resources and have teams stay together from project to project.

There is also a desire to have designated client resources. We find this particularly troublesome because there is "real" work and daily demands to keep the business running. When possible, try to schedule an Agile audit during a time when business activity is slow. Alternatively, ask your client whether mornings or afternoons have fewer time constraints on your key contacts and work directly with your contacts when their "real-job" time demands allow for collaboration with the auditor. During several Agile audits for an international insurance company, we were only able to have a designated audit liaison from the audit customer assigned to audit. If this is all you can get, take it, but realize that it will impact the audit deliverables because you are working through a middleman to get answers and evidence. To compensate for the lack of a designated business expert, we limited the scope of these Agile audits to ensure that the team could complete the audit within the two-week time frame. A small word of caution: expect interruptions when collaborating with your audit client and have empathy when meetings need to end sooner than expected.

 AGILE AUDIT PLANNING STEPS

So, let's assume the "gang is all here" and is motivated and dedicated to completing the Agile audit. We have five core steps for planning Agile audit engagements as follows.

Step 1: Hold the Sprint Planning Meeting

Sprint planning initiates the Sprint by laying out the work to be performed for the Sprint. This resulting plan is created by the collaborative work of the entire Agile audit team, which includes representatives from the audit client. The Agile team may also invite other individuals (i.e., subject matter experts) to attend the Sprint planning meeting to provide insight and advice. The Sprint planning meeting is a technique we recommend for every audit, not only Agile audits. One of our telecommunication clients holds a half-day collaboration meeting to plan each Agile audit. This meeting, facilitated by the Scrum Master, attended by the Product Owner and the Delivery Team, including audit customers, is part information sharing, part brainstorming, and part planning control tests for the highest risks. This collaboration meeting eliminates the traditional entrance meeting and is the Sprint planning meeting. Over time, audit customers witnessed how their attendance impacts the course of the audit and, because of the value-add, they actually attend the meeting. This Sprint planning meeting approach resolves the problem of poor attendance at entrance meetings and reduces pressure on the auditors to feel like they are business experts.

In Agile auditing, explicitly leveraging the Scrum framework, all Agile team members attend the Sprint planning meeting. The following actions occur during the Sprint planning meeting (Schwaber and Sutherland 2020):

- The Product Owner provides background information and perspectives from the client or customer.
- The Product Owner discusses why the Sprint is valuable by proposing how the audit (product) will add value. It is important for the Agile team to understand what the Product Owner wants its intent of the Sprint to be. The entire Agile audit team then collaborates to define the Sprint Goal, which should be complete at the end of Sprint planning.
- The Product Owner discusses the Product Backlog and current prioritization based on the most recent Product Backlog refinement meeting.
- The Product Owner clarifies the user stories.
- Other attendees, including the Scrum Master, subject matter experts, and stakeholders, in attendance may also provide information to help the Agile team clarify the user stories.
- The Delivery Team Members (i.e., auditors and audit clients) ask the Product Owner questions to clarify the anticipated user stories' expectations and requirements.
- The Delivery Team Members and Scrum Master refine user stories.
- The Delivery Team Members determine which user stories will be included in the next Sprint depending on the Product Backlog prioritization, the effort needed to complete each user story, and related user stories.
- The Agile team members, including the auditors, audit client, Scrum Master, and Product Owner, agree on the coming Sprint's user stories.
- The Agile team members articulate the value propositions, objectives, and scope for the coming Sprint.
- The Delivery team identifies and allocates tasks to team members (using the estimated effort required, Sprint duration, and team resources).
- The Agile team members agree on acceptance criteria, including documenting their understanding of the definition of done (see as follows).
- As the Delivery team perform the Sprint, they keep the Sprint Goal in mind (the why). If the work turns out to be different than they expected, the team collaborates with the Product Owner to negotiate the scope of the Sprint Backlog within the Sprint without affecting the Sprint Goal.

You may be asking, "How long does this meeting take?" For a two-week Sprint, the meeting lasts approximately four hours (two hours or less per week of Sprint length). To increase attendance, we recommend scheduling this meeting during the previous Product Backlog refinement meeting. Remember, in Agile auditing, the Agile team intends to move together from one Sprint to the next. While the core Agile team moves together, there may be new players in the Agile audit, and scheduling the meeting in advance allows the new players an opportunity to attend the Sprint planning meeting. You will also find that adding a tentative agenda, including the user stories and agenda item time frames, increases attendance. Breaks and refreshments may be needed for long meetings. You want participation by other team members, including audit clients and stakeholders, to provide transparency on the audit process and allow early answers to questions most auditors are asked at some point during the audit. For example, "why are you testing x control?" and "how long will this audit take?"

Step 2: Agree on the Definition of Done

Optimally, during the Sprint planning meeting, the team members will collectively agree on the definition of done. The Agile audit team determines the definition of done, which can change for each Agile audit. And the Agile audit is only done when the team satisfies the agreed definition of done. As Stephen Denning said in *The Age of Agile*, "to ensure there is no ambiguity with what we mean by 'done,' we are talking about being 'done-done!'" (Denning 2018). The definition of done includes answers to the following questions:

- What does success look like for the Agile audit?
- What are the activities necessary to complete the audit?
- What should we include on our "done checklist"?
- Do we need to check everything off the "done checklist"?
- Who determines we are "done"?

The definition of done provides the most value for the Agile team when it is publicly displayed in a central location, preferably a room where the team meets face-to-face for standing meetings, or on the team's workflow management and collaboration tool. For Agile audits, done means the team is ready to present its results to the Product Owner, typically during a Sprint review meeting. (See Chapter 11, Implementing Agile Auditing: Communicating Agile Audit Results.) The team should have some certainty that the Product Owner will approve the results. Technically, if the Agile audit is working as intended with constant inspection, the Product Owner would already have some idea of the results. Before the Sprint review meeting, if something specific concerned the Product Owner, the Product Owner would discuss the matter with the Scrum Master, who would inform the team members. For an Agile audit of the financial close-the-books process, the fourth Agile audit for the same Delivery Team, the team included the following on their "done checklist":

- All project taskboard tasks were moved to the "done" column.
- Test steps were completed.
- Audit evidence was returned.
- Workpapers were fully documented.
- Peer reviews of workpapers were completed.
- Review notes were cleared.
- Findings were communicated to process owners.
- Findings were added to the audit findings tracker.
- Lessons learned (retrospective) was scheduled.

Because the team worked together, they felt confident they could plan the Agile audit and complete the audit to meet this Definition of done. During the team's first Agile audit on accounting policies, the Definition of done included "place incomplete tasks on the Product Backlog" as the team anticipated that they were not able to plan the audit with enough precision to complete all tasks in the allotted duration. Additionally, for that first Agile audit, the Definition of done also included "lessons learned meeting held." Notice the change from the first to fourth audits. The team learned how to plan what they could complete with enough precision that they felt all tasks could be completed. They also decided that waiting until the lessons learned was held was impractical and unnecessary. The Definition of done was different for each audit.

Step 3: Agree on the Definition of Ready

During the Agile planning phase, preferably in the Sprint planning meeting, the Agile team also creates the Definition of ready. The Definition of ready is the set of criteria necessary to start working on an iteration or Sprint. The purpose of defining when the team is "ready" to launch the iteration is to prevent back-and-forth discussions and rework. It empowers the Agile team to delay starting the audit if the criteria are not met. Examples of items on an Agile audit of Emergency Preparedness Response Definition of ready included:

- Audit liaison has been identified.
- Audit test steps have been approved (incredibly helpful for by-the-book auditors conforming to IIA Standards).

- Daily meetings have been scheduled.
- Initial documentation request items have been received.
- Pre-scope meeting was held with audit leadership.
- The Product Owner or chief audit executive (CAE) has approved the Agile audit scope (while this approval was in writing to conform to departmental requirements, the "approval" is not really Agile).
- Project canvas has been completed.
- Project taskboard skeleton has been prepared.
- High-level walkthroughs have been completed.

There are many variations on the Definition of ready seen through the years. Below is a sample of additional items included in other Definitions of ready:

- Audit client expert designated and briefed on Agile auditing.
- Sprint Review scheduled.
- Sprint Retrospective scheduled.
- Videoconferencing enabled.
- RCM completed.
- System access to key client systems granted.

Step 4: Determine Your Project Tasks and Create Your Taskboard/Sprint Backlog

Your project tasks likely include items on a current project checklist, and the project tasks will consist of the procedures and test steps needed to complete the audit. We prefer a very detailed set of tasks. We use preprinted Post-its for manual taskboards or we copy and paste from previous Agile projects, using one of the many taskboard technology solutions for standard items found on a project checklist.

To be flexible, the Agile audit team identifies test steps as it gains additional knowledge. For Agile audits, developing test steps in response to new knowledge is preferred rather than identifying and approving all test steps before beginning fieldwork. Therefore, the approval of audit test steps goes hand in hand with the developing of the test steps.

To provide an example, one client began a two-week Agile audit of investment valuations with a Sprint planning meeting. In addition to determining the Definition of done and Definition of ready, they also decided to create their project taskboard. There were approximately 20 standard tasks immediately added to the taskboard that must be completed in every audit per their quality requirements and, since time was severely limited, the auditors knew they needed to start testing immediately. The Sprint planning meeting attendees agreed that the number-one risk was investments with manual prices determined by models rather than by pricing agencies. The first task/ test step, "identify model developers and assess qualifications," was assigned to auditor Z, who stated that it would be completed before the next Daily Scrum. The second task was "obtain a list of pricing model revisions by date and review related implementation testing results to determine if testing was thorough and any bugs were resolved prior to implementation." Auditor D, who had system development experience, agreed to complete this step by the next Daily Scrum. During the next Daily Scrum, auditor Z reported that the test was complete with no exceptions and the related workpaper was completed and ready for peer review. Auditor D reported that the test was completed and there was one bug that remained open. Thus, another task was added and assigned to Auditor D that read, "Discuss unresolved bug with implementation tester and developer to determine the significance of the bug and remediation plans." Each Daily Scrum resulted in adding anywhere from four to six tasks to the taskboard. The Product Owner was in attendance and saw the changes and additions to the taskboard daily; as no objections were posed, the changes were deemed approved.

Most Agile audit teams continue to apply the waterfall approach of approving the audit program and audit test steps at one time. Using the waterfall approach requiring approval of all test steps before fieldwork begins is not meant to imply that the entire audit is static or that the audit tests can't be changed. We are still doing Agile, after all, and Agile audit teams recognize that a predetermined audit test or audit program may not be the final test or audit program executed. Remember, Agile is different from how we usually work. Typically, we perform the approved audit program for the duration of the audit. Ordinarily, we don't consider what's changed within the organization, changed with the evidence, changed with the people, or even whether the risks changed.

In Agile auditing, as we gain additional information, the needs of the audit and organization change. As we learn more about controls, known control weaknesses, and identified errors or failures, audit test steps will change. Changes in direction and approach are expected to allow for a more flexible and responsive Agile audit. We can adapt to what we're looking for through frequent inspection of the tasks, audit tests, and program backlog.

Step 5: Prepare the Project Canvas and Other Planning Documents

The project canvas is a project control document that is highly useful for Agile projects. It is supposed to be a one-page summary of the Agile audit that is provided to Agile team members and stakeholders. See Table 9.1 for an example of a project canvas and content suggestions. We see the project canvas used more commonly today and initially excluded it from our methodology. We felt that it was another document created for the sake of creating a single document that includes other elements captured in other audit planning workpapers. Our advice now is simply, don't create extra work. If you want to use a project canvas, eliminate the redundant planning workpapers. We do like some elements of project canvas templates we've seen, including:

1. The business background, including alignment to the organization's strategy, business objectives, risks, metrics, and performance indicators.
2. Project drivers that state the value proposition for the audit and the reasons it's on the audit plan.
3. The Agile audit value proposition provides a statement on the value of doing the Agile audit for that area. It is sometimes a selling point for selecting an Agile audit over a traditional audit or continuous audit. For some Agile teams, the value proposition is used instead of audit objectives.
4. Related business areas and cross-functional business impact.
5. Key stakeholders.
6. Key systems and technology, including the audit history of the systems.
7. Project scope states what is needed to achieve the value proposition or audit objective.
8. Sprint description, which is often a description of the risks and controls under evaluation in the Sprint and a subset of Sprint Backlog items.
9. Agile team members.

Recall the five activities of Scrum projects. At this point in the Agile audit, we only needed one Sprint planning meeting and maybe a couple of daily meetings. Some internal audit shops continue to use traditional waterfall tollgate (a gate or tollgate is a standardized control point where each project phase is reviewed and approved to continue with the next phase) meetings, such as preplanning and planning meetings, with audit leadership before the Sprint planning meeting. Exercise caution with the number of meetings you have. Remember, transparency is fundamental to Agile. Except under

TABLE 9.1 Project Canvas

About the Business/ Business Highlights and Concerns	Project Drivers	Cross-Functional Impact
■ Business objectives ■ Business risks ■ Management concerns ■ Known issues/errors ■ How does the business area align with the organization's strategy? ■ What are the business objectives? ■ What are the risks to the business achieving its objectives?	■ Why is this project important to the business? ■ Why is it on the audit plan? ■ What are the drivers from the risk assessments? ■ What is the value-add to the enterprise? ■ Business strategy/ critical linkage ■ Control environment **Value Proposition** ■ What is the value of doing an Agile internal audit in this area? ■ As a result of this project, we will. . .? ■ Metrics we hope to improve	■ Critical IT systems/reports supporting and monitoring the business process ■ Compliance considerations ■ Financial reporting/impact

Key Stakeholders	Metrics/KPIs	
■ Who is most concerned about the value of the project? ■ Cross-functional: Who is most impacted?	■ Key metrics used by the business to measure the achievement of its objectives ■ What are the measures of success for the audit? ■ Audit timeline and target dates ■ Sprints to complete the project (Sprint 1, 2, 3, 4, . . .)	

Project Scope	Risk and Control Log	Core Project Team
■ What is needed to achieve the project objectives? ■ What are the areas to be concluded for the project?	■ Business risks and controls ■ Identify and prioritize the Sprint Backlog ■ Define project Sprint time frame	■ (RACI) Responsible, Accountable, Consulted, Informed ■ Project champion (audit client) ■ Product Owner (PO) (Partner/ CAE/Director) ■ Scrum Master (SM) ■ Audit Scrum Team ■ Development team (DT) auditors/audit team (AT) ■ Agile team (PO, SM, DT/AT)

extreme circumstances, such as fraud or other confidential matters, there should be few occasions where auditors meet in private to discuss the audit.

AGILE JARGON

Okay, it is Agile jargon time again. In Agile, the term **Sprint Backlog** is a specific, focused list of tasks ranging from two hours to two days to complete during an increment. Agile team members identify and record the tasks on the Sprint Backlog to track the specific deliverables needed to complete a user story from the Product Backlog. We discussed the user stories and Product Backlogs in Chapter 8, Implementing Agile Auditing: The Audit Planning Process. The Sprint Backlog template often includes the user story, story point rating (as discussed in Chapter 8), level of effort required to complete, assigned resources, and velocity.

The Sprint Backlog in an Agile audit would be the audit program and audit test steps. In some Agile audit methodologies, the audit program is the "audit backlog," which is an example of hybrid jargon (i.e., a term that combines both Agile and audit jargon). The Agile audit team determines the test steps and tasks needed to complete a Sprint. The team is empowered and self-managing, so they may add or remove steps on the Sprint Backlog as needed. We use the Sprint Backlog to prepare the audit project taskboard (also known as a Kanban board), which includes all identified activities and tasks from the Sprint Backlog. You can learn more about Kanban in Chapter 14, Exploring Kanban Agile Auditing.

The **project taskboard** is a visual tool to track the team's progress, determine the level of effort to complete, indicate the Sprint's current status to a stakeholder, and monitor scope. Agile practitioners recommend that tasks range from two hours to two days to complete. We opt for a detailed project taskboard including to-do tasks for each audit test, the related workpaper, and the corresponding workpaper review. Admittedly, our task durations may be as short as 15 minutes, but we include them because we don't want to forget them and it makes no sense to maintain a separate team to-do list.

We create a project taskboard instead of a separate Sprint Backlog. The project taskboard provides a visual reference point during the daily meeting, though most Agile teams do not adjust the project taskboard during the daily meeting. We prefer to have the team members who are accountable for completing a step manage the project taskboard during the daily meeting, so they are actively moving tasks through the taskboard columns (to-do, in-progress/doing, completed/done). The Scrum Master should inquire about obstacles if tasks get stuck in the in-progress column.

If there are incomplete tasks when the project reaches the Agile end date and the team communicates the audit results (Sprint Review), unfinished tasks are discussed and approved by the Product Owner or moved to a new Sprint. The framework recommended to most Agile audit shops requires either a project taskboard or the Sprint Backlog, but not both. Using one or the other reduces duplication of effort and redundant documents.

Agile audit teams must exercise caution when determining which user stories or objectives they will complete during a given Agile audit based on the best available knowledge and estimates of the level of effort to complete. Even in traditional audit project management, we advise a "promise low, deliver high" mentality to make sure we don't promise more than we can deliver. Keep that in mind during your Sprint planning meeting; the Agile team selects audit deliverables and creates the Sprint Backlog. (See Appendix C for a time-lapse Agile Audit Example).

Now that we have covered how to plan Agile audit engagements when implementing Agile auditing, we briefly discuss resolution of some of the problems discussed earlier in Chapter 5.

USING AGILE AUDITING TO SOLVE ENGAGEMENT PLANNING PROBLEMS

In Chapter 3, Traditional Audit Engagement Processes and Practices, we presented conventional methods and techniques used in assurance and attestation engagements. These methods and practices contribute to many problems throughout audit engagements. Do you recall the long list of the issues from Chapter 5, Why Agile Audit? If not, let's refresh the memory for the problems related to the engagement planning phase:

- Poor time budgets/estimates to complete audits
- Unreasonable audit deadlines
- Poorly defined supervisor expectations
- Uncommunicated audit leadership expectations
- Audit clients not attending entrance meetings
- Unable to plan audits thoroughly
- Too many assumptions based on procedures when determining test steps
- Unclear audit test steps
- Scope limitations by audit clients

Following, we provide solutions focusing on the first bullet, "poor time budgets/estimates to complete audits." In doing so, we help set the stage for solving the additional engagement planning problems.

Poor Time Budgets/Estimates to Complete Audits

This problem starts at the top and stems from imperfect information regarding the time taken to complete prior similar audits. The CAE sets individual audit engagement budgets during annual audit planning. In Agile auditing, instead of developing a plan without an adequate understanding of the scope of the audit project, competencies of the auditors, and level of effort needed to complete the audit project, the collaborative Agile team determines what they will be able to accomplish in a set time frame.

Following are examples of contrasting processes for the time estimates and budget for traditional audit environments and Agile audit environments. The first example is for a new audit, sales practices, and the second is for a repeat audit, accounts payable.

New Audit: Sales Practices

Traditional audit planning:

Based on the CAE's risk assessment of auditable entities, the CAE determines that sales practices are the highest-priority auditing area in the coming year. A similar audit does not exist, so the CAE pulls out the dartboard of hours to complete high-risk audits, ranging from 600 to 1,500 hours, lines up on the line, and aims. Thankfully, the CAE remembered to get the right dartboard since there is another dartboard for medium-risk audits and another dartboard for low-risk audits. Annually, using a specific dartboard, the CAE updates the hourly ranges on the dartboard based on the actual number of reported audit hours for each risk group.

The CAE throws the dart, and it lands at 850 hours. The budget is now 850 hours for the high-risk audit, and the CAE states that the preliminary scope includes sales procedures, sales staffing, sales compensation, writing proposals, and delivering sales pitches. The CAE continues this process for the remaining audits until the scheduled engagements consume the total available hours' audit team. Okay, maybe that is a little exaggerated; we've never actually seen a dartboard of audit hours. Or perhaps this is better than the process used in audit planning by some CAEs.

Agile audit planning:

Based on an evaluation of the organization's first strategic goal, increasing sales proposals and acceptance rates, the CAE and senior executive determine the risks that could significantly impact the goal. The risks identified are inefficiencies in the proposal writing process, staffing shortages on the sales team, and failing to receive requests for proposals that provide enough time to prepare and deliver sales proposals. The audit department applies dynamic risk assessment and data-driven risk assessments to audit planning.

The auditors gather data from emails, the mail receipt and distribution center, the enterprise resource planning tool, and the customer relationship management system to compare the number of requests for proposals to the number of proposal responses and determines average turnaround time. The auditors also review macro-level data on salesperson salaries and bonuses compared to competitors and regional salaries. During the Product Backlog refinement meeting, the data analytics team states that the company has a 62% proposal response rate, with an average of 59 days to deliver a proposal. Furthermore, the average salesperson's compensation is in line with regional salaries and just under the competitor group.

The Agile team agrees that if the proposal writing process is efficient, the sales team could overcome staffing shortages and achieve quick proposal turnarounds. The Agile team determines the specific scope, proposal writing, and tasks for the two-week Agile audit Sprint. After the Agile audit is complete for the proposal writing process, the Agile team reviews the Agile audit results and the remaining identified sales risks to determine if reevaluation is appropriate or if the Agile team should move on to another higher priority risk to audit.

Repeat Audit: Accounts Payable

Traditional audit planning:

The CAE determines that accounts payable needs to be included in this year's audit plan based on the risk assessment and audit cycle requirements for the auditable entities. The most recent accounts payable audit recorded 573 hours. The CAE assumes the same audit team will complete the audit, even though the audit activity experienced a 23% turnover in the last year, and anticipates a learning curve that should reduce audit time by 10%. The CAE sets the estimated hours at 515 hours. The preliminary scope includes the vendor master list, invoice payments, aged invoices, open purchase requests, and accounts payable procedures.

Agile audit planning:

The CAE uses a risk universe and defined risk assessment to prioritize risks. The risk assessment is updated quarterly to reflect macro and internal environments. Due to a global pandemic, the company is struggling to generate cash sources. Customers are not paying receivables in a timely manner, investment markets are dry, and debt vehicles are unavailable. The company needs to continue to serve existing customers on prepaid annual subscription plans. The company relies on nearly 100 vendors and suppliers for day-to-day operations. Daily continuous auditing trend analysis on the aging of accounts payable shows increases in the average number of days to pay vendors. At the Product Backlog refinement meeting, the Product Owner shares the above concerns and information, and the Agile team agrees an Agile audit of accounts payable is needed. As the Agile team receives answers to questions, the Agile team determines that the Agile audit should focus on vendor management and vendor relationships, not the accounts payable processes, payments, balances, and aging. Considering cash constraints, we need to keep the vendors and suppliers performing services for existing customers, even if we are slow to pay them. The Agile audit team needs to determine if the organization is proactive regarding managing vendor relationships, including negotiating vendor and supplier contract terms. The Agile team identifies the specific scope and tasks for the two-week Agile audit. After the Agile audit is complete for vendor relationship management, the Agile team reviews the Agile audit results and the remaining risks related to accounts payables, contracting, capital budgeting, treasury management, and accounts receivable. The review of the related areas and assessing those areas determines if there is another related risk that will form the next Agile audit or if a higher-priority risk needs audit's attention.

From the previous two examples, you get an idea on how Agile can solve the engagement planning phase additional problems. Since the Agile team is involved, it is able to identify the specific scope and tasks that can be completed in the two-week Agile audit, eliminating unreasonable audit deadlines characteristic of traditional audit planning. Moreover, since the team is self-managing, it can set and define the team expectations, which eliminates poorly defined supervisor expectations. Audit leadership expectations are communicated during the Product Backlog refinement meeting and clarified in the Sprint planning meeting as appropriate. Furthermore, the constant inspection during the Daily Scrum allows the team to reevaluate and respond to new information. Since collaboration with clients is essential in Agile auditing, the audit clients attend the meetings and are involved throughout the audit. As a result of continuous planning, audits are planned based on actual circumstances, and plans are flexible to deal with unanticipated changes. With audit clients involved in daily communications, erroneous assumptions about client procedures relied on to determine test steps can be almost immediately corrected, and unclear audit test steps adjusted. Finally, using up-to-date risk assessments which continue to be discussed as the audit progresses eliminates client scope limitations from the beginning of the Agile audit.

NUGGETS

Once the Agile team selects the user stories from the Product Backlog and obtains clarification from the Product Owner, the Agile team begins planning the Sprint. The Agile team is a self-managing team where team members are selected based on their specific knowledge and expertise. The Agile team should evaluate the knowledge of the team resources and assign team roles and Sprint tasks. The audit leadership can change the organizational alignment structures to facilitate creating self-managing teams. Once a self-managing team is formed for a product, the intent is for the team to move together from Sprint to Sprint to improve efficiencies and estimate Sprint workloads with precision.

There are five core steps for planning Agile audits:

1. Holding the Sprint planning meeting
2. Agreeing on the Definition of done
3. Agreeing on the Definition of ready
4. Determining project tasks
5. Preparing the planning documents

The Agile team identifies the tasks required to completely satisfy the user stories selected for the Agile audit or Sprint. The Agile audit team may elect to record the tasks in a Sprint Backlog or project taskboard. The project taskboard visually tracks the tasks' progress from not started, to in progress, to complete until all tasks are complete or the Sprint time limit has expired. As you consider your methodology, determine what you can do to facilitate creating self-managing teams, what planning steps your Agile teams will complete, and what Agile audit planning tools and documents your teams will use.

We've always emphasized the importance of planning an engagement well to eliminate unnecessary tests and reduce rework. The difference between the traditional engagement planning process and planning Agile audit engagements rests on the Agile mindset of doing what is right for the customer. The Agile mindset is addressed in Chapter 6, Creating the Agile Mindset. To do what is right for the customer, auditors must be aware of customer needs and apply an adaptive approach to engagements. Agile allows freedom and doesn't require planning the entire audit before you start testing. The planning process, like the rest of Agile auditing, is iterative.

CHAPTER TEN

Implementing Agile Auditing: Executing the Agile Audit

 ## TESTING WITH THE AUDIT CLIENT

Okay, these next thoughts may blow your mind. But remember, these are options, and you may need to be creative to ensure that you conform to your professional standards. Your ability to do Agile auditing well depends on your appetite to:

- Test controls with the client,
- Create minimally acceptable documentation,
- Leverage available technology, and
- Remain vigilant about sticking to the selected scope.

In traditional audits, it is almost unheard of to share the audit program with the audit client. What is the big deal about sharing an audit program, anyway? Are we worried about the audit client going through the entire population of transactions to make sure all the right things happened, all documents are in order, all signatures are visible? If the client wants to do that, great! That's what we want the business to do all the time. If being audited reminds them of what they should do as part of their day-to-day process so they avoid the scurry of activities to prepare for the audit, so be it.

> In Agile auditing, the audit client likely helps create the Sprint Backlog. That does not mean that the audit client determines the audit scope or that auditor objectivity is impaired. It does mean they helped the auditor gain knowledge quickly, informed the auditor of controls, and possibly explained how they might test the controls.

In Agile auditing, the audit client likely helped you create the Sprint Backlog. That does not mean that the audit client determined the audit scope or that auditor objectivity is impaired. It does mean they helped the auditor gain knowledge quickly, informed the auditor of controls, and possibly explained how they might test the controls. Sometimes the audit client is already testing controls, which may be a management control in and of itself! It also means that they already know what you are looking for, so why not look at it together? The auditor still draws their conclusions and reaches their own opinion, so objectivity is not impaired.

So, what does testing with the audit client look like? Well, before we answer this, let's look at a traditional audit to identify opportunities to improve the testing process, enhance efficiency, and reduce waste. While the following scenario can be almost any audit we have worked on, we selected a repeat audit of Mortgage Originations. We started by reviewing written procedures and performing a real-time walkthrough of a new mortgage application. Based on this test of one transaction, we confirm that the expected controls are in place. Then we ask for a population of all mortgage applications for the past year. Then we waited nearly one week before finally receiving the population. We were not aggressive in requesting the population sooner because we were also completing another audit at the same time.

When we initially received the population via email, we were too busy working on something else to verify the population and select our sample. Luckily, the population provided included all the necessary data elements and we were able to verify its completeness by comparing the file we received to a management report of mortgage applications for the same time period. We selected our sample and requested the audit client to pull the sample for us. Then we waited.

When the audit client provided the sample evidence and supporting documentation a few days later, we scanned through the items to confirm that the audit client provided everything, or at least that it looked like we had the requested evidence. We sorted the applications by "approved" and "denied," as each had different criteria. We started testing the first application against predetermined criteria, expectations, and attributes. While we expected some exceptions, we were surprised when we discovered that not everything was in perfect order with all "t's crossed and i's dotted." We collected the exception items, made copies of them for our workpapers, informed the audit client via email, and requested that we meet to review the exceptions. We provided a specific list of the sampled items containing exceptions. A follow-up email and phone call finally resulted in a scheduled meeting to discuss the exceptions. The email responses from the client felt as if the client was preparing for battle, possibly because we said the code word "exceptions," which they know means audit finding.

The meeting began by discussing the first exception, and the audit client informed us that there was another document we needed to resolve the exception; they committed to find it in their records and email it to us. We moved to the next exception, and as it turns out, we didn't notice that the attribute was met but was on a different page than where we expected to find it. We reviewed the remaining exceptions, and for most of them, we expected to receive some additional documentation via email after our meeting. Then we waited.

We received the email with some, but not all, of the expected documentation with a comment that the evidence existed but it just couldn't be located, and they needed another week to find it. Then we waited.

Okay, you get where we are going, and we haven't even started talking about writing the workpaper, receiving review notes, clearing review notes, and so forth. Maybe this is an extreme case. What can you do to improve this process? What opportunities do you see to reduce waste? If you answered these questions, you are already practicing Agile, and you haven't even finished reading this book. Congratulations!

TESTING WITH THE AUDIT CLIENT
- You get the population while you are doing the walkthrough.
- You verify the population with the client immediately.
- You pick your sample while you are with the client.
- Together, you pull the sample and start reviewing the audit evidence.
- The testing is completed during the initial meeting with the client.

Okay, let's answer our question, "What does testing with the audit client look like?" First, you are working with a dedicated audit client, so you also get the population while you are doing the walkthrough. You verify the population with the client right then and there. You pick your sample while you are with the client. Together with the client, you pull the sample and start reviewing the audit evidence. Sure, some evidence may not be immediately available, but you are likely able to review most of the items in the initial meeting with the client.

The preceding description is exactly what happened during an Agile audit of Production Billing for a manufacturing entity with offshore manufacturing facilities. The dedicated audit customer attended the Sprint planning meeting and provided various details of the relationship and contractual expectations with the offshore facility. One of highest-priority risks included overbilling on production hours. The day after the Sprint planning meeting, the auditor and audit client met and started reviewing a control chart of billed hours compared to production output for the preceding six months. Management reviewed this report regularly and the audit test was to ensure that management control was performed adequately. During the review, we identified four days where the number of billed hours was out of the tolerable range. We asked the audit client if they had inquired about the deviation. Confidently, the client said yes and after searching their emails, the client found support explaining the conditions surrounding the discrepancy for three of the four days. The emails included several members of upper management in the discussion and conclusion. The fourth discrepancy was resolved by a peer and we were told there was a billing adjustment, but the details were unfamiliar to our key contact. We were directed to the peer and were able to obtain evidence supporting the adjustment in the hours charged; the adjustment resulted in a $400 credit and process change to mitigate future errors during shift changes per the contract. The related audit workpaper was written in real time during the discussions with the audit client and their peer and included much of the same information provided above. The workpaper was submitted for review to the Scrum Master and the task was moved to "Done" on the taskboard during the following Daily Scrum. [Note: this was one of our first Agile audits. In hindsight, we still had the testing mindset of a traditional audit. Upon seeing there were only four exceptions, we could have communicated that overbillings did not appear to be as risky as we thought and discontinue testing.]

Executing the Agile audit in this manner allows the client to see missing attributes at the same time you do. Observe their response, listen to their explanation, collect additional evidence if it's available, and remember your professional skepticism. Since the client simultaneously sees the same exception you do, you can get their agreement on the facts and reduce future battles and debate. Suppose you, the Agile auditor, misinterpret the evidence. In that case, the audit client is there to educate you on how to read and understand the evidence and clarify any potential exceptions before you leave their desk. We encourage you to write your workpaper in real time while you are looking at the evidence. Your audit client, who is sitting there with you, can read what you are recording in your workpapers, and you can get immediate Agile team member or peer sign-off that the workpaper is accurate. Thus, you eliminate the need for subsequent supervisory approval, which doesn't exist in Agile because there is no audit manager or lead to review your workpapers anyway.

 ## WORKPAPER DOCUMENTATION IN AN AGILE AUDIT ENVIRONMENT

For my auditor friends who just got a little uncomfortable reading "there is no supervisory approval" and are probably about to jump out of whatever you are sitting on to find us, let us explain. Your professional guidance may say something like the IIA's Standard 2340, *Engagement Supervision*: "Engagements must be properly supervised to ensure objectives are achieved, quality is assured, and staff is developed" (Institute of Internal Auditors 2017a). Let's not forget the related interpretation to IIA Standard 2340: "The extent of supervision required will depend on the proficiency and experience of internal auditors and the complexity of the engagement. The chief audit executive has overall responsibility for supervising the engagement, whether performed by or for the internal audit activity but may designate appropriately experienced internal audit activity members to perform the review. Appropriate evidence of supervision is documented and retained." Do you remember when we said you might need to get creative to implement Agile auditing? Here's an opportunity for creativity. Reread the standard and its interpretation. It gives some flexibility:

- Supervision depends on audit experience: in Agile auditing, we are trusted to be competent and exercise due diligence. Also, consider that you are collaborating with the audit client, who is an expert.
- Supervision depends on engagement complexity: in Agile auditing, we are managing complexity by breaking down the engagement into small increments, thus decreasing complexity as compared to a traditional audit.

- Supervision can be performed by or for the audit activity: the audit client conducts a peer review of the workpaper for the audit activity.
- Evidence of supervision is documented and retained: Add a column on your Sprint Backlog template that says "peer review of workpaper" and ask your peer reviewer to initial it or just indicate the date of the review. Again, we are trusted to exercise due diligence, and if we say that something was performed, our word should be sufficient. However, since the standard said we need to retain documented evidence, a checkmark, date, or initial kept somewhere in the audit files should suffice.

Maybe this interpretation and our chosen action is a mistake. It is okay. Try it. See if it works. If you fail, change your approach. Adapt. Be Agile!

To ensure that peer reviews meet our needs and we have the appropriate documentation instead of the "comprehensive documentation" maintained for traditional audits, we must intentionally determine how much documentation is minimally acceptable. Being minimally acceptable is a challenging concept for many auditors. Thinking back, there was one particular auditor who overdocumented every workpaper, and even when audit supervisors identified the irrelevant information in his workpapers, the auditor refused to remove it because it provided background context. In one specific case, the auditor submitted a 14-page workpaper narrative on a test the auditor completed during a walkthrough. After the auditor reluctantly removed extraneous information and cleared all review notes, the workpaper was just over three pages. Do you have any idea how long the auditor spent documenting that one-hour walkthrough?

To establish your definition and expectations for minimally acceptable workpapers in Agile auditing, consider the following: how much time are you willing to sacrifice providing assurance on governance, risk management, and controls by spending more time documenting your work? For the past few years, we've been working on convincing all audit teams that average workpapers are good enough. Maybe your Agile team could create a grading system for your workpapers to help auditors learn what must be included in the workpapers and how much is too much. For example, maybe you state that the desired grade is a "C workpaper," not a "C+" and not an "A." Could you describe what a C workpaper looks like? Would you be okay with C workpapers?

In one of our classes, the CAE agreed that C+ would be acceptable, and the class identified the criteria that must exist to get a C+. The CAE agreed with the minimally acceptable standards considering the cost/benefit relationship of creating the alternative A workpapers the team was accustomed to creating. Two years later, when we returned, the big joke was, "when will a C+ ever really be acceptable?" We understood that the auditors diligently used the workpaper grading scale we created in the class to document their workpapers. They were intentional about not doing anything that would constitute an A workpaper. Still, when the auditors submitted their workpapers for review, to clear the review notes, they had to create A workpapers. Within months of reaching the C+ workpaper agreement, the auditors were back to perfecting their workpapers to an A grade to satisfy the CAE. This cost them time and meant they were sacrificing more risk-based assessments and delivery of value to their organization to create perfect workpapers that *might* be used in the next audit or reviewed by regulators.

 ## MANAGING SCOPE CREEP

Inevitably, at some point during the Agile audit, the auditor, the audit leader, CAE, or the audit client will want to add something to the engagement scope. The Agile team's answer is "no!" or at least, "not in this Sprint, so let's add a user story to the Product Backlog and reevaluate it during our next Product Backlog refinement meeting." Yes, Agile audits are supposed to adapt, but remember, you are also balancing adapting with producing tangible results in a short time frame. If you start adding to the scope and start adding more user stories to your iteration, you will miss your deadline. You must be strong, have courage, and remember that you are an empowered team committed to achieving a specific goal. If the scope addition is more important than the current, committed scope, the Product Owner can choose to terminate the Sprint. Sprint terminations, or discontinuing a Sprint after it starts, should be rare.

The team members' most valuable tool to stay in scope is the daily meeting or, in the Scrum framework, the Daily Scrum. Agile team members are accountable to each other. The daily meeting focuses on progress toward the Sprint Goal and produces an actionable plan for the next day of work. This creates focus and improves self-management. During the daily meeting, Delivery Team Members and the Scrum Master should be alert to anything that sounds like scope creep, and team members must have the courage to ask questions to determine if a task is out of scope. The Scrum Master facilitates conversation during the daily meeting. The Scrum Master also ensures that only the Agile team members in attendance get to speak during the meeting, even if other stakeholders or users attend the daily meeting.

The hardest part about being a Scrum Master is cutting off an interested party who is not on the Agile team, particularly when they are a senior leader in the organization. Be polite, offer an alternative (such as using a parking lot list to be discussed after the daily meeting) to using the daily meeting to discuss their issue, and follow up with the interested party as promised.

You may recall that inspection is a critical pillar in the Scrum framework. While we are executing the Agile audit, we continuously self-inspect and expect inspections by others. We inspect to make sure people are doing what they promise to do during our daily meetings, and that upcoming tasks are necessary and within scope. As we are completing our tests, we are inspecting our work for accuracy and completeness. A great way to inspect the Agile audit team's work is through checking workpapers, even before they are complete. Reviewing draft workpapers ensures that the audit team's work is moving in the right direction.

If you've ever led an audit, you have probably received all of the workpapers two days before fieldwork is due to be completed. When this happens, it's nearly impossible to inspect or review all the workpapers using the required level of care, before the audit deadline. Typically, we miss our audit deadlines, or we don't do a good job inspecting the workpapers (yikes!). Agile requires more frequent and timely inspection.

 ## AUDIT FINDINGS

Whether you refer to the differences between what you expected to see (audit criteria) and what you saw (the condition) as a finding, issue, control weakness, audit comment, observation, deficiency, reservation, process improvement opportunity, or any other term of endearment, discrepancies are inevitable in business processes. Nobody and no process is perfect. When and how you communicate them in Agile auditing is different when compared to traditional auditing.

For some audit teams, audit findings become findings only after all the fieldwork is completed and after the "boss" agrees that it is a finding. In those audit shops, auditors delay communicating possible findings until the finding is drafted. This isn't our preferred approach, primarily because we practice Participatory Auditing (see Chapter 17 for a description of Participatory Auditing), but we know it occurs.

Other audit activities accumulate and review a list of potential audit report comments (PARC) with the audit client periodically during status meetings. The PARC is managed, and some items may be cleared or removed from the PARC as additional evidence is provided to resolve potential findings. It is also managed to identify which items in the PARC will be reported in the final audit report based on residual risk and risk appetite assessment.

Audit findings are communicated differently in Agile auditing. Audit findings may not be communicated to the audit client at all because the audit client discovers the issues simultaneously with the auditor's discovery of findings; as part of the Agile audit team, the client reviews the evidence along with the auditor. This is one of the greatest benefits of Agile auditing because auditors and audit clients do not debate the facts. Additionally, in Agile auditing, the Agile team (including the auditor and the audit client) articulates the finding details, which saves time debating over word choices in written documentation and communications of findings.

The articulated finding details are documented in real time in the audit workpapers. An Agile audit shop may choose to include in the audit work-papers the customary elements of audit findings: criteria, condition, cause, and effect or potential effect as specified in paragraphs 6.17, 6.19, 7.19, 7.21, 8.116, and 8.118 of the Yellow Book (U.S. Government Accountability Office 2018). They may also choose to include recommendations as noted in paragraph 9.18 of the Yellow Book: "Auditors should provide recommendations for corrective action if findings are significant within the context of the audit objectives." We recommend this approach in traditional auditing as it aids in bringing clarity to the details of findings. Note, we have referred to these elements as "customary," as the majority of the audit teams we have dealt with have in one form or another adopted them. However, there are differences between standards specifically noted here from the Yellow Book and the IIA expectations for quality of reports – although, when you think about it, the differences are really not that different. The standards are all about ensuring proper communications. The IIA IPPF has several standards on report writing. However, there is no specified model required for the presentation of audit results or reports. IPPF Standard 2410, *Criteria for Communicating*, states "Communications must include the engagement's objectives, scope, and results According to Standard 2420 – *Quality of Communications*, 'Communications must be accurate, objective, clear, concise, constructive, complete, and timely'" (Institute of Internal Auditors 2017a). The content and level of detail should be determined by the needs of the audience. Therefore, different organizations use different content and formats. The IPPF supplemental guidance, the Practice Guide, "Audit Reports, Communicating Assurance Engagement Results," points out that the structure of a report often includes among other components, a "Statement of facts (condition, criteria, cause, effect/risk)," as well as "Audit recommendations (corrective action to mitigate the risk identified in the observation)." To ensure that you adhere to the professional standards, remember the acronym TAC⁴O, which stands for Timely, Accurate, Clear, Complete, Concise, Constructive, and Objective. This is a great mnemonic technique for aspiring CIA candidates.

At one of the IIA's conferences, the CAE of LinkedIn at the time shared a novel concept. His team did not write extensive audit reports. Instead, they issued "bug fixes." A bug fix is a simple communication used in software development and testing to inform someone that something doesn't work the way it should – a bug. We saw immediate opportunities to incorporate something like this into Agile auditing.

We mentioned this approach in one class; one participant adamantly stated that bug fixes violated IIA Standards because auditors must provide recommendations. We didn't get into the details during the course, but the IIA Standards do not require recommendations. Standard 2410.A1, *Criteria for Communicating*, states, "as well as applicable recommendations and/or action plans" (Institute of Internal Auditors 2017a). An Agile auditor could simply discuss or otherwise communicate the action plan to satisfy the IIA Standard.

To streamline writing audit findings, a technique successfully used by a mortgage origination company was to engage the audit client in performing specific testing as well as actually writing the finding. This was a very successful technique. The audit client was better able to identify the most effective language to ensure consensus on the weakness details and associated recommendations to mitigate or eliminate the issue. The audit team performed minor tweaks once the audit client provided their narrative of the weakness.

Another successful communication technique used in state government audits was to highlight in the audit report what was being done correctly by the process area or business operation. While communicating satisfactory performance is encouraged in the internal auditing profession by the IIA IPPF, specifically Standard 2410.A2, acknowledging satisfactory performance in engagement communications is often overlooked and usually does not receive the same attention as audit weaknesses. When we used this technique in our Agile audits, we gave the audit client positive affirmations (kudos) regarding the audit team's specific observations. In essence, the audit client was "kudified" (a term we coined, which became part of the clients' jargon). For example, we provided details and comments when the audit client was in the process of implementing (or had actually put in place) corrective actions even before the audit was finalized. This technique increased collaboration and client agreement on areas of weakness.

USING AGILE AUDITING TO SOLVE ENGAGEMENT EXECUTION PROBLEMS

You can use Agile auditing to solve the engagement execution problems discussed in Chapter 5, and listed here. We documented the Agile techniques that lead to solving some of these problems:

- Scope creep by auditors.
- Scope creep by audit leadership.
- Audit leadership changing audit direction in the middle of the audit.
- Scope creep by an audit client.
- Auditors getting placed on special projects during an audit.
- Data analytics failures.
- Often the failures occur because auditors do not understand the data. Completing analytics with the audit customer avoids this failure, as the customer is the expert on the data.
- Analysis paralysis when using data analytics.
- Wasted time waiting for audit evidence that doesn't exist.
- Wasted time waiting for audit client responses to emails.
- Audit clients providing irrelevant evidence.
- Audit clients providing incomplete evidence.
- Incomplete workpapers.
- Irrelevant information in workpapers.
- Retaining too much information to "prove" work performed.
- Workpapers do not support testing summary and conclusions.
- Perfecting workpapers.
- Unreasonable audit supervisor expectations.
- Nitpicky workpaper review notes.
- Too much time spent capturing hours worked on audits.

Let's consider audit scope creep, whether by auditors, audit leadership, or by an audit client. When determining the audit scope of the project, it is essential to remember the Agile Manifesto. Looking at the different audit objectives as epics versus stories and maintaining focus on the customers, after all, characterizes an organization that is ready to embark in the Agile way. Customers, as well as auditors, are working under the same mission, vision, goals, and values to help an entity succeed. Collaboratively, they can best agree on what type and level of assurance will deliver the most significant value to the organization. This is the first step in managing scope and occurs in the Sprint planning meeting. Staying focused on the agreed assurance throughout execution is essential to minimize scope creep.

Moreover, as we discussed earlier in this chapter, the team members' most valuable tool to prevent scope creep is the daily meeting, or in the Scrum framework, the Daily Scrum. Since the team members are accountable to each other, during the daily meeting team members and the Scrum Master are alerted to anything that sounds like scope creep and are empowered to ask questions to ensure they stay within scope. Furthermore, the Scrum Master ensures that even if other stakeholders attend the daily meeting, they do not present. Scope creep issues suggested by these non-Agile Team Member attendees are reduced or nearly eliminated.

Let's consider a few more ideas to solve the engagement execution problems listed earlier:

Problem	Solution
Analysis paralysis when using data analytics	Setting a time limit on each task requires the Delivery Team to reassess their progress and evaluate the cost/benefit of additional analysis.
Wasted time waiting for audit evidence that doesn't exist	Performing the sampling and testing in real time with the client coupled with early agreement on what constitutes an exception avoids searching for or waiting for evidence.
Wasted time waiting for audit client responses to emails	Due to the real-time collaboration, there are no emails requiring responses. Questions are asked and answered immediately.
Audit clients providing irrelevant evidence	Writing workpapers in real time with the audit client reduces the amount of time available and limits the amount of information that can be documented so that only essential information is in the workpaper.
Audit clients providing incomplete evidence	Audit clients and auditors see the information and reach a conclusion at the same time. Thus, there is no need to prepare for a battle to "prove" the results.
Incomplete workpapers	Simply put, the collaborative, real-time writing of the workpaper means you don't have time to perfect the workpaper.
Irrelevant information in workpapers	There is no audit supervisor, thus there cannot be unreasonable supervisor expectations. The expectations are set and agreed in the Sprint planning meeting.

(Continued)

Problem	Solution
Retaining too much information to "prove" work performed	In Agile, time is of the essence. We don't have time to perfect workpapers and we don't have time to nitpick irrelevant details of a workpaper, such as punctuation and spelling.
Workpapers do not support testing summary and conclusions	In Agile, we focus on meeting a deadline. Capturing hours is a non-value-added activity and is usually eliminated.
Perfecting workpapers	Setting a time limit on each task requires the Delivery Team to reassess their progress and evaluate the cost/benefit of additional analysis.
Unreasonable audit supervisor expectations	Performing the sampling and testing in real time with the client coupled with early agreement on what constitutes an exception avoids searching for or waiting for evidence.
Nitpicky workpaper review notes	Due to the real-time collaboration, there are no emails requiring responses. Questions are asked and answered immediately.
Too much time spent capturing hours worked on audits	Writing workpapers in real time with the audit client reduces the amount of time available and limits the amount of information that can be documented so that only essential information is in the workpaper.

We challenge you to continue to solve the engagement execution problems as you implement the Agile auditing framework.

NUGGETS

As previously stated, one of the significant differences in this framework is the level of collaboration with audit clients. Consider your appetite to perform audit tests with your audit client, write workpapers as you complete the audit work with your client, and have the audit client perform a peer review of the workpapers. Additionally, perform a cost/benefit analysis on the amount of time your team spends creating and reviewing workpapers compared to what they could be doing with their time (i.e., assessing more risk, providing more assurance, and adding more value).

Consider the following questions as well:

- Are you ready and willing to sacrifice audit workpaper perfection to add more value?
- What are you willing to establish as a minimally acceptable workpaper and audit documentation criteria?
- Will you be willing to leverage technology in your Agile audits, including collaboration tools, videoconferencing, project taskboard tools, and data analytics?
- Are your auditors willing to take accountability to set a scope they believe they can complete in a limited time frame?
- Will your Product Owners be willing to stick within an agreed-upon scope?
- Do your audit clients want to work collaboratively with you to get the audit completed within a short time frame?
- Are your Scrum Masters ready to help your Agile teams remain vigilant about sticking to the selected scope?

CHAPTER ELEVEN

Implementing Agile Auditing: Communicating Agile Audit Results

 REPORT WRITING

> *Why do we spend so much time writing audit reports?*
> *The painful truth is that sometimes we write the report for ourselves.*

Writing audit reports is undoubtedly our least favorite part of auditing, particularly since there is no standard language or structure universal to the profession. The IIA Standards require internal auditors to communicate the results of engagements; written reports are not required. Why do we spend so much time writing audit reports? Why write a report at all? The painful truth is that sometimes we write the report for ourselves. Before redesigning your reporting process for Agile auditing, consider the following:

- Why do you write a report?
- Who is your audience?

- Who reads your report?
- Who is your primary reader?
- What do your audience and primary reader know about the process area?
- What do your audience and primary reader know about the audit process?
- How much information do your audience and primary reader want regarding the audit?
- How much detail do they need?
- What do they use the report for once they receive it?
- What do they do with the report after the audit?
- What would happen if you didn't provide a written report?
- How would you communicate your results?
- Have you already shared your results before writing the report?
- If so, was your communication sufficient for the audit client and larger audience?

 ## DAILY MEETINGS TO COMMUNICATE "BUGS," DEFICIENCIES, AND FINDINGS

If you've practiced Agile auditing, your client already knows the errors and exceptions; they participated in identifying them. Your client's boss, if they attended the open daily meetings, already heard of the exceptions. The only thing you may need to do is summarize your results for the board and senior management.

 ## SPRINT REVIEW

Before communicating results, issuing an opinion, or providing a final report from an audit perspective, Agile audit teams hold a Sprint Review, as an informative session, with the team members, Scrum Master, and Product Owner. Remember, the Product Owner has final approval authority for the Sprint's completion based on the Sprint and Sprint Review information. The Product Owner also learns which Sprint tasks or user stories were not completed (this should be rare) and adds the incomplete items to the Product Backlog as a result of the Sprint Review. The Agile audit team also discusses the identified issues, resolutions, and corrective actions during the Sprint Review. The team presents the Agile audit's value proposition during the Sprint Review. Recall that the value proposition is an element in the project canvas. Thus, all Agile team members understand the expected value of the Agile audit. Three activities should not happen at the Sprint Review:

1. Decision making
2. Product Backlog refinement (this occurs shortly after the Sprint Review)
3. Commitment to the next Sprint (this happens during the next Sprint planning meeting)

We recommend Sprint Reviews for all audit projects, including traditional audits.

DO I STILL NEED A REPORT?

After working in an Agile audit environment, conducting daily meetings, and holding a Sprint Review, it is natural to feel like you have communicated the audit progress, findings, and opinions sufficiently. So, you are likely to ask, "Do I still need a report?" Maybe.

Making this determination largely depends on your ability to ensure that the right people hear your message, the stakeholders understand the organization's risks, and how by-the-book you want to adhere to your professional standards. It will also depend on your ability to communicate your new Agile auditing approach to those relying on your audit work and parties who evaluate your effectiveness as an auditor or audit activity.

A bank in Kansas City, Missouri, shared their successful approach to convincing regulators and external auditors that an "official" audit report was unnecessary. First, their procedure manual delineated the audit results communications process, including cross-references to applicable standards. Second, they held frank discussions with the regulators regarding the move to Agile auditing. Third, they provided the regulator examples of actual completed audits showing how results were communicated without an "official" report. Fourth, the regulators received the related workpapers for the original work performed and the workpaper of the testing performed to verify remediation of the exceptions communicated to prove that an official report was not necessary to get the audit customer to take the right actions. Last, the auditors maintained contact with the regulators prior to implementing significant adaptions to their Agile auditing approach to keep the regulators abreast of and comfortable with the methodology.

SPRINT RETROSPECTIVE

The final step in an Agile audit is holding a Sprint Retrospective meeting (lessons learned session) to help the Agile team become more efficient in the next Sprint. A Sprint Retrospective should be 45 minutes or less per week of Sprint length. This is a closed meeting for the Delivery Team Members. including the Scrum Master and Product Owner. With other audit teams, we've participated in lessons learned, which tended to become forums for complaining. Learning about Agile taught us a better way to conduct lessons learned exercises. In the Sprint Retrospective, two key questions drive the team discussions:

1. What did we do well so we can do it again?
2. What could we do better on the next Agile audit?

We like the star model derivative of the retrospective, which places experiences in one of five buckets/prongs: keep, do more, do less, start doing, and stop doing. In practice, we use sticky notes that we can move around the buckets based on discussions.

1. Discuss what should we keep doing. We start with what we should continue doing by having team members brainstorm things that are working well and writing a sticky note for each. Then the team moves sticky notes to the second, "do more," or third, "do less," prong of the star.
2. Identify additional tasks that we should we do more frequently.
3. Discuss what should we do less of to create efficiencies.
4. Identify potentially inefficient or non-value-added tasks and place those sticky notes in the "stop doing" bucket.
5. List things that we should start doing to make the next Agile audit more efficient or to add more value.

 ## USING AGILE AUDITING TO SOLVE ENGAGEMENT COMMUNICATION AND REPORTING PROBLEMS

The conventional waterfall methods and practices applied in assurance and attestation engagements lead to various problems when communicating within audit teams, with audit clients, and in writing and presenting audit reports. We initially presented the following problems in Chapter 5:

- Poorly written audit findings
- Audit reports with too much "fluff"

- Audit reports that don't state the right message
- Audit reports that conceal what's wrong
- Audit reports that take months to write
- Audit reports with much internal back-and-forth between internal audit leadership
- Audit reports with much internal back-and-forth with audit clients
- Audit reports that anger audit clients
- Exit conferences with fiery discussions between auditors, audit clients, and executives

When using Agile auditing, you are time-bound to complete the audit in less than one month and preferably in just two weeks. Thus, there is no time for fluff or continuous back-and-forth between the Agile team and internal audit leadership or arguing with clients over findings or language. Collaboration with the entire team and adequately defining the meaning of "Done" minimizes reporting problems.

One of our clients successfully eliminated all of these problems by developing a template for audit results communication. This template was a maximum two-page summary of the results. What is impressive is that the client often completed the results template. Thus, it eliminated the banter that is so often prevalent in communicating results. I know what you are thinking: What about the accuracy of the communication and auditor independence, and objectivity? Remember, the Product Owner exercises final approval of the Sprint's completion based on the Sprint and Sprint Review information. Also, ownership remains with the audit activity. It doesn't have to be as hard as we make it! There was agreement with the clients to keep it simple and use neutral words, stick to the facts, and ensure that the report stimulates action necessary to address the audit's issues.

One reality of auditing is that change is hard. Most of the teams we work with insist on writing a traditional audit report. Even those with mature Agile auditing methodologies still have a grueling audit report-writing phase of the Agile audit. It is unfortunate that we don't have many examples of Agile audit reports. In a perfect Agile auditing world, there would be no report. Perhaps a simple listing of expected corrective actions to track the necessary remediation follow-up and monitoring activities expected of auditors would suffice. We did present such a list to an audit committee who responded, "We really just want to know if there is anything we need to know about." When it comes to satisfying an audit committee, instead of giving them a lengthy report, it would be more Agile to list the audits and provide an opinion on each. For any audit the audit committee desires further explanation of, the

Product Owner would be well-versed to provide a verbal summary or the completed workpapers. How can you become more Agile in your report writing? We challenge you to implement a similar approach.

 NUGGETS

For your Agile audits, have you considered all your communication options to select your organization's best approach? Maybe your team can provide "bugs" each time you identify an exception or discrepancy. Perhaps your communication of Agile audit results could be limited to verbal discussions supported by an accessible issue tracking system that includes the expected corrective actions and implementation dates. Maybe you can completely forego writing a "report." If your professional standards require a report, what are the specific requirements? How can you make sure you meet *only* those requirements and nothing more, just the minimum expectation? Before you change your current process in favor of Agile auditing, consider all the options. Don't forget to consider your audience's needs. Would your audit clients be okay if they didn't receive a written audit report? Would your audit committee agree with this approach?

PART THREE

3

Special Considerations

CHAPTER TWELVE

Agile Auditing in the "New Normal" Environment (Remote Auditing)

 ## THE NEW NORMAL

The longer we sustain a change in the environment, the closer that new, changed environment becomes the usual way of doing something. "The new normal" (North America) is a previously unfamiliar or atypical situation that has become standard, usual, or expected (Oxford Dictionary 2020b). The term initially was used in a lecture cautioning economists and policymakers that industrial economies could revert to their most recent means after the 2007–2008 financial crisis (El-Erian 2010).

The 2020 global pandemic, COVID-19, is creating a new normal as we are writing this book. The pandemic tested the feasibility of Agile auditing in a virtual environment. The need for social distancing has challenged the management of all audit activities, including risk assessments, testing, and reporting. Communications within the audit teams and clients have moved primarily to a virtual environment. Organizations are being affected by restrictions on travel and requirements to stay at home, presenting practical challenges to any audit team attempting to complete an engagement.

This socially distanced environment is a perfect opportunity to embrace Agile auditing and technology to complete audits in a collaborative environment. Many Agile tools, such as project taskboards and daily meetings, help audit management and teammates follow work progress.

By and large, before the pandemic, Agile projects were designed to occur with face-to-face, in-person teams. Entire organizations redesigned their facilities to create open work environments to encourage collaboration needed in Agile projects. Pre-COVID-19, one of our clients moved all auditors out of their cubicles and assigned them lockers for their belongings. There were a limited number of cubes, offices, and small meeting rooms available for reservation daily. Without a reservation, you were working in a shared collaboration area. When COVID-19 came along, office buildings closed, libraries closed, and government authorities did not permit large group gatherings. What was an Agile team to do? Use technology!

Technology tools, including collaboration tools, taskboard tools, and videoconferencing, have been around for a while to aid in Agile projects. However, early Agile audit adopters weren't consistently taking advantage of them. Additionally, organizations have electronic systems and data for most of their processes and transactions, which aids in remote auditing and provides easy access to audit evidence. Moreover, most auditors have data analytics tools to extract, sort, filter, and analyze data. They probably should be a primary means of testing and concluding, especially in Agile environments.

We remember getting very excited when one of our clients said the team would meet via Skype, a popular videoconferencing and screen-sharing tool. Then we realized that their use of this fantastic tool was essentially a conference call. Nobody shared their video cameras or screens, and most participants used their mobile phones. We haven't had the chance to work with that client since COVID-19 started. However, on our last Skype call with them, we encouraged them to leverage all available technology and technology features for their Agile auditing.

Technology, from videoconferencing to data analytics software used to extract data, identify anomalies, exceptions, and nonconformance with expectations and criteria, help enhance efficiencies in the Agile auditing process. Data analytics aficionados are rejoicing in the audit profession as auditors are finally embracing data analytics techniques, machine learning, and robotics process automation as essential means of analyzing evidence and drawing conclusions.

We are in a world of unprecedented change, with disruptive technologies changing how we operate in all industries and professions, including auditing. As Richard Chambers states in *The Speed of Risk*, "To remain relevant in a global business environment of increasing competition, technological advances, and downsizing, internal auditors must act tactfully as agents of change – and embrace the potential risks associated with innovation" (Chambers 2019). When we think of innovation, names like Apple, Alphabet, Amazon, Microsoft, Samsung, Huawei, Alibaba, Tesla, and Facebook come to mind. So how many of these companies apply Agile methodologies and practices in one or more functions beyond IT? In other words, how many of these companies are using Agile in Human Resources (HR), Marketing, Sales, Audit, and other business departments? Nearly all. According to a study conducted by Organize Agile, which included corporations from 19 countries, almost half of the organizations have been using an Agile methodology for three years or longer. Of these, 80% use Scrum as their Agile methodology (Consultancy.eu 2020).

As noted earlier in Chapter 5, when discussing Agile's benefits, one of the top reasons for using Agile is improving flexibility amid a rapidly changing environment. Agile has been around since early 2001. However, the adoption of Agile has been slow in some disciplines, including auditing. *Crossing the Chasm* by Geoffrey Moore (Moore 2014) provides a simple model based on the technology adoption curve that divides technology users and organizations into five categories distinguished by their unique psychographic profile. It describes the market penetration of any new technology product in terms of progression in the types of consumers it attracts through its useful life. The first group is the **Innovators**: a tiny group that pursues new technology products aggressively even before a formal marketing program has been launched. Next are the **Early Adopters**. Like innovators, they buy into new technology very quickly. However, they are not technologists like innovators; they rely on their instincts. They are highly motivated to leverage the advantages they see in the new technology. The next group is the **Early Majority**. This group shares some characteristics of the early adopters, but a sense of practicality strongly drives them. They also are likely to be followers and do what others are doing (everyone is getting in the ocean, I think it's safe to go in, let's go!). The penultimate group is the **Late Majority**. This group does not care if everyone is getting in the ocean (they also probably don't like sharks!). They do not like change and are very risk-averse. Finally come the **Laggards**. This group doesn't want anything to do with new technology for any reason (see Figure 12.1).

As you can see in Figure 12.1, there are cracks or gaps between each group, with the largest gap being between the early adopters and the early

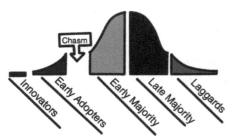

FIGURE 12.1 Agile Auditing Adoption Life Cycle
Source: Illustration by Carmen Catlin. Adapted from Moore (2014).

majority. Moore refers to the big gap as the chasm. He explains that the smaller gap between innovators and early adopters indicates that early adopters, not being technologists, cannot readily transfer technology into significant new benefits. Moore further explains that getting through this initial gap shows that the new technology enables some strategic leap forward that was not possible previously to appeal to the nontechnologist early adopters. Moreover, the gap between the early and late majority exists because the late majority is unwilling to change. At this point, the technology, product, or service offered needs to be made increasingly more comfortable to adopt for it to be successful.

So, what does this have to do with Agile auditing in the new normal? If you think about it, it reflects how different disciplines have adopted Agile. Some claim Agile adoption has not truly crossed the chasm, and some claim it is entering the late majority. Regardless of where Agile auditing is placed on the Agile auditing adoption life cycle diagram, change is here. Not adopting a more flexible and collaborative approach could mean the demise of nearly any audit shop. As you embark on your Agile auditing journey, think about Moore's simple adoption curve and apply it to your organization as a way to reach greater market penetration and acceptance of a new way of conducting audits.

EXISTING TECHNOLOGIES

Virtual Conferencing

Collaboration tools such as taskboards and videoconferencing have been around for a while. Virtual meetings are real-time interactions that happen over the internet or via a conference call with participants from anywhere on the globe. Platforms such as Skype, Zoom, and Microsoft Teams create an efficient means of sharing and exchanging data and information in real time without participants being physically located in the same place. These platforms also allow individuals to see each other, increasing communication effectiveness because you can observe nonverbal cues missed with email communications and traditional audio-only phone calls. Additionally, most platforms allow screen sharing, a valuable tool in the new normal, remote auditing world. Auditors can watch the customer perform on-screen actions to complete transactions and processes.

What's more, some organizations are slow to adopt the full functionality of the platforms. For example, people are hesitant to share their videos, and available recording options are not often used, as just mentioned with the example of one of our clients meeting via Skype. As individuals become more comfortable with the technology, many predict organizations will opt for more videoconferencing and reduce regular face-to-face meetings. Our clients often ask us to share our techniques for having successful virtual conferences. We have included some of our successful practices here.

Before we share our techniques, we want to take into account our new normal environment. In many situations the entire family is operating from home (virtual class learning with multiple children in different grade levels with both parents working from home offices). Keep in mind the team's needs for creating a work-life balance. Can a nonparent Team Member carry more on its plate? It is important for the team to bond together and ensure that all members have each other's backs.

Techniques for Effective Virtual Conferencing

Before the meeting:
- Determine the purpose of the meeting and who needs to participate.
- Be mindful of participant time zones when setting up the time for the meeting.
- Develop an agenda, including opportunities for participants to engage, and include set times for speakers.
- Work with the presenters to prepare materials.
- Conduct meeting dry runs as appropriate, especially for more involved and complicated presentations.
- Share the agenda, connection information, and handouts in advance and send a reminder just before the meeting.

- Keep meetings short, preferably under an hour, unless you are doing a 15-minute Agile standup meeting.
- Add stimulating and interactive content to keep participants interested.
- Develop and place ground rules in the chatbox for participants to see.*
- Choose appropriate technology based on meeting purposes and participant needs. Keep in mind any special needs and make sure the audio technology is suitable for participants to hear clearly (e.g., a high-quality headset, microphone, or speaker). Also, consider the following questions when choosing the technology: Do you need to record the meeting? Do you want participants to interact by phone, on the computer, or via the chat function?
- Consider the demands of team members who may be simultaneously parenting and coordinating virtual learning sessions for their children.

Develop a backup plan for different situations, including technical malfunctions, internet connectivity issues, or power outages.

*Ground rules:
When you are at a conference, even a virtual one, you are not alone! There are many factors to consider. How formal should participants be? Setting expectations for conduct during virtual conferences is a best practice for all organizations in the current work environment.

- Turn away from email for the short duration of the meeting.
- Before speaking during the meeting, state your name and speak loudly and clearly.
- Use the mute/unmute button.
- Specify the dress code for participants, if applicable.

During the meeting:
- Speakers should use their webcams or post their photos.
- Consider your body language.
- Talk to the camera, not the picture.
- Request that participants virtually raise their hands or use the chat function to respond, to prevent multiple participants from speaking simultaneously.
- Use polls to ask participants questions, as appropriate.
- Monitor the chat and be attentive to participants' needs.

After the meeting:
- Follow up on actions agreed upon.
- Provide a link for the recorded meeting, when applicable.
- Check with participants and request feedback, recording feedback in lessons learned.

Training for meeting hosts:
- How to use the web application and tools used for the meetings.
- Keeping the screen at eye level.
- Background: Be aware of personal information or items you may not want to show on camera (i.e., books, religious icons, family pictures).
- Awareness of face touching, where to focus your eyes, reduce outside or family noises (dog barking and weed blowers come to mind!).

Data Analytics

Analyzing data in our audits to create business value is not a new concept. However, what continues to improve is technology, reliance, speed of the analysis, and quantity and data sources used for analysis. Data analytics (DA) is an essential tool for auditors to gain business insights and evaluate controls. It often ranks on the top three skills most desired of an auditor. DA has become increasingly important for organizations of all types and sizes. Agile auditing demands DA, especially under our new normal. We **emphadamantly** assert that auditors who don't gain DA skills will fade away. So, what are you to do if you are an auditor in a group of individuals whose DA skills are minimal? You develop DA skills! Following is an overview of DA basics to get you started. Unfortunately, we can't possibly include everything you need to know about DA, as that in itself requires a whole new book. As you read, we hope you will realize that, for the most part, you have been doing analytics without the fancy names and that expanding your skills is within your reach.

Auditors overrely on discussions with audit clients and on reviews of small samples to draw audit conclusions. Auditors need to rely more on testing entire populations of data or transactions to identify patterns, anomalies, exceptions, discrepancies, and outliers and then use other techniques to determine if the identified exceptions are evidence of larger problems. There are many opportunities to leverage data analytics in the new normal remote auditing world to reduce business process owners' and audit clients' demands.

So, let's talk basics. As described by Stippich and Preber in their book *Data Analytics* (Stippich and Preber 2016), the term *data analytics* is the process of gathering and analyzing data and then using the results to make better decisions. They further state, "The 'American Institute of Certified Public Accountants' (AICPA) defines data analytics for external audits as 'the science and art of discovering and analyzing patterns, identifying anomalies, and extracting other useful information.'" Further, Stippich and Preber point out that this definition also applies to other audit professionals, such as internal auditors. They note that the IPPF Standard 1220.A2 states, "in exercising due professional care internal auditors must consider the use of technology-based audit and other data analysis techniques" (Institute of Internal Auditors 2017a).

Why do we need to use DA, especially in the new normal? One reason is that it reduces auditor bias. J.J. Sutherland said it well when he wrote, "data doesn't care about your opinion" in *The Scrum Fieldbook: A Master Class on Accelerating Performance, Getting Results, and Defining the Future* (Sutherland 2019). Unless someone is intentionally manipulating the data, DA tells a factual story.

So, what has been keeping the audit profession from leveraging more data analytics? One reason is the belief that the available data is not useful. Our friend and data analytics guru, Joe Oringel of Visual Risk IQ, has said numerous times, "don't let bad data keep you from doing good data analytics. Even bad data can tell you a lot about an organization and its process." Another reason is not knowing where to begin. Data analytics is a process that starts with determining your business question. John Tukey, a notable mathematician and pioneer in data analytics, encouraged identifying exploratory and confirmatory questions (Tukey 1980). Exploratory questions are broad general inquiries that are open-ended in nature; for example, how many completed transactions did we have last month? Confirmatory questions are specific inquiries directed to acknowledge the existence or nonexistence of something and are typically closed-ended questions. For example, were there any transactions approved by terminated employees? To identify good questions, you must be an excellent critical thinker. Critical thinking is a crucial skill for data analytics; it is also one of the nine attributes of outstanding internal auditors (Chambers 2017b).

In addition to thinking about questions as exploratory or confirmatory, auditors can think of data analytics questions focused on the past, present, or future. Data and questions focused on the past provide hindsight on what already happened (**descriptive** analytics) or why something happened (**diagnostic** analytics). Another view to starting DA leverages DA descriptions provided by Thomas Davenport, a well-known pioneer on data analytics in the academic arena. Davenport describes data analytics as providing information on what happened (past), what is happening now (present), and what will happen (future). Davenport also describes data analytics as providing insight on how and why something happened (past), what's the next best action (present), and what is the best or worst that can happen (future). Davenport's descriptions align with other data analytics types – determining what will happen in the future (**predictive analytics**) and providing a specific course of action or correction (**prescriptive analytics**) (Davenport and Harris 2017). *We further discuss these analytics during the Data Analytics Process topic later in this chapter.*

DA is more than collecting tons of data and cramming it in reports that few people understand. Let's start by explaining some of the DA key terms (also included in the Appendix A: Glossary of Terms at the end of this book). The terminology in this list comes (in part) from the IIA's Global Technology Audit Guide (GTAG), "Understanding and Auditing Big Data" (Institute of Internal Auditors 2017b). It is a shortlist of terms that, in our opinion, should be of most use to those of you less familiar with DA. For those of you who have become DA experts, feel free to skip this section.

The 3 Vs of Data (aka Big Data):

■ **Volume** is the amount of data created, including structured and unstructured (see "Variety" below).
■ **Velocity** is the speed at which we produced data. As technology use grows, the amount of data created grows exponentially.
■ **Variety** refers to the type of data format, **structured** and **unstructured**. Structured data is effortlessly organized and formatted and can be searchable in a relational database. Structured data is what we are familiar with and have been using in our audits for years. Examples include names, addresses, dates, and identifying figures such as social security and credit card numbers. Unstructured data, categorized as qualitative data, has no predefined model and cannot be processed and analyzed using conventional tools. Instead, it requires nonrelational tools to analyze, and this is a big part of what is new for auditing. Examples include text, audio, video, social media activity, and surveillance imagery, including GPS and facial recognition. It is much more challenging to process, organize, and analyze.

Other notable Vs of data include:

■ **Veracity.** Content quality and accuracy, the truthfulness of the data. Remember, auditors also need to consider whether the data collection was ethical and legal and how the data is being stored and protected!

- **Variability.** A summary statistic representing the amount of dispersion in a data set, i.e., the extent to which data points deviate from the mean and each other; is typically measured by range, mean, variance, and standard deviation.
- **Visualization.** The ability to translate vast amounts of data into simple-to-understand and presentable graphics and charts to gain insight from the analysis. An excellent reference to "enable you to shift from simply showing data to storytelling with data" is the book by Cole Nussbaumer Knaflic, *Storytelling with Data* (Nussbaumer Knaflic 2015).
- **Value.** Generated when new insights translate into actions that create positive outcomes.

> To take advantage of DA to its fullest potential, including using "big data," organizations need to invest in creating the proper environment.

To take advantage of DA to its fullest potential, including using "big data," organizations need to invest in creating the proper environment. Creating this environment starts with training and retraining existing staff, hiring and retaining skilled personnel, and ultimately implementing a DA program suitable for the organization, including acquiring and implementing DA technologies appropriate for its analysis needs. Before you spend a single dollar, start simple, and use existing tools (MS Excel, Access, or other Audit Command Language [ACL] your organization might already have). Also, you need to leverage your current insights and understand what skills and knowledge your team already possesses.

Data Analytics Process

Following is a synopsis of the DA process. You can consider this process as your recipe for starting DA. You will most likely realize that you are already performing many of these steps, even if you are not using advanced technologies for your analysis.

Before you even get started, you need to understand the organization's mission, vision, goals, values, and objectives. Having a good understanding will help identify the critical questions you will be asking in your audit. From the start, it is crucial to establish a clear understanding of the expected benefits you will derive from your analysis and link it to your audit plan.

1. *Decide on the goals and objectives (determine your business question).* Defining objectives may first require significant data collection and analysis. Step 1 is also known as framing the business problem statement. It is a clear, succinct explanation of what the problem is and why it is justifiable. It describes specific issues the business is facing and ideas on how to address them. In this step, you address the five questions of who, what, where, when, and why. To determine your business question, you need to know the data: Does it exist? What skills does your team have to analyze and interpret results? Auditors need to know if the required data exists or not, or is unavailable. Knowing this will help set priorities and improve future data. Also, there are times when you will develop the question without knowing enough about the problem or what information you have. Exercise caution with trying to develop the question without necessary information. This can lead to solving a problem that was not a problem in the first place (it could be a symptom of the problem). Now you can determine what you are testing.

2. *Determine what you are measuring and how to measure it.* Generally, measurements refer to designating numbers to indicate different variables' values. This step is also known as framing the analytics problem statement. You are rewriting the business question in this step to determine how to proceed. It is a translation of the "what" of the business into the "how" of the analytics problem. Here you will answer questions such as what results do you want? Who will take action? What do they need? At this point, you should also determine success metrics (key performance indicators as well as critical success factors). This step will help you determine the approach you will use to analyze the data. What will be your inputs and outputs? What are your assumptions about the analytics of the problem? For example, do you expect all the data to have a positive or negative trend? Do you expect exponential growth? You will define success and get input from the client on agreement of success factors. What criteria will you measure against? How will you know there is something wrong?

3. *Obtain your data.* Now that you know what types of data you need for your analysis, you can determine whether you can gather the data from existing databases, considering data internally as well as externally produced. Suppose data is not available or is insufficient. In that case, consider if this may be an audit finding or if you can collect new data. You also need to know how the data was created and collected. It will help with understanding whether there are limitations, biases, or abnormalities in the data. Understanding how the data was created and collected can also help

you better know how to clean the data and conduct the proper analysis. The more relevant data you can acquire, the better correlations and more significant actionable insights you will achieve.

4. *Clean your data.* This a foundational element of the data analysis process. Some data is better than no data. However, junk or incomplete data may generate incorrect results, mislead the auditors, and cause significant credibility issues. Data cleansing aims to create data sets that are standardized and uniform to allow proper business intelligence and access for whatever data analytics tools you are using. It also helps find the right data for your particular query. Cleansing prepares the data for analysis by correcting syntax errors, removing irrelevant data, standardizing data sets, and correcting other issues in the data such as empty fields, missing codes, and duplicate data points. There are different data-cleansing methods, depending on how the data is stored and what questions you are trying to answer. Data cleansing can be tedious and is often a reason why auditors abandon DA. Cleansing data can take a considerable amount of time; we've heard estimates that it can take 80% or more of the time spent performing DA. Working with your client from day one will help you get the data you need faster.

An essential aspect of substantially reducing the need for data cleansing starts at the data collection point. For data created by the organizations (internally created data), the organization needs to develop a data-driven culture and implement programs to teach all employees how to accurately collect, work with, and make decisions based on high-quality data. A lack of data literacy skills can be very costly for an organization.

An excellent example of low data literacy was discovered during Ceciliana's audits of a large grocery store chain. During the audit, Ceciliana noted that sales of carbonated beverages (which were subject to sales tax) had substantially declined for the past year, and sales of fruit juice (which are exempt from sales tax) had increased drastically, resulting in the retailer incurring a much lower tax liability than in previous years. The retailer explained that since the overall sales had not declined, he concluded it was a good thing, remaining unaware of the problem. Unfortunately, the retailer was still liable for the tax on sales of the carbonated beverages, whether collected or not from his customers. This mistake caused the retailer thousands of dollars in additional tax plus interest and penalties. Upon closer review, Ceciliana noted that cashiers were using new sophisticated point-of-sale cash registers with rather complicated keypads. The keypads were small, challenging to read, and listed beverages in consecutive order. When pressing the button for carbonated beverages, a tax was added to the bill. However, no tax was added or collected for fruit juice sales, which, based on its placement, was the button that was being used for nearly all beverage sales, carbonated or not. The cashiers had become aware of the input error and didn't think much about it, as the price for all beverages was similar. If these employees had been equipped with the proper data literacy skills, they would have been able to see that they were collecting erroneous data, and could have quickly stopped the error that turned into bad data and a large tax liability.

5. *Determine your approach (select methodology)*. In this step, you will summarize and visualize the data. It is an essential step in data analytics, as people often understand pictures better than words. For example, with graphics and images, you can see the different variance measures indicating the data distribution around the mean. Auditors can use tools including Microsoft Excel (MS Excel) and standard spreadsheets or more sophisticated tools dedicated to analyzing large volumes of data using preprogrammed macros and scripts.

One of our Agile seminar attendees who worked for a financial institution shared an example of how they used MS Excel to solve a contentious issue from the past audit during their Agile pilot implementation. They were looking for just one exception to the credit limit approval process to meet the criteria established to indicate that controls were not working as intended. Using a simple data validation tool in MS Excel, they tested the entire population for the audit period. They discovered over 30 instances where approvals were not in conformance with the established criteria. They were able to stop the testing and immediately provide accurate results of the exceptions and solve the prior audit dispute. The test from start to end was completed in a couple of hours compared to a few weeks in the prior audit, including extracting the data. Moreover, additional investigation based on the testing results disclosed that one manager had made these 30 approvals to gain favorable treatment from the financial institution clients. You can imagine what the end of the story was for this manager! Our seminar attendee informed us that their financial institution was pleased with the Agile pilot results and planned to implement their Agile methodology.

The selection of the method will also depend on what question you are trying to answer. As noted earlier, the different analytics – descriptive, predictive, and prescriptive – answer different questions. As described in James Evans' book, *Business Analytics*, descriptive analytics answers "What happened?" and answers to this question are usually descriptive statistics (Evans 2016). These include charts and graphs such as histograms and scatter plots as well as information such as the mean, median, mode, variance, standard deviations of distributions of data, and cross-tabulations, and are based on historic data. The majority of audits start with descriptive analytics, which is the most commonly used and most well-understood type of analytics. Auditors and business process owners use the data to understand past and current business performance to make informed decisions and summarize data into meaningful charts and reports. This data can further be drilled down to make specific queries, review business performance, find problem areas or areas of opportunity, and identify trends or patterns in data (Evans 2016).

"Predictive seeks to forecast the future by examining historical data, detecting patterns or relationships in these data, and then extrapolating these relationships forward in time" (Evans 2016). An example would be predicting the response of different customer segments to an advertising campaign. Predictive analytics can be beneficial to auditors. It can predict risk and find relationships in data not readily apparent with traditional analyses. Predictive analytics can help detect hidden patterns in large quantities of data to segment and group data into coherent sets to detect trends. For instance, a bank manager might want to predict the chances that a loan applicant will default or alert a credit card customer to a potentially fraudulent charge. Predictive analytics help answer questions such as: What will happen? What do we expect? What is the risk of X or Y? (Evans 2016).

Prescriptive analytics addresses questions such as: Which route should our drivers use to minimize gas cost? Should we change our plans if a natural disaster closes a supplier's factory, and if so, by how much? Prescriptive analytics uses **optimization analysis** (finding optimal problem parameters subject to constraints) to identify the best alternatives to minimize or maximize some objective. It can determine the best pricing and advertising strategy to maximize revenue or the best mix of investments in a retirement portfolio to manage risk (Evans 2016).

So how do you choose an appropriate methodology? Some of the factors to consider are:

■ *Time.* Some models will take more time and work than others.
■ *Accuracy.* Some models influence the accuracy of the results. Earlier, we discussed the quality and readiness of data and the accuracy needed to meet the success factors agreed upon with the business process owner.

- *Relevance.* Is the methodology going to provide results in the scope of the audit?
- Data availability and readiness.
- Team members' availabilities and skills.
- The popularity of the methodology, as some methodologies are better known and thus more acceptable.

6. *Select your software tool.* Keep it simple and use the tools you already have. There are different software tools to help you with your DA, including spreadsheet, statistical, optimization, and simulation systems. At our conferences, participants often ask us, "What DA tool do you use or recommend?" There are too many to recommend one in particular. Our preferred tool is the one that would be the optimal one – the one that best fits the task at hand at the desired price. There are many factors to consider, including:

- Business and analysis objectives
- Cost
- User-friendliness and training required
- Features desired
- Type of analytics needed
- Integration with existing legacy systems
- Sources and types of data
- Scalability
- Customization
- Collaboration required
- As auditors, we cannot forget security

Though we are not endorsing it, many of our clients use MS Excel with its advanced features. It has proven to be the most economical and most accessible for auditors. They are already familiar with it and have the tool on their desktops.

MS Excel has many advanced features, from the input of external data from different sources (e.g., Access, Web, SQL Server, and other databases) to analytic features within its multi-table database. Power pivot allows for storage of millions of rows that do not have to be loaded on your actual spreadsheet but rather on separate spreadsheets. MS Excel also has add-on tools such as power queries, which allow you to read the data from various sources. Another useful feature is its visualization tools, Power View and Power Map. So, if you have been using Excel to filter or sort data or to create graphs, you have been doing DA, and you might not have known it! One part of being an Agile auditor is to learn how to use the tools you already have. Learn how to write algorithms, functions, and macros in MS Excel. You will soon be close to performing machine learning operations and creating tools that can help automate some of your processes, such as slicing and dicing MS Excel errors.

There are downfalls with any tool. MS Excel has its pitfalls that you must be aware of, including version control, lack of control, inadequate security, vulnerability to fraud and corruption, susceptibility to human error, and don't forget about regulatory compliance problems.

7. *Model testing and deployment.* Here you get to run your model, verify that it is working as intended, and validate that it is providing accurate results. If results do not meet expectations, additional modeling and testing may be necessary. Remember that a problem may be solved using more than one methodology. Accuracy may vary depending on the methodology selected. Sometimes it is enough to place the data on a chart and perform simple statistics computations to solve it. DA is a journey. Some have suggested that selecting the appropriate DA model is a combination of science and art.

8. *Optimize, optimize, and optimize again.* The DA process is iterative and can sometimes lead to continuous improvements, improving audit results and the business and the value of the data itself.

We have barely scratched the DA knowledge available. However, we hope we have planted some seeds with this information and have provided you the foundations to get your DA journey started.

Now that we have provided an overview and synopsis of the DA process, we can't forget that it is also essential to have a solid understanding of statistics. Auditors need not become data scientists, statisticians, or business analysts to stay relevant. However, brushing up on statistics is something you need to do to become a better auditor. Yes, STATISTICS – don't get too excited! We know just how hard it is to get started with DA without a statistics foundation. Learning or relearning statistics might seem like a daunting task. Trust us; it is not, if you take it one step at a time. The benefits of refreshing or bringing this knowledge back into our brains are endless and highly rewarding. Following is a summary list of what we consider some of the essential statistics topics to get you going:

- Normal distribution
- Variability (including range, mean, variance, and standard deviation)

- Difference between continuous and discrete variables
- Sampling distribution
- Central limit theorem and application in practice
- Hypothesis testing for means and proportions
- Z-score and Z-tables
- *t*-score and *t*-tables
- Statistical significance
- Confidence intervals

As you have seen from the DA process described earlier in this chapter, business analytics is a union of three critical disciplines, none of which is new. They have been taught and used for many years: statistics, business intelligence and information systems, and modeling and optimization (traditionally, in operations research and management science).

So, what is stopping you? As auditors refresh and enhance their knowledge and application of statistics, they will also increase their ability to perform DA and to apply the different technologies discussed in the next section.

 ## NEW TECHNOLOGIES AND AGILE AUDIT

As part of being Agile, all audit professionals need to embrace next-generation methodologies and technologies and develop the new skills necessary to stay relevant and add value to their organizations. We cannot stop progress or the introduction of new technologies.

As part of being Agile, all audit professionals need to embrace next-generation methodologies and technologies and develop the new skills necessary to stay relevant and add value to their organizations. We cannot stop progress or the introduction of new technologies. Undoubtedly, new technologies will result in the automation of many jobs now and in the future. Innovative, Agile start-ups are pushing out the laggards, which presents excellent opportunities in this digital revolution. The audit profession has forever changed and will continue to change at incredible speeds via the introduction of new technologies, including robotics process automation, machine learning, and artificial intelligence. Following is an overview of these technologies and how they are being applied to today's world, making it more Agile. We hope that this overview will elucidate and inspire you to continue your Agile audit journey and seize these technologies to help you along.

Robotic Desktop Applications, Robotics Process Automation, Machine Learning, and Artificial Intelligence

When we first started hearing these words, we were puzzled. We wondered what they meant, the differences between them, and how they might affect the way we audit today and in the future. Well, the future is here! These technologies are affecting how we audit around the world. Likewise, every organization's internal control structure implementing any of these technologies is also affected, impacting risks to their business objectives and therefore, how we audit.

Over the past several decades, technologies including **robotic desktop automation (RDA)**, **robotic process automation (RPA)**, **machine learning (ML)**, **artificial intelligence (AI)**, and other software advances have enabled the automation of many routine tasks. These advances go beyond email junk or spam filters, spelling and grammar checkers, and GPS locators. They have evolved into self-driving cars, drones, planes, and facial recognition videos. We are far from being experts in any one of these technologies. However, as part of becoming Agile and performing Agile auditing, it has been crucial for us to become familiar with these technologies and understand their applications and impact on the audit world. These technologies are evolving every day. This is why introduction of these technologies in this book will be at a high level with a focus on becoming more Agile ready. We hope it sparks a fire and a desire to learn more about them and expand your use of them in your everyday fun life of auditing the Agile way!

First, let's start by providing a little history from one of the most trusted "voices" for engineering, computing, and technology information worldwide, the Institute of Electrical and Electronics Engineers (IEEE). The IEEE is the world's largest technical professional organization dedicated to advancing technology for humanity's benefit (IEEE 2020). According to the IEEE Standards Association, starting around "2010, a new type of technology emerged that is neither an operating system nor an application but is a platform built to provide digital process automation that mimics human operations in a digital environment. This new technology can use single or multiple applications or systems through the standard human interface layer (HIL) in the same way a human operator would. Early uses of this new technology have replaced rote or strictly transactional processing previously performed by humans. With the addition of increasingly sophisticated rules engines, analytics, machine learning, and cognitive computing, these technologies are now capable of performing human tasks. These tasks include assessment, reasoning, decision making, and probabilistic or deterministic process fulfillment. Collectively, this capability, when deployed in the modern enterprise, is 'intelligent process automation'" (IEEE 2020).

This "new technology" jargon can be mentally and visually confusing for many of us. For example, using the word "robotics" may conjure up Will Robinson's Robot images in the 1965 television series *Lost in Space*. For those of us who are millennials, it brings up images of the Rambler-Crane Series Robot in the 1998 *Lost in Space* movie. What is the origin of using the word "robotics" in these technologies? According to Tom Taulli, author of *The Robotic Process Automation: A Guide to Implementing RPA Systems* (Taulli 2020), the term *RPA* originated in 2012, coined by the chief evangelist for Blue Prism, Pat Geary. Taulli points out how this term can be confusing as you separate each word. He explains that, for example, the word robotic does not refer to a physical robot. Instead, it is about a software-based robot (or bot) that can automate human actions in the workplace, generally for white-collar applications in clerical and administrative functions.

Differences between RDA, RPA, ML, and AI

Figure 12.2 shows the differences and relationships among these technologies in an automation continuum. As we move from left to right in the automation continuum, the technology becomes more complex and more costly.

RDA tools are installed on a single computer for one user for processes that only involve one person, one desktop, and the applications that live on the desktop. RDA helps users handle simple repetitive tasks (process-driven) and involves a person playing an active role (manual involvement). Take, for example, a call center. The call center representative receives a call and needs to retrieve the customer's information necessary to manage the inquiry, order, or complaint. Instead of the representative having to manually retrieve the data from various applications (or, as previously done, from different hard copy file cabinets and file folders), the RDA assists by gathering this information. Meanwhile, the call center representative speaks with the customer. How? The representative provides the RDA with input information such as the account number or the customer's last name to extract the information needed.

RPA tools are installed on a server or in the cloud and work with applications used by the whole department or organization. RPA allows multiple users with different permissions to work together in the same process that can span across the organization. With RPA, there is no human giving instructions

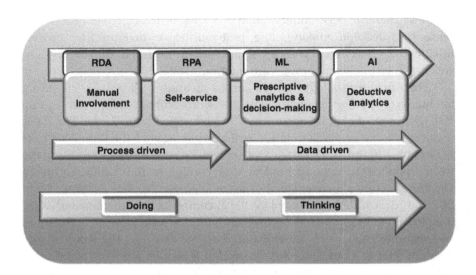

FIGURE 12.2 Automation Continuum

as to when to collect the information. There is no user interaction. The design of the RPA is entirely self-sustaining.

An example would be if you needed to update a large number of customer records. Let's suppose the customer record can only be open by one call representative at a time. You would not update all customer records in the middle of the work shift, potentially disrupting many call center representatives' call flows. The open record the representative was already working on would not be able to be updated. Thus, you would create an automatic (no user interaction) "automation" to update the records when the work shift had ended, such as in the middle of the night. Starting this automation could begin in various ways (self-service) depending on your system. A Windows Scheduler might start the update at a specified time each night. This automation (the robot) would start from the task scheduler and complete the required record updates when the call center is closed.

Neither RDA nor RPA can make cognitive decisions. Therefore, they are limited to routine processes, such as record retrieval or record updates.

According to Tom Taulli in his book *The Robotic Process Automation Handbook*, RPA is relatively easy to implement. Unlike some of the more traditional business applications such as enterprise resource planning (ERP), RPA generally does not involve burdensome implementation and integration. RPA is software that sits on top of existing IT systems and is reasonably easy for a person to use. It doesn't require knowledge of complex coding. Therefore, the IT department does not have to be involved as much for the support. RPA also does not require extensive training of IT personnel. It also applies to RDA though installed on a single computer, as stated earlier. Some of the more common automated tasks these two technologies can perform include: reading and writing data, moving files and folders, copying and pasting data, filling in forms, and extracting structured and semi-structured data from documents. Practically any high-volume, business-rules-driven, repeatable process qualifies for this kind of automation.

Let's move from RPA to ML and AI. Machine learning is a subset of artificial intelligence. It is a method of data analysis that automates analytical model building. It is a branch of AI based on the idea that systems can learn from data, identify patterns, and make decisions with minimal human intervention. ML is where a computer can learn and improve how it operates by processing large amounts of data without being explicitly programmed. ML is one of the first forms of AI and makes use of traditional statistics. However, it gets exciting and rather complicated with even more advanced algorithms when it comes to AI. AI is broader than ML. AI is about making machines "intelligent" using a variety of approaches.

> If we think of AI as machines "thinking" the way humans think, then we can think of ML as machines drawing conclusions from information in the same way humans do, by taking in information, identifying relationships and patterns in the data, and developing a model of how it thinks the world works. Machine learning happens when a machine produces a predictive model. (Poisson 2020)

RDA, RPA, ML, and AI technologies grow from simple process-driven automation to human-intelligent-data-driven.

Issues to Consider When Implementing These Technologies

As organizations continue implementing these new technologies, they need to be aware of the risks they present, including the following:

- **Type of data** – Recall the two types of data, structured and unstructured. RDA and RPA primarily use structured data, which represents a small fraction of all available data in an organization.

- **Bias** – Data might be biased toward particular groups. "Bad data can contain implicit racial, gender, or ideological biases. Many AI systems will continue to be trained using bad data, making this an ongoing problem" (Taulli 2020).
- **Causation** – Just because there is a relationship or correlation between two variables, it does not mean that a change in one variable caused the change in the other variable (causation). We have to be aware of patterns we discover and analyze these patterns, ensuring we derive accurate conclusions.
- **Common sense** – As individuals, we can use "common sense" (I'm not saying we all have it!). However, common sense is a difficult challenge with AI because of the ambiguity of terms. The lack of useful data for the infinite possibilities that exist is yet to be defined.

How Are These Technologies Affecting Audit, and How Can We Use Them to Become More Agile?

Understanding how an organization uses these technologies and their impact on its risk profile is crucial for audit professionals. The way we audit is drastically changing. First, auditors must understand the different risk exposures and internal controls related to these technologies, including access security, change management, and the IT environment's governance. Therefore, auditors must methodically examine the different technologies (RDA, RPA, ML, AI) as their organizations are adopting them.

The success of the implementation of these technologies depends heavily on adequate internal controls. As part of the organization having "audit readiness," managers must be prepared to demonstrate to auditors how each of the technologies adopted works and offer documented evidence and audit trails of automated controls and performance measures. Further, organizations implementing technologies such as RPA will be more likely to have control activities that lead to favorable outcomes and enhanced audit readiness. RPA can include features that will enable improved management monitoring, enable self-audits by different departments in the organization, and enable better reporting, resulting in faster problem or error resolution and better information for management as well as potential opportunities. In turn, RPA technologies can help auditors evaluate controls more quickly and more effectively, leaving more time to examine other risk areas.

The audit process can benefit substantially from the introduction of these technologies in various audit tasks. Audits can be completed faster and more efficiently through automation of specific audit processes, allowing auditors to perform more complex tasks, including examining business processes and associated risks and controls, and more effective detection of fraud or other irregularities in real time.

As you can see from our brief introduction to these technologies, data is the starting point, then information and knowledge, ultimately helping organizations make better-informed decisions. As we continue to move to a more Agile way of working and implement Agile auditing, we cannot underestimate the impact of small improvements. Saving 10 to 20 seconds for every task, even something as mundane as using cut-and-paste actions or autocorrect for our written communications may seem trivial. But it is anything but trivial when we scale it across thousands of steps and multiple employees across the organization. The impact can save us months or years!

RECIPE FOR STARTING DATA ANALYTICS (DA)

In summary form, here are the steps from the data analytics process explained in this chapter, along with a few ingredients to give you a good start to using DA in your Agile auditing journey:

Before you start, you must understand the business, then:

1. Decide on the objectives (determine your business question)
2. Determine what you are measuring and how to measure it
3. Obtain your data
4. Clean your data
5. Determine your approach (select methodology)
6. Select your software tool
7. Run and test your model
8. Optimize, optimize, and optimize again

If you elect to use MS Excel to get started with your DA process, here are some knowledge areas needed to build a foundation to perform DA (this is a limited list):

- Basic understanding of creating formulas and how rows and columns reference cells
- Formatting techniques to create worksheets and graphs, including conditional formatting

- VLOOKUP and XLOOKUP
- What Ifs
- Create pivot tables; use multiple tables and charts to create dashboards and represent data visually using pivot charts

For auditors experienced with Excel who regularly employ its more complex capabilities and want to further their knowledge of Excel shortcuts and tricks, an excellent resource is Bob Umlas's book, *This Isn't Excel, It's Magic!* (Umlas 2007). Although written in 2007, Umlas's book contains excellent tips, including everything from advanced filters to data cleansing tricks.

In addition to knowing the DA steps and statistics and using DA tools such as MS Excel, successful auditors who want to continue to grow their DA skills need to have strong mathematics and technology knowledge, excellent communication skills, business savvy, grit, critical thinking and problem-solving skills, adaptability, courage, and passion.

NUGGETS

Agile audit in the new normal requires us to adapt and embrace disruptive technologies to be prepared to deal with global changes, including the 2020 COVID-19 global pandemic, which caused this new normal. The disruptive technologies, including virtual conferencing, data analytics, robotics process automation, machine learning, and artificial intelligence are not only making Agile auditing easier, but their implementation is vital. As organizations embrace these technologies, the way we audit is drastically changing. Auditors must gain a clear understanding of these technologies, including their different risk exposures and related internal controls, as well as access security, change management, and IT governance.

CHAPTER THIRTEEN

Lean and Agile Auditing

 ## WHAT IS LEAN?

Lean focuses on reducing waste, specifically related to inputs. To perform Lean correctly, you need to measure motions, steps taken, and time spent on activities. You also measure the distance between steps. The first time we heard of Lean techniques, we searched the internet to learn more. We came across a random video on the web about someone trying to be efficient with household chores and how they measured the amount of time it takes to wash dishes and decided that paper plates were the way to go. Well, let's take that idea in a different direction.

Imagine your family uses a dishwasher to wash dishes. In your home, the requirement is that every dish goes immediately into the dishwasher once the meal is complete. You have four family members in your home, and they are each responsible for their personal dishes. Think about how many steps each family member takes three to six times a day, from the table to the dishwasher and from the food prep area to the dishwasher. That is a lot of steps! How many times is the dishwasher door opened? How many times are the drawers pulled out and pushed in? How many times did someone have to realign the wheels of the drawer because they got off track?

Now think about how the dishes are arranged in your dishwasher – scared yet? How many times did you find yourself rearranging someone else's dish so yours would fit? How many times do you think others did the same thing to your dishes? How many times did you rearrange dishes to make sure they were cleaned properly?

Okay, the dishwasher is full, and you add the soap and start the wash cycle. How long do you spend, how many steps do you take unloading the dishwasher, inspecting the dishes along the way, and creating a pile of dishes that need to be rewashed? How many movements were required for you to put all the clean forks with the forks, clean spoons with the spoons, knives with the knives, and so on? How long did it take you to reload the pile of dishes that need to be rewashed?

And the cycle repeats itself every day. Add up all the motions, steps, time, and distance. Now, think! Innovate! Is there a better way that may take less time to load the dishes and place them in their proper location once they are clean?

Imagine if at each meal, one person was designated to collect all the dishes and place them in the sink. Family members leave dishes in the sink until the day's end. One person puts the dishes into the dishwasher each evening unless the sink is overflowing intraday, necessitating interim loading. Each family member rotates putting the dishes into the dishwasher, but only after receiving proper training on loading a dishwasher to maximize use of space and minimize rewash. Plates are positioned in the same direction and bowls are placed in the same direction and the tines of the dishwasher shelves neatly separate everything. Spoons are in one slot, handles up. Forks are in a separate slot, handles up. Knives are in another slot, handles up. Glasses and cups are sorted. The dishes are loaded; the person who loads the dishwasher adds the soap and starts the wash cycle.

When the cycle is complete, another designated family member unloads the dishwasher by grabbing the spoons' handles with one hand and the forks with the other hand and places them in their resting place. The knives come out next and are placed in their proper spot. The plates and bowls are gathered and stacked and placed in their location. The glasses and cups are put away. How many motions and steps are required now? How much time did the process take? How much distance was traveled? This unloading process is used in our home, and a 10-year-old girl can unload a dishwasher in two minutes (on a grumpy "why do I have to do the dishes today?" day) or less.

 ## ELIMINATING WASTE USING AGILE AUDITING

Kanban principles are applied in Lean as well as Agile disciplines. Many recognize Taiichi Ohno, a Toyota industrial engineer in the 1940s, as instrumental in creating Kanban and inspiring Lean manufacturing. Ohno identified the following "seven wastes" you can use to evaluate your audit processes (Dumas, La Rosa, Mendling, and Reijers 2013):

1. Delay, waiting, or time spent in a queue with no value-added
2. Producing more than is needed
3. Overprocessing or undertaking non-value-added activity
4. Transportation
5. Unnecessary movement or motion
6. Inventory
7. Defects in the product

With a comprehensive review of our audit processes, we can eliminate waste through our Agile audit framework.

■ We are eliminating delays and time spent waiting for audit evidence.

For example, think back to the unique approach of working side-by-side with your audit client to review samples instead of waiting for evidence and emails (as discussed in Chapter 10). This side-by-side collaboration is our typical approach to executing the Agile audit. Another example of eliminating this type of waste is that every meeting starts precisely on time, and participants better show-up on time because we will not repeat. We will not go back, and we will not prepare meeting summaries and minutes, which would waste more time and would produce more documents than necessary.

■ We minimize documentation, specifically in workpapers.

An internal auditor student in one of our Agile auditing classes made an excellent case for only documenting the problems when completing Agile audits. This minimal approach to documenting is a very creative interpretation of IIA guidance, but a valid one. IIA Standard 2330, *Documenting Information*, states: "Internal auditors must document sufficient, reliable, relevant, and useful information to support the engagement results and conclusions." (Institute of Internal Auditors 2017). The student's argument was since the Agile audit report could be limited to include only exceptions, the workpapers that must support the conclusions (the exceptions) would only need to document the exceptions. This minimal documentation approach means that if all sampled or tested items met the criteria, there would be no need for a workpaper or other documentation. In our Agile auditing practices, we haven't gone to this extreme – yet!

- We are eliminating non-value-added activities.

  A non-value-added activity is one that the audit client wouldn't pay for or a step that wasn't done right the first time. One example is auditor timekeeping. Could you imagine giving your audit client an itemized bill that includes a line item for "timekeeping activities"?

- We are minimizing movement (unless we're trying to get our daily steps in!).

  In Agile auditing, we try to co-locate whenever possible to minimize auditor back-and-forth movement between the audit client's area and the auditor's workspace. We ask for a designated space in the audit client's area to complete the Agile audit. We've done this since 1997, before Agile auditing was even a concept. A former boss constantly challenged us if we were at our audit desks by saying, "if you are at your desk, you are not auditing." In the designated space, we brought in flipcharts and chalkboards (we didn't have many whiteboards back then), removed most of the chairs, and set up camp. Now, this space primarily serves as the place where we proudly and visibly display our Kanban board and hold our Sprint planning meetings, daily standup meetings, Sprint Reviews, and Sprint Retrospectives. Remember, in our Agile audit framework, most of our actual work is performed with the audit client, at their workspace, including documenting audit workpapers.

- Potential product defects are eliminated through the collaborative approach of working with the client to review samples and being transparent with our work, documentation, and conclusions. Our daily standups are open to any stakeholder. When we describe what we are doing that day, it could include working with the audit client to write any issues or potential audit report comments, assuming we are writing an audit report.

  Now turn your attention to your current audit process. Do you have any waste? If not, contact us and tell us your secrets. Are there any obvious unnecessary steps you can eliminate? Are there any steps you can automate? How much time will you save?

NUGGETS

Lean is a waste reduction and elimination approach, which means you must start by understanding your current process, a Kanban concept, to determine where you have waste. Through its design, Agile auditing helps eliminate waste related to five of the seven wastes identified by Ohno. Where can you eliminate waste? What are some techniques you can embed in your Agile audit process to help reduce waste?

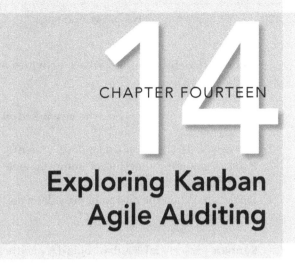

CHAPTER FOURTEEN

Exploring Kanban Agile Auditing

 ## WHAT IS KANBAN?

In the book *Essential Kanban Condensed*, the authors describe Kanban as "a method that shows us how our work works" and "the alternative path to agility" (Anderson and Carmichael 2016). Kanban originated from Lean manufacturing and was made popular by Toyota. In the Japanese language, Kanban means a sign, signal card, tally, or large visual board. Some consider Kanban as a subset of Lean. Kanban has similarities to Lean and to other Agile frameworks. Officially, "Kanban is a method for defining, managing, and improving services that deliver knowledge work, such as professional services, creative endeavors, and the design of both physical and software products. It may be characterized as a *'start from what you do now'* method – a catalyst for rapid and focused change within organizations – that reduces resistance to beneficial change in line with the organization's goals" (Anderson and Charmichael 2016).

The Kanban Method is inspired by the original Lean-manufacturing system and has been adapted specifically for knowledge work. It emerged in the mid-2000s as an alternative to the Agile methods prevalent at the time (Project Management Institute 2017).

Kanban visually identifies where activities are in one of four different stages (Ries 2018).

1. *Backlog.* These are items ready to be worked on but for which work has not yet started.
2. *In progress.* All the items under development.
3. *Build.* Combining developed items in step 2 to create a customer-ready product.
4. *Validation.* When the customer provides a positive response or acceptance of the product.

Kanban uses visual Kanban boards, or other visual tools, to track the items or activities in each stage. Practitioners recommend having no more than three items or activities in each stage at one time. This aids in increasing productivity by allowing the Kanban team to receive feedback from the customer, make adjustments to their process, and proceed with the next item without reworking completed tasks.

Kanban is the only framework that creates a feedback loop specific to delivery risks (see Chapter 2, What Is Audit?, for more details on delivery risks). Another difference is that Kanban does not have any required roles and does not create new positions. Kanban allows individuals in existing positions to describe their functions as service request managers or service delivery managers. The service request manager is similar to the Product Owner in Scrum. The service delivery manager ensures that the flow works well enough to deliver the product to customers and facilitates key meetings, similar to a Scrum Master in Scrum.

 ## WHEN CAN I USE KANBAN?

Kanban's application to professional services and knowledge work deems it a preferred method for performing audit services. As noted in the preceding section, Kanban starts with what you do now (your existing workflow, a "start where-you-are" approach). Kanban teams document their understanding of the current process, including existing tasks, roles, and responsibilities, and identify incremental improvements to the ongoing process. Kanban is easier to adopt than other methods because it recognizes that many humans don't like change. One Kanban principle is that Kanban teams must agree to pursue improvement through change; another principle is that every Team Member can lead an improvement. Improvements are focused on the work itself to reduce process starts, work in progress, and process stops by emphasizing continuous flow through a system. As discussed in the About the Authors section, Ceciliana ran the preparations for her marvelous child's wedding using an Agile approach and putting into use a Scrum Board with the headings "Backlog," "To Do," "In Process," "Verified," and "Done." Scrum Boards are similar to Kanban boards, as both use Agile methodology to plot the workflow and track the project status from beginning to end. However, Scrum Boards tend to be more methodical, requiring more prep time and organization while Kanban boards provide the team with more flexibility with less organizational structure. Moreover, Scrum uses Sprints to complete the job, while Kanban does not.

KANBAN PRINCIPLES APPLIED TO AGILE AUDITING

Kanban has its own set of principles, values, and practices. Kanban has nine values, as follows (Project Management Institute 2017):

1. Agreement
2. Balance
3. Collaboration
4. Customer focus
5. Flow
6. Leadership
7. Respect
8. Transparency
9. Understanding

The following exemplifies application of these principles to auditing:

- **Agreement** – Everyone (the audit committee, audit management, auditors, and audit leadership) is committed to improvement.
- **Balance** – Recognize and balance varying viewpoints, competencies, and capabilities among auditors and audit clients.
- **Collaboration** – Work together effectively to complete the audit by a specified deadline to provide timely insight and assurance.
- **Customer focus** – Maximize value to customers, whether internal or external to the organization, by providing constructive feedback and information to help mitigate risks, correct weaknesses, and achieve goals.

- **Flow** – Work continuously as a team and avoid bottlenecks in determining and approving audit tests, receipt of evidence, workpaper reviews, and audit report reviews.
- **Leadership** – Lead at any level; everyone can lead, inspire, and contribute to continuous improvement, including new auditors, audit staff, and audit customers.
- **Respect** – Consider others, value others, and strive to understand viewpoints of audit clients, mature auditors, and audit staff.
- **Transparency** – Have honest, clear, open-door communications within the audit team and with audit clients and leadership.
- **Understanding** – Start with the current process, tasks, roles, and responsibilities documented in your audit methodology. Create a process map of your current flow. Evaluate the current audit process and look for opportunities to improve.

As you review the Kanban values and their relationship to auditing, are you asking, "Am I already doing Kanban?" Maybe. We thought the same thing until we looked a little deeper into some of our professional process flaws and mindset, including:

1. I haven't started with the required thorough understanding of our audit workflow because that's not my job.
2. We haven't looked for continuous improvement opportunities because we've become comfortable with the way things work.
3. We haven't let team members self-manage around workflow. Admittedly, some auditors would spend all day, every day, performing walkthroughs, learning about business processes, understanding objectives, identifying and assessing risks, and avoiding, at all costs, writing audit reports. Right?

 ## MANAGING WORKFLOW, THE KANBAN WAY

> Applying Kanban in auditing helps manage typical workflow-based flaws and challenges.

Applying Kanban in auditing helps manage typical workflow-based flaws and challenges. For example, consider the traditional audit planning process when audits are structured with quarterly end dates. The typical audit project work-flow begins with a strong start. Auditors are excited to start working on their next engagement. We arrange the kickoff meeting, hold interviews and per-form walkthroughs with process owners, and request populations, samples, and evidence. Then we wait.

Because we wait so long, we start another audit or pick up some extra work. When the audit client provides the requested evidence, we are mid-stride in another effort and fail to check the evidence to verify that we have what we requested. When we finally get around to looking at the evidence on the first audit, we inevitably discover that the evidence isn't what we needed or is incomplete, so we clarify or modify our request and wait some more.

We move onto another project, and then when we return to the first audit, we are unmotivated and may even procrastinate. We look at the quarterly deliverable date, and just like the Dad in the movie *The Incredibles*, we say, "I have time." Another month goes by, and we realize we need to get the audit done. We perform our evidence review, test our samples, and under-estimate the work remaining. Some of us may also tell our audit supervisor we are "almost done."

But wait, you still need to document your workpapers, which may take double the amount of time you spent performing the walkthrough or com-pleting your testing. You finally document your work, and so do your other team members, and now the audit supervisor is stuck reviewing all the work-papers days before the reporting deadline. Does this sound familiar?

Well, Kanban solves this challenge by managing the work-in-progress flow to achieve a constant, continuous flow instead of the strained workflow and substantial end-of-audit time demands described above. The audit super-visor, under Kanban, would be best advised to prioritize the audit work. The priority may be audit tests of controls for the highest risks; then, we prioritize those tests requiring more data or longer lead times to obtain the evidence. Early in the process, auditors are provided simple, defined policies and stated expectations and rules for work items and deliverables. Auditors understand that a certain percentage of audit tests must be completed with workpapers submitted in a timely manner for review each week. Even better, auditors may be assigned different days of the week to submit their workpapers). The coolest part of Kanban for the audit team is in the first weeks of the audit. The audit supervisor can dig in, get dirty, and complete audit tests too. Team collaboration was achieved!

Audit supervisors commit to completing workpaper reviews and providing feedback to each auditor, perhaps within 24–48 hours of receiving completed workpapers. This staggered workflow avoids bottlenecks by limiting work in progress to a manageable level. Workflow is consistent and smooth throughout the audit life cycle.

Kanban values state that everyone is a leader, anyone can act on continuous improvement opportunities, and everyone is committed to improving the process. To facilitate actions on these values, supervisors set up a feedback loop. We do this by holding daily Kanban meetings to coordinate work activities and encourage each Team Member to identify three improvements or changes to the current process. Auditors are empowered to experiment with the changes and can adjust as desired.

 ## NUGGETS

There are many frameworks and approaches to Agile project management, from Scrum to Kanban. The Agile Manifesto and Agile principles establish a foundation to build an Agile approach for your organization, regardless of which framework you select. Kanban is an Agile method based on making visible otherwise invisible knowledge work. Making work visible on the Kanban board ensures that the team works on the right amount of work at the right time and can deliver. Kanban has nine values: agreement, balance, collaboration, customer focus, flow, leadership, respect, transparency, and understanding. These Kanban principles apply to Agile auditing. Kanban starts with "what you do now." Improvements are then pursued through evolutionary change, which happens over time, based on experience and understanding. Both Scrum and Kanban are complementary from the perspective of improving the business. As you continue your transformation, continue to look at the recipes to determine your methodology. And again, don't be afraid to adjust the ingredients!

CHAPTER FIFTEEN

Merging Risk-Based Auditing and Integrated Auditing with Agile Auditing

Let's first visit the definition of risk. The Institute of Internal Auditors (IIA) defines risk as "The possibility of an event occurring that will have an impact on the achievement of objectives" (Institute of Internal Auditors, 2017a). ISO 31000-2018 defines risk as "the 'effect of uncertainty on objectives,' and an effect is a positive or negative deviation from what is expected" (International Organization for Standardization 2018). According to the U.S. Government Accountability Office (GAO), "Risk is the possibility that an event will occur and adversely affect the achievement of objectives" (U.S. Government Accountability Office 2014). COSO defines risk as "the possibility that an event will occur and adversely affect the achievement of an objective" (Committee of Sponsoring Organizations of the Treadway Commission [COSO] 2013). As can be seen by these definitions, risk has different meanings to different people and organizations. Some emphasize the general impact without emphasizing a positive or negative effect, and some emphasize the adverse effect.

Nonetheless, it is essential to note that the consistent theme emphasizes "the impact on organizational objectives." A foundation of this chapter is that risk-based auditing (RBA) is a conscious effort to understand the organization and its objectives as well as the risks that can have an impact on the organization's ability to accomplish its objectives.

STOP CREATING KITCHEN SINK AUDITS!

In our first two-day Agile auditing course in Albuquerque, New Mexico, most of our attendees were there because they were curious. Some thought the topic was new enough to entertain them in their quest for continuing education credits. Some attendees' bosses "volunteered" them to attend. Others were just there for free lunch. We had approximately 30 people in attendance, and participants were seated in a U-shape configuration so they could all see each other. We selected this setup to allow participants to share thoughts, commentary, and questions openly and frequently. One attendee sat to the immediate left at the top of the U, closest to the projector screen. This gentleperson was a mature individual with white hair, who wore glasses that they fiddled with through most of the first day. I remember looking over at this individual throughout the first day and wondering, is this person getting it? Does this person understand? What's the hurdle that I see in this person's eyes? Was this individual forced to be here? Why does this gentleperson appear so frustrated?

Well, at lunch on the second day, we finally learned the answer. This attendee came up to the buffet line and shared a little about their audit experience. This individual worked exclusively for governmental entities and was currently auditing a public utility. The attendee said, "Raven, I just had my aha moment. For the past day and a half, I've been thinking that you're crazy. There's absolutely no way to get the audits done that I'm doing today in two to four weeks from planning through reporting. And that was my aha. I can't get the audits that I do today done in two to four weeks because I still think I need to audit everything since it may be years before I go back." Why did this individual think this? Because in their mind, they hadn't realized that every Agile audit had to identify and focus on specific, essential risks. The attendee thought they would attempt to complete their current audit, including everything, while excluding nothing. The attendee was afraid that the audit might miss something that could be wrong if they eliminated anything, even the smallest inconsequential control or attribute test. These thoughts, perceptions, and attitudes create what I like to call the "kitchen sink" approach to audit. The kitchen sink audit includes everything because it could be years before you come back to review that area. You simply cannot complete kitchen sink audits in two to four weeks.

Before we left the buffet line, I asked the auditor to share their aha moment with the class. This gentleperson agreed, and when class resumed, I turned it over to the attendee to share their thoughts with the class. I then asked what the number-one risk was for their most recent audit. The attendee thought for a moment, stated the risk, and I asked, "If you just focused on that one risk and tested the key control(s) for that one risk, could you complete an audit from planning to reporting in two weeks?" Their reply was, "Yes!" As I looked around the room, I could see other light bulbs turning on, as others were having their own aha moments. It was a good training day.

The kitchen sink approach to auditing came to me in 2017 while attempting to finish a delicious ice-cream meal, called the Kitchen Sink Dessert, at Beaches and Cream, a restaurant at Walt Disney World's Beach Club Resort. It has no fewer than 28 ingredients! Yes, you read correctly; it is an ice-cream sundae with 28 ingredients served in a dish that is shaped like a kitchen sink, complete with a faucet and handles. The reality is, I only wanted one flavor of ice cream, a banana, almonds, maraschino cherries, and a little whipped cream. However, my daughter insisted we go for the entire dessert and suggested I could just scoop out what I wanted. Imagine making your way through a pint of whipped cream, a jar of cherries, chocolate chips, peanut butter chips, chocolate sprinkles, cupcakes, brownies, candy bars, cookies, and 20 other ingredients to finally find the coffee ice cream. The dish was so full that the whipped cream and several different toppings were spilling out of the kitchen-sink dish.

This was a dessert dish that was so full that it was impossible to finish. Ever more difficult than finding the ice cream, many audits are designed to be difficult to find what the auditors are looking for. But while you are there, and since you can, or really since you just can't avoid looking at something, because what if something is wrong with the one thing you decide not to look at, you just add more stuff to test. You keep adding until the audit is overflowing like the whipped cream spilling over the side of the kitchen sink.

We didn't finish the dessert, not even close, even after sitting there for 30 minutes, and we eventually got a separate dish just to remove all the extra stuff we didn't want. Who knows, maybe Disney decided that someone might want a specific topping one day. Since Disney had it in the soda shop, they might have thought, "Might as well put it in the dessert; someone may want it someday." Just like our audits, we add extra, unnecessary, undesirable topics to our audits because we can, so we "might as well."

We should also mention that these massive, overflowing audits somehow still end up with scope creep. We eventually find another topic, or two, that we need to include since we aren't returning to audit that area anytime soon. Suddenly, you end up with 30 toppings, as our kitchen sink had with the addition of two more jellied candies that aren't in the recipe. (If you are curious, you can find the complete recipe in the Disney Park Blog, "Kitchen

Sink Dessert Recipe at Beaches and Cream at Disney's Beach Club Resort" link: https://bit.ly/Disneykitchensink.)

 ## WHAT IS RISK-BASED AUDITING (RBA)?

> RBA links internal auditing to the organization's overall risk management framework.

RBA links internal auditing to the organization's overall risk management framework. It is a conscious effort to understand the business. Identify the business objectives and the risks that affect the business's ability to accomplish the objectives, assess these risks, and determine the audit scope based on the assessed risks. Identify the controls, assess the adequacy of control design, evaluate control effectiveness, provide assurance that the risk management processes manage risks effectively, and communicate the potential risks that remain if they are beyond management's risk appetite. Simple, right?!

RBA aims to improve audit efficiency and effectiveness by focusing on the activities that contribute to managing risk concerning organization-wide goals. RBA increases the organizations' accountability by ensuring transparency, validating essential internal control, and allocating resources to manage critical risks. Moreover, RBA is required by both the Red and the Yellow Book standards. IPPF Standard 2010, Planning, states that "The CAE must establish a risk-based plan to determine the priorities of the internal audit activity, consistent with the organization's goals" (Institute of Internal Auditors 2017a). Further, the Yellow Book specifies in part, under paragraph 8.35, that: "A written audit plan provides an opportunity for audit organization management to supervise audit planning and to determine whether: . . . the audit plan adequately addresses relevant risks (U.S. Government Accountability Office 2018).

Extreme Risk-Based Auditing

Audits are projects with defined start and end times and the time to complete audits using the Agile framework is short. "Extreme RBA" goes an extra step. We incorporate RBA as a project focusing on the highest risks that affect the organization's ability to accomplish its objectives. There are a few turning points that make RBA extreme. It is *extreme* because we have seldom seen audit shops do all of the following:

1. Annual organization-wide risk assessment (Agile auditing requires regular updates). RBA plans need to be dynamic and nimble. Thus, audit activities update their audit plans quarterly, monthly, or at the beginning of each new project, to ensure they focus on the areas of highest risk to achieving the organization's objectives.
2. Engagement-level risk assessment (gather information; perform data analytics; identity objectives of the process under audit; identify the risks; leverage the risk registers' identified risks to aid in risk identification and assessment, and assess inherent risk impact and likelihood for each risk).
3. Go/No-Go. If a risk isn't essential to achieving business objectives, we shouldn't be auditing it – if it isn't risky, we don't look at it. Go/No-Go is a concept we learned from our client, Zurich Financial Services. If our assessed risk is low, we "No-Go" the audit at that time and can revisit it later if risks have changed.
4. Write a risk-based finding if the controls are inadequate, or improperly designed, to mitigate risk to an acceptable level. We do not need to test the effectiveness and execution of the controls, since we've determined that the controls are not adequate.
5. If controls appear to be adequate, we perform a test of control effectiveness, and if management's controls pass based on a predetermined pass rate (likely one that doesn't expect perfection), that is great; no additional testing is required.
6. If controls fail, you may decide to forego substantive testing to allow the audit to evaluate additional risks, and you proceed to communicate the risk-based finding.

CAN I STILL COMPLETE INTEGRATED AUDITS IN AGILE AUDITING?

> An integrated audit takes a global approach.

You definitely can! An integrated audit differs from a nonintegrated audit regarding the scope, overall complexity, depth, and breadth of coverage. An integrated audit takes a global approach and looks at several aspects, including financial, operational, regulatory, IT, compliance, and fraud risks and objectives.

It is important to remember that an Agile audit is flexible and iterative in its design. Rather than rigid audit plans, continuous updates to audits, projects, and tasks are prioritized based on risks and needs. RBA, which is pivotal in an Agile audit, provides the perfect setting for completing integrated audits. As we discussed in Chapter 4:, What Is Agile Audit?, an individual Agile audit focuses only on necessary and enough processes to address the evaluated risks, and it adapts to the entity's changing needs and new information. Evaluation of risks does not occur in individual silos. Instead, a holistic approach considers the relationship between all aspects of the organization from information technology, financial, compliance, and operational controls in establishing an effective and efficient internal control environment. From the start, Agile audit challenges auditors and audit clients to determine the value to be delivered by any particular audit. It prioritizes audits based on importance and urgency as well as readiness to perform the work. Agile audit adds value by centering our value proposition on business objectives and business risks. The best value propositions are created only after understanding what the audit customer wants and needs, and considers the organization as a whole. An Agile, integrated audit evaluates the interplay between financial, operational, compliance, and technology processes on achieving control objectives.

 ## NUGGETS

RBA links internal auditing to the organization's overall risk management framework. RBA starts with comprehensive risk-based planning, enabling the internal audit activity to focus its limited resources on the highest risks to achieving organizational objectives, which goes hand in hand with Agile auditing. Raven's extreme RBA reduces the amount of testing, depending on whether controls appear to be adequate or not. If controls fail, you may decide to forego substantive testing to allow the audit to evaluate additional risks, and you proceed to communicate the risk-based finding.

In an integrated audit, you take a global approach and look at financial, operational, regulatory, IT, compliance, and fraud risks, which is a match with Agile audit, being flexible and iterative. Rather than rigid audit plans, continuous updates to audits, projects, and tasks are prioritized based on risks and business or organizational needs. Still, Agile audit, while using an integrated audit approach, focuses only on necessary and enough processes to address the evaluated risks, and it adapts to the entity's changing needs and new information.

CHAPTER SIXTEEN

Building the Auditor Toolbelt and Self-Managing Agile Audit Teams

 AGILE AUDITING AS A TOOL

At the beginning of most of our classes, we discuss the importance of building an auditor toolbelt. Auditors must be equipped with the right tools to competently perform their jobs and complete audits with the right level of due professional care. Think of a plumber or handyman or carpenter; while they have their favorite tools and universal tools, some tools are needed to perform specific jobs. The professionals must know of and know how to use the tools to perform particular tasks efficiently and effectively. Can you imagine a plumber trying to clear a deep clog with a screwdriver? Funny though! The plumber needs a drain auger (plumber's snake) in good working order, and they need to know how to use it.

Before we get too far ahead of ourselves, take a look at or think about your current audit strategy and long-range plan. Assess how it works with or against Agile auditing. For example, suppose you have prepared your team members to manage themselves and have provided training on time management, project management, managerial skills, leadership skills, and stress management. In that case, you are closer to having and being comfortable with a self-managing team. You also need to consider the organization's culture and your audit team subculture. We talk more about culture in Chapter 17, Preparing Your Organization for Agile Auditing/Creating the Agile Culture.

> To be Agile-ready, auditors need to build their audit toolbelt with essential knowledge, skills, and abilities. The Agile framework is one tool to include in your belt. it may even become your favorite tool!

Think of Agile auditing as a tool that you can use when applicable; it may even become your favorite tool. We have other tools that work with Agile auditing, including the IIA and Yellow Book Standards, data analytics, machine learning, automated workpapers, and data visualization.

Auditors need to be prepared for the unforeseeable today and in the future and develop the skills to enhance success. The IIA report "On Risk 2021" addresses organizational approaches to risk management, including internal audit fit. This report reveals that internal audit provides minimal assurance on two of the C-suite's top three risks. These two risks are talent management and disruptive innovation, giving the lowest ratings to personal knowledge and organizational capabilities related to those risks. It further says that this incomplete coverage may be due to limitations on resources, *skills*, or work scope (Institute of Internal Auditors 2020).

SKILLS NEEDED TO BE AN AGILE AUDITOR

In Chapter 12, we discussed Agile auditing in the new normal. We recognized that we are in a world of unprecedented change, with disruptive technologies changing how we operate in all industries, including auditing. We have all read similar statements in the media and our professional publications. Moreover, we recognized Richard Chambers' statement regarding auditor relevance as stated in his book *The Speed of Risk* (Chambers 2019), "To remain relevant in a global business environment of increasing competition, technological advances, and downsizing, internal auditors must act tactfully as agents of change – and embrace the potential risks associated with innovation."

In Chapter 4, we discussed the core skills needed to implement and perform Agile audits successfully. These skills included: communication, collaboration, leadership, trust-building, time management, conflict management, and negotiation. The following are additional attributes that, when learned and applied, will make you an exemplary Agile auditor:

- Change agents
- Getting agreements
- Effective presentations
- Emerging risks related to sustainability and how sustainability fits into the organization's operational and strategic priorities
- Knowledge of new technologies. Chapter 12 discussed some of these technologies, including data analytics, robotics desktop applications, robotics process automation, machine learning, and artificial intelligence. We also provided suggestions on brushing up your knowledge of statistics as well as MS Excel.
- Business continuity and crisis response
- Effects of economic and political uncertainties on the likelihood of achieving organizational objectives

According to Richard Chambers, based on one-on-one interviews as well as a global survey of approximately 300 CAEs, the professional attributes of outstanding internal auditors include the following (Chambers 2017b):

- Ethical resiliency
- Results focus
- Intellectual curiosity and open-mindedness
- Dynamic communication and inspirational leadership
- Insightful relationships
- Critical-thinking skills, business acumen, and technical expertise

BECOMING AN INTEGRATED AUDITOR IN AN AGILE AUDIT WORLD

In Chapter 15, we discussed the merging of risk-based audits and integrated auditing with Agile auditing. We explained how we can still complete integrated audits using Agile auditing. An integrated audit takes a holistic approach, looking at the objectives and risks from different aspects, including financial, operational, compliance, regulatory, IT, and fraud. Therefore, auditors must sharpen their business acumen knowledge and embark on a continuous learning process. We don't mean that the auditor must be an expert on all topics. The team collectively should have the necessary skills to perform the audit. As stated in the IIA Standard 1210, *Proficiency,* "Internal auditors must possess the knowledge, skills, and other competencies needed to perform their responsibilities. The internal audit activity collectively must possess or obtain the knowledge, skills, and other competencies needed to perform its responsibilities" (Institute of Internal Auditors 2017a). This standard further says that internal auditors are encouraged to demonstrate their proficiency by obtaining appropriate professional certifications and qualifications.

During our combined 50-plus years of audit experience, we have known auditors from all backgrounds and professions. For the most part, we have seen that auditors come from a business and accounting background. However, we have also seen successful auditors from engineering, biology, medicine, psychology, economics, political science, and other liberal arts. The beauty of auditing is that it does not discriminate, and anyone with a curious mind has the power to "fall in love" with this profession. Raven and Ceciliana are not the only ones who have become passionate about this profession, making it a part of their daily lives.

When you think about it, there is so much you need to learn, not only from a business standpoint. There are other vital skills to learn, such as leadership, interpersonal skills, technical skills, a real sense of curiosity, persuasiveness, a service-oriented mind, a thirst for knowledge, an open mind with a global perspective, and a deep desire to add value. An integrated auditor is an auditor of the future who owns these qualities. These auditors will also be individuals who are willing to supplement the training they receive from their organizations by investing their own time and money in learning and training. Chapter 3 provides a recipe for building auditor knowledge and skills and explains how to create a proficiency gap analysis. Consider adding this recipe to your toolbelt to keep track of the skills you have, those you need, and those you want.

USING SCRUM VALUES TO CREATE SELF-MANAGING AGILE AUDIT TEAMS

The Scrum values, when applied to audit, can create practical and efficient self-managing Agile audit teams. Let's review and discuss the values.

■ **Commitment** – The Agile audit team must be committed to and pragmatic about achieving the objective. Each Team Member must be committed to performing their job competently and efficiently at a consistent, steady pace. The team needs to be committed to helping each other, adapting when needed, improving whenever possible, and raising obstacles quickly.

- **Courage** – Each Team Member must have the courage to speak up, admit failures, try a new approach, and accept new roles. Team members need to be brave and honest. Team members also need to embrace failure. Using the best information available to you at a given point in time, you will make the wrong decisions in the iterative approach to the project, and you will have failures. Share your failures, fail fast, and make the necessary adjustments.
- **Focus** – Once the team is clear on the requirements, only tasks and activities that directly relate to meeting the requirement should be selected and completed. Team members are accountable to one another to evaluate each task and identify any task that is unnecessary.
- **Openness** – Each Agile audit Team Member should openly and honestly share their work, progress, and obstacles. Team members should keep an open mind about how the work will be completed, share suggestions, and accept feedback.
- **Respect** – Team members need to respect each other, their client, organization resources, different views, diversity, and each individual's knowledge, skills, and competencies.

One of our conference participants shared that their audit department implemented a "Team Commitment Declaration." The purpose was to help the team become more unified and work with greater harmony. By signing the declaration, each Team Member would commit to specific values and principles to working together as a team to continually improve and add value to their organization. After implementing this declaration, the team's coherence, harmony, and accountability grew. Some commitment declaration elements included the following:

- Integrity – I have committed to the highest degree of ethical conduct in the performance of my work. The integrity I exhibit establishes trust and provides the basis for reliance on my judgment.
- Objectivity – I exhibit the highest level of professional objectivity in gathering, evaluating, and communicating information.
- Confidentiality – I respect the value and ownership of information.
- Competence – I apply the knowledge, skills, and experience necessary in the performance of my work.

- Accountability – I am responsible for my performance and work product.
- Commitment to quality – I continuously improve my services' accuracy, reliability, usefulness, and timeliness.
- Teamwork – I utilize my skills and abilities collaboratively to achieve organizational goals. I am committed to supporting my team to achieve success.
- Personal development – I am committed to helping my team members develop knowledge, skills, and abilities. I will continuously pursue education, training, and professional opportunities. I am responsible for my growth.
- I will treat others the way they want me to treat them.
- I will recognize that everybody makes mistakes and will learn from them and expand my perspective and knowledge.

If you haven't yet, you might consider incorporating key values into your Agile team or auditors' duty statements. It is a way to instill these values into everyone's mind and get a solidified commitment.

 ## BENEFITS OF DEALING WITH SELF-MANAGING TEAMS

Team members' roles within a self-managed team are more fluid than in a traditional hierarchical team structure. There is typically greater discretion over work and work hours, which tends to increase an individual's motivation and performance. What is more, team members tend to have greater freedom to balance each other's skills. In an article in *The Journal of Technology Studies*, Robert Howell discusses the benefits of self-directed teams (Howell 2001). Some noted benefits include: cost savings, innovation, quality and service improvement, increased loyalty and commitment to the team and the organization, greater collaboration, lower absenteeism, improved decision-making, increased productivity, improved customer satisfaction, and higher motivation.

 ## CAUTIONS OF DEALING WITH SELF-MANAGING TEAMS

Following are forewarnings about self-managing teams:

1. Managers must be ready to release control, let go, and let the team manage itself in a way the team members feel is best.

2. Setting up the team can be difficult, particularly if the organization doesn't already have an established culture of using self-managed teams. Different departments in the organization might find it challenging to collaborate with other areas of the organization if they have different work styles and practices. Team members could become apprehensive if they feel their responsibilities may increase. Moreover, the team leaders may feel that their roles are threatened by having some responsibility taken away from them.

3. Each Team Member must be ready to hold every other Team Member accountable. Consider the daily meetings. Today, one of your team members says they will work with the audit client to write the workpaper on the testing they completed the day before. At tomorrow's daily meeting, they say again that they will work with the audit client to write the workpaper on the testing they completed, now two days prior. Team members must be prepared to say, "I thought that was your update yesterday; what happened?" There may be a justifiable reason, an obstacle that the Scrum Master can help remove. Failure to honor their commitment could also result from the auditor having a low-production day, not feeling well, or having procrastinated.

4. Duplicate communications may occur at the beginning of the Agile audit since a clear communication protocol is still in process of being established.

5. As with any team, there is the potential peril of a lollygagger or freeloader. Suppose a Team Member is not meeting his responsibilities. One Team Member can have an impact on the entire team's work and productivity.

Planning, preparation, ongoing communication, and follow-up are necessary for a transition toward self-managed teamwork. For a self-managed team to remain successful, its members must be tolerant of others' errors. They must be willing to learn and allow others to learn, as well. Finally, trust between the team members is a critical foundation for successful self-managed teams.

 NUGGETS

To be Agile-ready, auditors need to build their audit toolbelt with essential knowledge, skills, and abilities. The Agile framework is one tool to include in your belt. Other tools that work with Agile auditing are the IIA Standards, Yellow Book, Generally Accepted Auditing Standards (GAAS), and skills such as data analytics, machine learning, automated workpapers, and data visualization.

What are some of the principles and values you might include in your "Team Commitment Declaration" or auditors' duty statements? What are some of the challenges you might encounter in building a self-managing team? What additional skills do you need or want to learn to become an integrated auditor in an Agile audit world?

CHAPTER SEVENTEEN

Preparing Your Organization for Agile Auditing/Creating the Agile Culture

Is your organization already embracing Agile practices or ready to embark on its Agile approach? How about you? Are you ready to start your Agile auditing journey? An Agile transformation requires more than just adopting new practices and implementing a new framework. It requires a transformation of behaviors, norms, and a complete mindset across the entire organization. The entire organizational culture needs to adapt and become more Agile. But what is Agile culture? Agile culture is about behaviors, attitudes, values, and beliefs.

> Culture is dynamic, not static. Everyone in your organization creates your culture by what they think, say, and do each day. Culture is lead from the top down, but it comes to life from the bottom up.
>
> – Jon Gordon

WHAT IS CULTURE?

John P. Kotter (chairman of Kotter International, a Harvard professor, and a well-regarded thought leader on the subject of leadership and change) defines culture as the "group norms of behavior and the underlying shared values that help keep those norms in place" (Kotter 2012). During one of our seminars, a student defined it plainly as: "It is the 'vibe' in here." We create culture either intentionally or unintentionally. The culture of an organization is vital to its long-term success. It impacts the treatment of employees and clients and how we conduct business. The culture of an organization can dramatically affect productivity, work dynamics, innovation, and communications.

Before you can change an existing culture, you need to measure the culture at all levels. You need to perform a culture assessment, which doesn't mean that you need to perform a human resource–driven survey of all employees. It means that you need to evaluate the various elements that create cultures. Start this assessment by agreeing with your stakeholders on what a healthy culture looks and feels like. Then agree on the culture the stakeholders want in the organization. Look across your organization and evaluate the following:

- The organization's mission, vision, goals, and values (MVGV)
- The tone at the top, middle, and bottom
- Corporate values – are they in alignment with the actions of specific departments and business areas?
- What are the expectations of senior management and the board compared to what happens?
- How is accountability determined?
- Existence of policies and procedures – are they up to date and followed?
- Conflict of interest and risk management policies, job descriptions, training and certifications, and strategic plans – are they current and communicated?
- Code of ethics and code of conduct – are they established, communicated, followed, and in alignment with the MVGV?
- How are reporting and oversight handled?
- Communications and information flow between all levels in the organization – are communications transparent?
- Compensation policies and structure – do they align with the MVGV?
- Who are the customers, and how are they treated?
- What is the sense of urgency level? Is everything urgent?

Although this list is rather lengthy, it is not all-inclusive. What other areas or aspects of your organization could help you measure the culture within your organization? Now that you've begun, you will have a better idea of your organization's culture and how it perceives the auditors.

CHANGING OTHERS' PERCEPTION OF AUDITORS

Somehow, auditors got a bad rap. Maybe it was created by audit generations of yore. Maybe the auditor just before you contributed to a negative perception of auditors. It doesn't matter; what matters is that you understand the perception. Moreover, understand that negative perception will impede progress on becoming Agile and doing Agile audits.

To start changing perceptions, you must identify and understand current perceptions. Perform a brand audit of your audit activities. The concept of a brand audit was first introduced to Raven by Thomas M. Bohn, president and chief executive officer for ACG Global, Association for Corporate Growth, in Chicago, Illinois. He indicated that it was something every auditor should do for themselves. Tom's ideas moved Raven so much that she now recommends that every audit department perform a brand audit, particularly when changing processes and strategic direction, to ensure that the audit department meets the customer's needs. To perform a brand audit of audit, you must determine the following:

- How do people feel when they hear "the auditors" or "the audit team" or "the audit department"?
- What do they think when they see you?
- What do they do when they learn that they will soon meet with the auditors to discuss their processes?
- Who influences your brand?
- What do audit clients and stakeholders believe is the audit's value proposition?
- What do people believe is the role of an auditor?

Compare the results with the brand you want. Did the results reflect the identity you want, the beliefs and values you live by, the behaviors you desire in your auditors, the skills you want your auditors to demonstrate, and the environment you want to create when you perform your audits? If you haven't thought about the brand you want, take a look at Richard Chambers' book *Trusted Advisors* (Chambers 2017b). In his book, Chambers shares the top attributes needed to excel as an internal audit professional and be the go-to person within the entity. You need to know what brand you want and where you stand in your audit clients' hearts and minds to determine whether you need to change their perceptions. If you need to change perceptions, identify the brand you want and the perceptions you want others to have, and create your roadmap to move perception in the right direction.

PARTICIPATORY AUDITING

For years, we've practiced Participatory Auditing (also known as participative auditing). At this point, remembering who coined that term is beyond recollection. Participatory Auditing involves your audit client's direct participation in the audit. Instead of being the unwilling auditee, the audit client is part of the audit team from the start of the audit project, if they choose to be. Our Agile audit framework embeds Participatory Auditing. The audit client is part of the Agile audit team from day one.

Throughout our careers and during our teaching engagements, we have seen examples and heard countless stories where client participation in the audit in one form or another leads to superior quality, agreement, and satisfaction by all involved. The purpose of a recent research paper published by the *Asian Review of Accounting* was "to determine the role of client involvement in the audit process and client psychological comfort in influencing client perceptions of audit quality" (Sampet, Sarapaivanich, and Patterson 2019). The research concluded that "Both client level of involvement and psychological comfort impact their perceptions of three dimensions of audit quality: service quality, independence, and competence. Audit quality, in turn, is strongly associated with overall client satisfaction" (Sampet, Sarapaivanich, and Patterson 2019).

Following is a sample list of how our audit clients participate in audits:

- At the daily meetings, clients attend and have an open exchange of viewpoints on challenging issues.
- During the annual organization-wide risk assessment and periodic updates, business process owners provide information and updates on issues they are currently working on and also share plans as well as any lessons learned.
- During the engagement-level risk assessment, clients help by providing information and reports, including results of their reviews and any data analytics they performed.
- During the audits, clients help conduct testing with guidance from the auditors. They have taken the initiative to assist in writing the audit findings. This level of participation can raise eyebrows regarding independence and objectivity. See Chapter 18 for tips on successful external quality assessments in an Agile environment.

These are just some of the many examples we have witnessed during our careers. How do you achieve this kind of participation? What are some actions you can take to get the ball rolling?

We advocate that the client's participation starts with your acknowledgment and, more importantly, the audit client's, that you cannot do the audit without them. Also, remain humble and tell the client that you are not an expert in their area. Tell them what you do know, what you've read to prepare, what classes you've taken, and similar areas you've audited to establish credibility. However, do not pretend you know the process as well as they do. Remember, they are the ultimate expert, and they need to know you know this.

INFLUENCING A CULTURE THAT SUPPORTS AGILE AUDITING

We know that forcing change doesn't work when people don't believe in the change or believe it is optional. If the change is implemented under these conditions, the change, if any, is temporary. We have seen temporary changes time after time when process owners implement audit recommendations; they don't believe it will help them mitigate risks and achieve objectives. What happens then? The next time you audit this same process, you will likely run into the same findings!

> One way to influence culture is to share positive experiences of others!

So how do you influence culture without forcing people? One option is to share the positive experiences of others. Consider this from a *Harvard Business Review* article:

> New Agile methodologies – which involve new values, principles, practices, and benefits and are a radical alternative to command-and-control-style management – are spreading across a broad range of industries and functions and even into the C-suite. National Public Radio employs Agile methods to create new programming. John Deere uses Agile practices to develop new machines, and Saab to produce new fighter jets. Intronis, a leader in cloud backup services, uses Agile methods in marketing. C.H. Robinson, a global third-party logistics provider, applies Agile to human resources. Mission Bell Winery uses Agile practices for everything from wine production to warehousing to running its senior leadership group. And GE relies on Agile to speed a much-publicized transition from a 20th-century

conglomerate to a 21st-century 'digital industrial company.' By taking people out of their functional silos and putting them in self-managed and customer-focused multidisciplinary teams, the Agile approach is not only accelerating profitable growth but also helping to create a new generation of skilled general managers." (Rigby, Sutherland, and Takeuchi 2016)

Perhaps these examples spur thoughts on diverse opportunities for Agile methods and provide ideas on encouraging your organization to use Agile.

The Influence of the Grateful Agile Leader

The "Grateful Agile Leader" is a new suggested radical alternative to command-and-control-style management and is vital in influencing a culture that supports Agile. "Grateful leadership is a style of leadership that is somewhat newer than other styles of leadership" (Parente 2019). Leaders who exhibit the "attitude of gratitude" can be highly influential and motivate others to improve performance. We first discuss this management style in Chapter 7, noting that each of the three roles in Scrum can adopt this style, as titles are not necessary.

> "A culture of Grateful Leadership starts with leaders who are inspired by a profound sense of personal gratitude."

To influence culture, auditors may need to change the organization's perceptions of auditors and audit activities. Imagine the impact the audit activity and auditors alike can have by adopting a grateful leadership style. Judith W. Umlas (author of *Grateful Leadership* and founder of the Center for Grateful Leadership) has created a powerful movement that is sweeping organizations worldwide and, in particular, organizations implementing Agile methodologies. This Grateful Leadership movement recognizes a culture of acknowledgment that delivers rewards on every organizational level. In her book *Grateful Leadership, Using the Power of Acknowledgment to Engage All Your People and Achieve Superior Results,* she provides best practices to guide employee engagement, motivation, staff retention, and increased productivity (Umlas 2013). Umlas explains that "A culture of Grateful Leadership starts with leaders who are inspired by a profound sense of personal gratitude." She further explains, "By creating a culture of appreciation throughout their organization, in which people truly feel valued, these leaders motivate their followers to strive for continuous improvement and always greater results.

This, in turn, promotes a positive environment and the overall well-being of both the leaders and their followers. In such cultures, employees and other stakeholders feel valued and appreciated, and they want to stay" (Umlas 2013). Moreover, Umlas provides a framework and a foundation to create or enhance a culture of appreciation and acknowledgment, which she calls the "5C's" (consciousness, choice, courage, communication, and commitment), which set the stage for the Seven Principles of Acknowledgment.

In Chapter 7, we describe the three Scrum roles. We discussed that the Scrum Master is a servant leader of the Scrum Team. The 2020 update to the Scrum Guide has changed the words around from a "servant leader" to "a leader who serves." This update is intended to help focus on the leadership role of the Scrum Master to help achieve the project goals. The term *servant leader* was coined by Robert K. Greenleaf in his book *Servant as Leader*, published in 1970. He proposed that the best leaders are servants first. The essential tools included listening, persuasion, access to intuition and foresight, and pragmatic measurements of outcomes (Frick 2004). The Servant Leadership style is well known for its great fit with Agile. The purpose of the Grateful Agile Leader is to use the structures of both Grateful Leadership and Servant Leadership to lead with an Agile approach.

Applying the servant leader's objective to enhance and increase teamwork and personal involvement and becoming a Grateful Agile Leader is a powerful way to influence people and culture. A culture of gratitude has the potential to:

- Create a participatory environment
- Empower the Agile team and the entire organization by sharing the decision-making process
- Focus on building a foundation of trust
- Encourage collaborative audit engagements

Another way to influence people is simply to involve them in the change. Ask for their thoughts and opinions. Ask for their suggestions. Listen to them. Alistair Cockburn, one of the 17 authors of the Agile Manifesto, asserted that Agile is gaining momentum. A culture of listening is needed to support Agile development's continued advancement and bring the laggards on board (Cockburn 2019). See Chapters 2 and 12 for a discussion of laggards and crossing the chasm and the identified groups of technology adopters. When you listen to people, you build greater buy-in. To listen to people, especially around sensitive topics like disruptive changes such as Agile auditing, you must "start with the heart." Start with heart is a concept from *Crucial*

Conversations that teaches that when you are addressing difficult topics, you start with three questions (Patterson, Grenny, McMillan, and Switzler 2012):

1. What do you want for the other person?
2. What do you want for yourself?
3. What do you want for your relationship with the other person?

Let's use these questions as a tool to help you influence a culture that supports Agile auditing.

What Do You Want for the Other Person?

From our perspective, we want the other person to love auditors and look forward to hearing feedback on their processes, controls, and risk management practices. We want the other person, our audit clients, to work collaboratively with us and share knowledge and information freely and fearlessly. Your answer may be different.

What Do You Want for Yourself?

We want to be liked and viewed as trying to help the organization accomplish its objectives while managing risks using intelligent internal controls. We want less resistance to audit requests. We want to waste less time waiting for evidence.

What Do You Want for Your Relationship with the Other Person?

We want the audit client to acknowledge us in the hallways, cafeteria, and the gym. We want them to pick up the phone and call us whenever they have a question or want to float a new idea or control.

But what if the people in your organization don't want the same thing as you? What if they don't want to collaborate with you? You need to determine why they don't want to collaborate. Cockburn recognizes that to move Agile out of system development and information technology and into other parts of an organization, we must tackle culture and address how to run organizations with radical transparency (Cockburn 2019). Answer these questions:

▪ Why don't people freely share their problems with auditors?
▪ Why do audit clients insist on reviewing questions before audit interviews?

- Why do clients take extraordinary time to provide procedures and documents they use daily?
- Why do audit clients argue the black-and-white facts provided by their evidence?
- Why don't most auditors get invited to social gatherings with coworkers?
- Why don't audit clients want to develop relationships with auditors?

If you think about the answers to these questions or the root cause of all these problems, it comes down to this: audit clients aren't sure if they trust the auditors or, worse, they may even fear for their promotions, bonuses, and jobs, depending on how auditors present their conclusions. Perhaps your audit client has been punished as a result of a prior audit. How do you influence increased trust and reduced fear? By being transparent and honest and honoring your word. If you've ever told an audit client "everything looks good" just before you left their office from an audit interview and then ended up with an audit finding on the topic you were discussing, in the client's mind, you weren't honest, and you didn't honor your word. In other words, you can't be trusted. If you think there were times when auditors couldn't be trusted, or similar scenarios happened in your organization, it is time to perform reconnaissance and remediation activities.

 ## IDEAL CONDITIONS FOR AGILE AUDITING

A few years ago, two clients contacted us to facilitate Agile auditing training. During our intake process, we steered the clients in a different direction because their reasons for electing Agile auditing were not strong enough, in our opinion, to sustain such a transformation. Reason one was because everyone else is doing it. That is never a good reason to do anything. In our talks on ethics and ethical erosion, we point out that just because everyone is doing something doesn't mean it's right and doesn't make it right for you. Reason two was because they thought it would solve problems with audit committee oversight of internal audit processes. If your audit committee or the governing body doesn't understand what you do or doesn't give you enough time on the board agenda, Agile can't solve your audit committee problems. If these are your reasons for implementing Agile auditing, reevaluate the need to use Agile auditing before beginning your journey. We're sure other reasons would justify your reconsidering venturing down the Agile auditing journey. Let us know your audit team's initial decision against Agile auditing if you've been down that path. Table 17.1 illustrates favorable and unfavorable conditions for Agile auditing:

Some say that the organization's culture is its DNA – the core identity of the organization. Culture changes are not easy but are necessary for Agile initiatives to succeed. We once heard that to change a culture, a company needs a rapid turnover of 50% of the workforce. Maybe that is true; maybe it is an exaggeration, but Stephen Denning stated it best: "changing a culture is thus a large-scale and long-term undertaking, involving many players" (Denning 2018). Denning also identifies three frequent mistakes in trying to change the culture:

1. Overuse of the power tools of coercion and underuse of leadership tools
2. Failure to use leadership storytelling to inspire people to embrace change
3. Beginning with a vision and a plan, but failing to put in place the Agile management that will cement the behavioral changes

We have personally seen two of these mistakes in action. The first was an attempt to implement Agile auditing from the bottom up. A small team of auditors at a large utility company went "rogue," as one manager put it, and started influencing peers to adopt Agile auditing. Every time auditors implemented an Agile practice, they were struck down by either the audit leadership or the peer reviewer. It was a fruitless exercise and one from which the instigating auditors did not recover. To avoid this, whenever you have a great idea, do your research, develop a well-orchestrated marketing plan, and work to get leadership buy-in before you begin.

Our own client experience was the second time we witnessed a failure in implementing Agile auditing. A visual roadmap laid out the vision. There was a long-term plan to roll out the entire framework, with checkpoints and adaptations built into the roadmap. Unfortunately, it did not succeed: there was too much time between the phased roll-out; too little communication on the desired changes; not enough interest in the voluntary training to educate the masses on the Agile audit framework; and thus, not enough action to change behaviors to make Agile auditing a sustainable approach. It is great to plan, but avoid overplanning and underdoing.

Crucial to the success of Agile is an environment in which failure is not viewed as a negative factor. As we noted in the Preface to this book, failing and failing fast is a collective mindset in Agile disciplines. It is okay to fail. Failure

TABLE 17.1 The Right Conditions for Agile Auditing

Condition	Favorable	Unfavorable
Organizational Environment	Organizations, audit clients, and stakeholder preferences and solution options change frequently.	The organization is stable and predictable.
	The organizational focus is doing what is right to deliver value in a fast-paced, competitive arena.	The organizational focus is high-volume, mass production.
	The first line of defense and executives understand the roles and responsibilities in risk management and internal controls.	The perception in the organization is that controls are unnecessary and inefficient.
Audit Client Involvement	Close collaboration and rapid feedback are feasible.	Audit clients are unavailable for constant collaboration.
	Audit clients discover what they want/need as the audit progresses.	Requirements are clear at the outset and will remain stable.
Innovation Type	Problems are complex, solutions are unknown, and the requirements are not clearly defined.	Similar problems have occurred before, and the solutions are clear to resolve the problems permanently.
	Goals and risks change.	Goals and risks are stable.
	Creative approaches to managing risk and timely insight on risk management are essential.	Innovation, creative thinking, and risk management assurance are unimportant.
	Organizational activities are highly creative and encourage discovery projects.	Organizational activities are highly administrative and repetitive.
	Cross-functional collaboration is vital to organizational success.	Organizational risk management is effective in silos.
Modularity of Work	Incremental assurance has value, and audit clients can use more timely feedback on issues identified.	Audit clients cannot resolve identified control weaknesses and other issues until the entire audit project is complete.
	Work can be broken into parts and conducted in rapid, iterative cycles.	Work products and audit results must be delivered all at once.
	Late changes to audit tests are manageable.	Late changes to audit tests are expensive or impossible to manage.
Impact of Interim Mistakes	They provide valuable learning.	They may be catastrophic.

Source: Adapted from Darrell K. Rigby, Jeff Sutherland, and Hirotaka Takeuchi, "Embracing Agile," *Harvard Business Review*, May 2016.

is even expected! Successful Agile projects are those that recognize failure quickly, through constant inspection, and rapidly adapt to identified failures.

> Creating a culture where people are afraid to fail leads to failure. Allowing people to fail and learn from failure ultimately leads to success.

– Jon Gordon

 NUGGETS

Be mindful of your teams' different situations and the complexities that may exist with their particular workloads. A "one-size-fits-all" solution for an organization rarely works well. Agile practices need to be tailored and adapted to account for the team's specific customers, risks, and unique circumstances. Kanban may be a better fit than Scrum, or in other circumstances, a blended approach may be preferred. It would be best to think about the best fit for the team and your organization and then continue to inspect and adapt as the team's performance improves. By incorporating adaptive thinking and a user-centered design approach, your organization can make incremental changes that will ultimately increase user satisfaction, a cornerstone of Agile values and principles.

A top-down transition may not be the best approach. Our preferred approach is having good support at the top and great excitement and enthusiasm at the bottom and middle levels and starting slowly by encouraging individuals to attend lunch-and-learn sessions to become familiar with key Agile concepts. Establish opportunities, such as a forum or roundtable, where people can share experiences and offer contributions. Share goals and objectives of implementing Agile clearly and visibly and seek input from participants to best approach the Agile transformation. An alternative may be to run an Agile pilot to get started, involving the most enthusiastic participants. This pilot will allow others to see results from the outside and slowly move to adopt Agile. Share your progress on the pilot's results, emphasizing your successes. Gaining buy-in at all levels will not necessarily be an easy process. However, it will likely be the essential success factor in your Agile transformation.

CHAPTER EIGHTEEN

Passing Your Quality Assessment Review in an Agile Audit Environment

Audit activities get audited too! In short, each group of auditors has expectations placed on them by regulatory and standards-setting bodies. Identify your regulatory body or standards-setting organization, start working with your reviewer, or participate in roundtables relevant to your audit group to discuss how you can conform to the Quality Assessment Review (QAR) expectations. We also encourage you to consult the appropriate standards and take the tips we provide here to ensure that you observe the standards. Following, we'll share what we know to help you pass your QAR, specifically for issues of most concern when implementing an Agile auditing framework.

As you have learned from reading this book, Agile auditing is an approach to deliver what customers need in a fast-changing environment. It assumes fixed resources and time, and variable scope; therefore, it is value-driven. In contrast, the traditional waterfall – predictive model – approach assumes fixed scope and variable resources and time; therefore, it is plan-driven. This chapter will cover the top four areas of most concern, as expressed by our clients and our conference participants, when implementing Agile auditing. They are:

1. Audit independence and objectivity
2. Audit planning

3. Audit documentation
4. Audit supervision

Although passing the QAR is critical, we must remember that the quality objective is not about doing just enough to pass. Instead, we must understand why the relevant authorities, such as the Institute of Internal Auditors (IIA), the U.S. Government Accountability Office (US GAO), the American Institute of Certified Public Accountants (AICPA), the Financial Accounting Standards Board (FASB), the Securities and Exchange Commission (SEC), other comprehensive basis of accounting (OCBOA), and the Generally Accepted Tax Accounting Principles (GATAP) detail such requirements. Understanding the "why" will help the entire Agile team ensure that the audit activity passes the QAR with flying colors!

> The QAR helps determine whether an audit organization's quality control system is in place, adequately designed, and operating effectively.
> We must adapt how we think about meeting the standards in an Agile auditing environment.

So, let's start with a reminder of the overall objective of the QAR. The QAR helps determine whether an audit organization's quality control system is in place, adequately designed, and operating effectively. A QAR provides stakeholders with assurance that an audit organization follows established policies and procedures and applicable auditing standards. We must adapt how we think about meeting the standards in an Agile auditing environment.

We first provide an overview of the standards used for the three types of audits covered in this book (internal, government, and external financial audits). Then we will cover the four areas we listed that are of most concern regarding your QAR when implementing Agile auditing.

 GOVERNMENT AUDITORS

Government auditors maintain and examine the records of government agencies (federal, state, country, city, and other local jurisdiction) and of private businesses or individuals performing activities subject to government regulations or taxation. Governmental audits include financial statement audits performed under Government Auditing Standards on entities such as states, local governments, not-for-profit organizations, and institutions of higher education.

In Chapter 2, we explained that government auditors can be external to the entity, department, or agency they are auditing (known as external auditors in the government environment) or internal to the entity, department, or agency they are auditing (known as internal auditors in the government environment). Moreover, in the United States, government audits adhere to standards published by the Government Accountability Office (GAO). The Generally Accepted Government Audit Standards (GAGAS), commonly known as the Yellow Book; Standards for Internal Control in the Federal Government, also referred to as the Green Book; and Financial Audit Manual, known as the Blue Book, are different standards for financial controls, operating controls, and enterprise risk management provided by the GAO.

Government entities, entities that receive government awards, and other audit organizations performing Yellow Book audits are required to use Yellow Book standards. The Yellow Book outlines audit report requirements, professional qualifications for auditors, and audit organization quality control. Auditors of federal, state, and local government programs use these standards to perform their audits and produce their reports (U.S. Government Accountability Office 2018). Government auditors may also follow the IIA Red Book. You will see both books used as applicable when we discuss the standards in this book.

Gene L. Dodaro, Comptroller General of the United States, notes in his Yellow Book opening letter, "Audits provide essential accountability and transparency over government programs. Given the current challenges facing governments and their programs, the oversight provided through auditing is more critical than ever. Government auditing provides the objective analysis and information needed to make the decisions necessary to help create a better future." Dorado also notes that the professional standards, commonly referred to as Generally Accepted Government Auditing Standards (GAGAS), provide a framework for performing high-quality audit work. These standards provide the foundation for government auditors to lead by example in independence, transparency, accountability, and quality through the audit process (U.S. Government Accountability Office 2018).

The Yellow Book covers four types of engagements. All engagements begin with objectives, which determine the type of engagement and the applicable standards. These engagements are financial audits, attestation engagements, reviews of financial statements, and performance audits (GAGAS Section 1.14).

The Yellow Book is a framework with a set of standards and guidelines. It is not prescriptive in terms of directing step-by-step actions for how to meet each standard. However, it provides basic requirements for what you need to do to meet the standards. When you consider the Agile Manifesto, meeting the standards should be easier. In our experience with QARs, there is flexibility in meeting the standards, as stakeholder needs and the purposes and responsibilities of audit activities vary across the profession.

The Yellow Book uses two categories of requirements, identified by specific terms, to describe the degree of responsibility imposed on auditors and audit organizations. The first category is unconditional requirements. Auditors and audit activities must comply with these requirements in all cases where such a requirement is relevant (look for the word "must"). The second category is presumptively mandatory requirements. Auditors and audit activities must comply with a presumptively mandatory requirement in all cases where such a requirement is relevant, with some exceptions (look for the word "should"). Additional application guidance provides further explanation of the requirements and guidance for applying them.

The Yellow Book requires each audit organization to establish a quality control system designed to provide reasonable assurance of compliance with professional standards and applicable legal and regulatory requirements. Specifically, GAGAS Chapter 5.84 requires an external peer review by reviewers independent of the audit organization at least once every three years. The first peer review should cover a period ending no later than three years from the date an audit organization begins its first engagement. The period under review is generally one year.

INTERNAL AUDITORS

Internal auditors around the globe follow the IIA's International Professional Practices Framework (IPPF). A QAR evaluates the internal audit activity's conformance with the IPPF's mandatory elements, specifically the Standards and the Code of Ethics, the Core Principles of Internal Auditing, and the definition of internal audit. Agile audit activities should begin by looking for the right independent assessor. Interview them and ask them if they have performed a QAR for an audit team that practices an Agile audit methodology. If not, that doesn't mean you can't use them; it means you need to work with them and educate them on Agile auditing.

The IIA Standards require audit activities to have a quality assurance and improvement program covering all aspects of the internal audit activity. This means that the quality assurance and improvement program must include both internal and external assessments. IIA Standard 1312 states, "External assessments must be conducted at least once every five years by a qualified, independent assessor or assessment team from outside the organization" (Institute of Internal Auditors 2017a).

EXTERNAL AUDITORS

External auditors first determine whether the organization's financial statements (often of public companies) follow Generally Accepted Accounting Principles (GAAP) or International Financial Reporting Standards (IFRS). The external auditor must form an opinion regarding the fairness of the financial statements, asserting whether the financial statements are free of material misstatement, whether due to error or fraud. Moreover, the resulting audited financial statements are relied upon by various external users such as investors, creditors, and government bodies. GAAP are widely used in the United States, whereas IFRS are widely used in countries outside the United States. External auditors for publicly traded companies are limited by regulations in their ability to engage in non-audit services for the same organization while serving as external auditors. Regulations such as the Sarbanes-Oxley Act address independence for audit firms and individual auditors. This act requires that the lead partner's position on an external audit engagement rotate at least every five years. Likewise, other rules intended to prevent perceived or actual conflicts of interest between auditors and the organizations they audit apply in many regulated industries.

AGILE AUDITING AND YOUR QAR

As explained earlier, an Agile audit is not a rigid recipe. Instead, it is an approach, a mindset based on values and principles established by the Agile Manifesto that we need to observe to be successful. It is a dedication to continuous improvement principles with a primary focus on helping others. Let's revisit the four Agile Manifesto values detailed in Chapter 6, with an audit focus emphasizing the areas of concern, to set the context of how to meet professional standards when using Agile auditing.

We are uncovering better ways of auditing through collaboration with the beneficiaries of our work. Through this work, we have come to value:

1. Working with people over processes and tools, while maintaining our independence and objectivity
2. Providing relevant and timely insights over extensive audit documentation
3. Client collaboration and relationship building over negotiating findings and numerous audit report iterations
4. Doing what's right and adding value over following a predetermined inflexible plan

Audit Independence and Objectivity – Working with People over Processes and Tool

Auditors implementing Agile auditing have expressed concerns regarding independence and objectivity. The Agile audit framework provides a structure and guidance for collaboration with audit clients, as they are part of the Agile team from the beginning of the Agile audit. Agile audits cannot move forward without the audit client. The framework focuses on adding value from the audit client's perspective by centering the Agile audit on the value proposition, which leverages business objectives and business risks, not audit risks.

Internal audit activities focus on the effectiveness and efficiency of communications among team members within each phase of audit engagements, planning, fieldwork, and reporting. This may include the use of various tools, such as the enterprise governance, risk, and compliance (GRC) software and internal audit software tools and templates. These tools and processes provide foundational elements for efficient communication of audit results. However, Agile purposely focuses more on relationships with increased face-to-face client collaboration. It recognizes that the human element of meaningful interactions improves communications and enhances solutions and auditor/client agreement. The tools, templates, and systems used by auditors may facilitate the audit process. Nonetheless, these tools do not necessarily create value for the client.

The IIA Standard 1100, *Independence and Objectivity,* states that "The internal audit activity must be independent, and internal auditors must be objective in performing their work." Standard 1110, *Organizational Independence,* notes that the CAE "must report to a level within the organization that allows the internal audit activity to fulfill its responsibilities. The CAE must confirm to the board, at least annually, the organizational independence of the internal audit activity." And Standard 1120, *Individual Objectivity,* states that "Internal auditors must have an impartial, unbiased attitude and avoid any conflict of interest."

The IIA's Implementation Guide 1110, *Organizational Independence,* states that:

> Organizational independence is effectively achieved when the chief audit executive reports functionally to the board. Examples of functional reporting to the board involve the board:
>
> ■ Approving the internal audit charter.
> ■ Approving the risk-based internal audit plan.
> ■ Approving the internal audit budget and resource plan.
> ■ Receiving communications from the chief audit executive on the internal audit activity's performance relative to its plan and other matters.
> ■ Approving decisions regarding the appointment and removal of the chief audit executive.
> ■ Approving the remuneration of the chief audit executive.
> ■ Making appropriate inquiries of management and the chief audit executive to determine whether there are inappropriate scope or resource limitations.

Therefore, the audit activity's organizational independence can be achieved whether a traditional waterfall audit approach or an Agile audit approach is used.

IIA guidance states that objectivity is an unbiased mental attitude that allows internal auditors to perform engagements so that they can believe in their work product and that quality is not compromised. Objectivity requires that internal auditors do not subordinate their judgment on audit matters to others. They must manage threats to objectivity at the individual auditor, engagement, functional, and organizational levels. IIA guidance also states that the auditor shall not participate in any activity or relationship that may impair or be presumed to impair their unbiased assessment. This participation includes those activities or relationships that may conflict with the interests of the organization.

The IIA's Implementation Guide 1120, *Individual Objectivity,* states that internal audit policy manuals might describe the expectations and requirements for an unbiased mindset for every internal auditor, and address matters such as:

■ The critical importance of objectivity to the internal audit profession.
■ Typical situations that could undermine objectivity, such as auditing in an area where an internal auditor recently worked; auditing a family member or a close friend; or assuming, without evidence, that an area under audit is acceptable based solely on prior positive experiences.

- Actions the internal auditor should take if they become aware of a current or potential objectivity concern, such as discussing the concern with an internal audit manager or the CAE.
- Reporting requirements, where each internal auditor periodically considers and discloses conflicts of interest.

Often, policies require internal auditors to indicate that they understand the conflict-of-interest policy and to disclose potential conflicts. Internal auditors sign annual statements indicating that no potential threats exist or acknowledging any known potential threats. To reinforce the importance of these policies and help ensure that all internal auditors internalize their importance, many CAEs will hold routine workshops or training on these fundamental concepts.

The CAE should consider potential objectivity impairments when assigning auditors to engagements and avoid assigning auditors with potential conflicts. Also, performance and compensation practices may impact auditor objectivity. If auditor performance appraisals are based significantly on client feedback, auditors may be inclined to "go easy" on the client, anticipating higher ratings, which may impair objectivity. Or, if performance appraisals are largely based on the auditor's ability to adhere to unrealistic time budgets, auditor objectivity may be impaired causing the auditor to cut corners or fail to expand testing or audit scope when necessary.

Therefore, auditor objectivity must be monitored and can be achieved whether a traditional waterfall audit approach or an Agile audit approach is used. In the Yellow Book, objectivity includes independence of mind and appearance when providing audits, maintaining an attitude of impartiality, having intellectual honesty, and being free of conflicts of interest. Likewise, maintaining objectivity includes a continuing assessment of relationships with audited entities and other stakeholders in the context of the auditors' responsibility to the public. The concepts of objectivity and independence are closely related. Independence impairments impact objectivity.

As to independence requirements for external auditors, standards require independence in mental attitude is to be maintained by all auditors in all matters relating to the assignment. Auditors must be without bias concerning the client. Independence recognizes sensible impartiality that recognizes obligation for fairness to management, the process owners, as well as anyone who may rely on the audit report. Clients and all users of the reports should maintain confidence in the independence of the auditors. Independent auditors should not only be independent in fact; they should avoid situations that may lead outsiders to doubt their independence.

The AICPA's Code of Professional Conduct also has provisions to guard against the presumption of loss of independence. "Presumption" is stressed because the possession of intrinsic independence is a matter of personal quality rather than rules that formulate specific objective tests. Moreover, the Securities and Exchange Commission (SEC) has also adopted auditors' independence requirements who report on financial statements filed with it.

Client interactions, collaboration, building business relationships, enhancing trust, and shared understanding with the clients allow for enhanced recommendations and communication throughout the audit, driving success and value for the entire process. Accordingly, when implementing Agile Auditing, auditors must maintain their independence and objectivity and document potential areas of concern. These actions are no different than when following the waterfall approach. However, because of enhanced communication and collaboration with the client, the audit activity should maintain greater awareness regarding perceptions of a lack of independence or auditor objectivity. With our Agile framework, ownership remains with the audit team. We recommend the audit activity's policy and procedure manual document the Agile methodology, including how independence and objectivity are to be maintained.

Moreover, each audit engagement can include a simple template that notes how independence and objectivity are maintained. This document can include any relationship, the time since the auditors last worked in that area if applicable, and other similar items that could raise any doubt about independence and objectivity. Also, a properly documented risk assessment can add support to independence and objectivity. In conclusion, we emphasize that independence and objectivity must be managed, but can be achieved regardless of an Agile audit approach or a traditional waterfall audit approach.

Audit Planning: Doing What's Right and Adding Value over Following a Preset Inflexible Plan

Planning is a vital aspect of Agile auditing. However, rather than conducting extensive planning upfront as in waterfall methodologies, Agile spreads this planning activity evenly throughout the project life cycle. High-level planning, however, is completed at the beginning of an Agile project and this planning is continuously elaborated upon throughout the project as new information becomes available in every Sprint. In Agile, planning occurs in every Sprint with a Sprint planning meeting, creating a better alignment between the work conducted and the associated risks. This continuous planning allows audit projects to begin more quickly and to remain flexible. If new information becomes available, the team can make necessary adjustments. Continuous planning also provides the project team with the ability to more quickly and efficiently adapt to changes and optimize plans as new information emerges. Risk-based planning is a requirement of Agile auditing.

The IIA's Implementation Guide 2201, *Planning Considerations*, states:

In planning the engagement, internal auditors must consider:

- The strategies and objectives of the activity being reviewed and the means by which the activity controls its performance.
- The significant risks to the activity's objectives, resources, and operations and the means by which the potential impact of risk is kept to an acceptable level.
- The adequacy and effectiveness of the activity's governance, risk management, and control processes compared to a relevant framework or model.
- The opportunities for making significant improvements to the activity's governance, risk management, and control processes.

The daily communications characteristic of the Agile audit framework facilitates an iterative process for addressing each of these elements on a regular, proactive basis. Further, planning in Agile is a daily routine. Daily communications occur with the Daily Scrum meeting, where the team discusses three things: As a Team Member, what did you do yesterday? What are you doing today? and What obstacles do you have? These meetings also serve to highlight any necessary adjustments to the engagement plan.

The Yellow Book does not contain requirements related to ensuring that the activity's plan of engagements must be based on a documented risk assessment. However, it requires a risk assessment to determine the audit organization's overall audit planning. It also requires individual audit planning. In Agile auditing, the plan is documented, but it is completed in iterations. All standards require documentation of audit planning.

GAGAS Chapter 8, Section 8.03 to 8.07, discusses planning requirements. In general, these sections state that in planning the audit, auditors must adequately:

- Plan the work necessary to address the audit objectives and document the audit plan.
- Plan the audit to reduce audit risk to an acceptably low level.

This guidance further states that auditors should:

- Assess significance and audit risk and apply these assessments to establish the scope and methodology for addressing the audit objectives. Moreover, it specifically states that planning is a continuous process throughout the audit.
- Design the methodology to obtain sufficient, appropriate evidence that provides a reasonable basis for findings and conclusions based on the audit objectives and reduce audit risk to an acceptably low level.
- Identify and use suitable criteria based on the audit objectives.

Flexibility is an important characteristic of Agile auditing. For example, in Agile audit engagements, Sprints are used to perform an audit. Splitting the scope into smaller subproducts, more iterations, and shorter lead times instead of a successive fixed schedule allows the team to always be aware of risks and new information affecting the audit. The CAE or its delegate must approve changes in the scope or audit work program. In Agile, we have seen approval of changes usually done by the Product Owner.

Audit Documentation: Providing Relevant and Timely Insights over Extensive Audit Documentation

In Agile auditing, less documentation doesn't mean *no* documentation. Because the clients and auditors are working together throughout the audit process, exceptions are discovered cooperatively and can be addressed by the entire team instantaneously. Robust conversations about poor control design will occur. Detailed discussions about poor control execution will occur as exceptions are identified. Relevant and timely insights are derived and communicated in real time. Process owners can collaboratively agree on remediation activities and timelines for implementation. Therefore, inherent in the Agile approach is less documentation is required.

The Yellow Book contains a requirement to report abuse when an auditor becomes aware of it. Another requirement for evaluating internal control in a government environment may also include considering internal control deficiencies that result in waste or abuse. However, the determination of waste and abuse is subjective. Thus, auditors are not required to perform specific procedures to detect waste or abuse in financial audits. Auditors may consider whether and how to communicate such matters if they become aware of them.

Audit activities should establish specific policies and procedures for performing audit engagements, including planning, documenting, executing the audit work program, supervision, and reporting. When Agile audit processes permit streamlined documentation, this should be addressed through guidance in audit activity policies and procedures.

Audit Report and Supervision: Client Collaboration and Relationship Building over Audit Report Negotiation

A frequent question asked during our Agile Auditing conferences is whether it is okay if the audit client reviews the work. Our response has been to ask the audience to show us the standard that disallows the audit client from reviewing the work. This topic has been controversial, as it implies that the client can review the work and act as "supervision." Here is where we get into the attribute standards versus the performance standards. The Quality Assessment Review places a big emphasis on the IIA's attribute standards – auditor independence and objectivity (IIA Standard 1100) are essential in fulfilling the auditor's role and responsibilities. By definition, the client whose work or activity is being audited is *not* objective with respect to their own work. Further, by definition, they're not objective with respect to auditor conclusions. Therefore, the client (auditee) might not be able to fill the shoes of an otherwise objective and independent reviewer of the audit work. IIA Standard 2340, "Engagements must be properly supervised to ensure objectives are achieved, quality is assured, and staff is developed," requires engagement supervision. Moreover, the interpretation of the standard states, "The extent of supervision required will depend on the proficiency and experience of internal auditors and the complexity of the engagement. The CAE has overall responsibility for supervising the engagement, whether performed by or for the internal audit activity but may designate appropriately experienced internal audit activity members to perform the review. Appropriate evidence of supervision is documented and retained" (Institute of Internal Auditors 2017a).

Continuous improvement and supervision are characteristic of Agile auditing. The retrospective meeting provides an overview of how the team is self-managed, how individuals are engaging, and lessons learned. In Chapter 7, we discussed the roles in Agile auditing. Ownership of the audit remains within the audit activity, and so does overall supervision within the self-managing Agile team. As explained in Chapter 1, auditing team members are a cross-functional, self-managing group of individuals possessing all the skills necessary to complete the Sprint tasks. The team has total authority on the exact approach to get its work done, estimate how long the work will take, create the work schedule, and manage their own time. The team is accountable for all aspects of the work. Supervision is built in, as audit leadership expectations are communicated during the Product Backlog refinement meeting and clarified in the daily meetings. We encourage you further to discuss this area with your external quality assessor. As you implement your Agile methodology, you will find that sometimes it is best to be safe and conservative; other times, you might want to push the envelope and expand your risk appetite.

 NUGGETS

> As you embark on your Agile journey, you will realize that meeting the standards is no different than when following the traditional waterfall audit approach. You might even realize that it is a less painful process with Agile.

As you embark on your Agile journey, you will realize that meeting the standards is no different than when following the traditional waterfall audit approach. You might even realize that it is a less painful process with Agile. It provides the necessary flexibility regarding the form and content of audits, depending on the audit activity's circumstances. In Agile auditing we:

- Work with clients from the beginning without relinquishing ownership and control of the audit scope. The clients are validated and empowered to share risk and control information and other concerns regarding risks to achievement of business objectives.
- Provide relevant and timely insights in small increments with the necessary documentation instead of extensive audit documentation that adds no value to the client or the audit process.
- Meet daily and hold Sprint Retrospectives; we enable continuous client collaboration and relationship building, creating opportunities for proper supervision and immediate communication of audit results.
- Plan according to the work we can complete in a specified time and adjust as necessary based on risks and time to complete the work.

CHAPTER NINETEEN

Nuggets for Agile Audit Success

We encourage participants to summarize their new or refreshed knowledge from our training courses by identifying three nuggets. A nugget can be anything meaningful to them – an idea, a question, something to research later, something to tell someone else, an aha moment, or even a thought related to the content discussed. We encourage you to identify your nuggets or key takeaways for each chapter. Through our Agile auditing journey, we've learned a lot, and there is more to learn. As adults, we learn from our own experiences and the experiences of others. In this chapter, we share some lessons learned along the Agile auditing journey.

Nugget #1: Create a roadmap.

Nugget #2: Socialize your desires, intent, and roadmap well before you start implementing or piloting Agile audits.

Nugget #3: Doing an Agile audit with an audit client in the middle of an Agile project doesn't work. In Agile, team members are dedicated to their projects. They don't have enough time to work closely with auditors when they are dedicated to another Agile project.

Nugget #4: Dedicate auditors to work on only the one Agile audit project. Have defined start and end dates for the Agile audit.

Nugget #5: Identify a dedicated audit liaison. Personally, audit liaisons are not my favorite concept. Often the liaison doesn't know the answers to the questions, and there are delays in getting responses as they try to find the answer. However, at least a dedicated audit liaison is dedicated to getting the answers, sometimes with relentless dedication.

Nugget #6: Empower the team to make decisions. As teams continue to work together and are given decision-making responsibilities, they will become more confident and will accomplish work faster.

Nugget #7: Create a culture of continuous improvement where failure is encouraged. Fail fast, and make the necessary adjustments.

Nugget #8: Start by focusing on the top risks.

Nugget #9: Perform small, incremental audits with a focused scope and frequent delivery of solutions. You can't do it all at the same time!

Nugget #10: Communicate, communicate, and communicate – remember, you can never overcommunicate!

Agile is quickly becoming the go-to approach for auditing. Being Agile means that we adapt to our environment and the business around us. Being Agile means that we improve our approach and evolve, so we do not become "Jurassic auditors." Let's keep an open dialogue about your Agile journey. We want to be with you while you grow as an Agile auditor, and we encourage you to stay in touch and connect with us. Thank you!

When faced with challenging opportunities, making the most difficult choices has resulted in the best and most permanent lessons learned and the most incredible achievements and progress.

– Ceciliana Watkins

Glossary of Terms

Agile: An ability to move quickly and easily in response to your environment.

Agile project management: An approach to project management based on a set of values and principles that breaks projects into smaller, incremental deliverables based on customers' needs and interests.

Agile Delivery Team: Team members who complete product tasks from the Sprint Backlog during a Sprint to deliver a product, also known as the Delivery Team.

Agile team: A cross-functional, self-managing group of individuals who have total authority on how to get their work done, estimate how long work will take, create their schedule, and manage their own time; includes the Delivery Team, Product Owner, and Scrum Master.

Artificial intelligence (AI): "The combination of cognitive automation, machine learning, reasoning, hypothesis generation and analysis, natural language processing, and intentional algorithm mutation producing insights and analytics at or above human capability" (IEEE Standard 2755-2017).

Audit: An evaluation of evidence to reach a conclusion on something.

Audit activity: A department, division, team of auditors, or other practitioner(s) that provides independent, objective assurance and consulting services designed to add value and improve an organization's operations. The internal audit activity helps an organization accomplish its objectives by bringing a systematic, disciplined approach to evaluate and improve the effectiveness of governance, risk management, and control processes. In this book we refer to the audit activity. An audit team is a subset of an audit activity (i.e., the audit team working on a particular engagement, as opposed to the entire audit department or function). "Audit shop" is sometimes used interchangeably with audit activity. Audit shop is commonly used in informal settings and at times is also used in professional literature, although our experience is that "shop" is considered by some to be a little less than professional, and denotes retail (e.g., a coffee shop or a gift shop).

Audit plan: The engagements from the audit universe that will be performed over a specified period.

Audit universe: A list of all potential engagements or auditable entities/units.

Auditing: The process of identifying, gathering, examining, analyzing, evaluating, and concluding on information to form an opinion on a specific topic.

Business agility: The ability to identify changes and risks from internal and external sources and respond to those changes promptly and appropriately, to deliver value to customers, and remain sustainable.

Chief audit executives (CAEs): Audit directors, general auditors, auditor generals, partners, and principals. The most senior leader who has overall responsibility for an audit activity.

Data analytics (DA): The process of examining large data sets to uncover hidden patterns, unknown correlations, trends, customer preferences, and other useful business insights. The end result might be a report, an indication of status, or an action taken automatically based on the information received.

Data mining: Finding meaningful patterns and deriving insights in large sets of data using sophisticated pattern recognition techniques. To derive meaningful patterns, data miners use statistics, machine learning algorithms, and artificial intelligence.

Data science: A discipline that incorporates statistics, data visualization, computer programming, data mining, machine learning, and database engineering to solve complex problems.

Data velocity: The speed at which data is produced.

Data volume: The volume of data in a single file or file system can be described by a unit called a byte. For example, 1 kilobyte (KB) = 1,000 bytes; 1 megabyte (MB) = 1,000 kilobytes; 1 gigabyte (GB) = 1,000 megabytes (the size of Beethoven's 5th Symphony); 1 terabyte (TB) = 1,000 gigabytes; 1 petabyte (PB) = 1,000 terabytes; 1 exabyte (EB) = 1,000 petabytes; and 1 zettabyte (ZB) = 1,000 exabytes (as much information as there are grains of sand on all the world's beaches!) (Williams 2012).

Definition of Done (DoD): A formal description of the state of the Increment when it meets the quality measures required for the product. When a Product Backlog item meets the DoD, an Increment is born. The DoD creates transparency by providing everyone a shared understanding of what work was completed as part of the Increment. Also, if a Product Backlog item does not meet the DoD, it cannot be released or even presented at the Sprint Review. Rather, it returns to the Product Backlog for future consideration (Schwaber and Sutherland 2020).

Delphi method: The method entails a group of experts who anonymously reply to questionnaires and subsequently receive feedback in the form of a statistical representation of the "group response," after which the process repeats itself. The goal is to reduce the range of responses and arrive at something closer to expert consensus. RAND Corporation developed the Delphi method in the 1950s, originally to forecast the impact of technology on warfare. (RAND stands for "research and development.") RAND is an American nonprofit global policy thinktank created in 1948 by Douglas Aircraft Company to offer research and analysis to the U.S. Armed Forces. The Delphi method has been widely adopted and is still in use today (RAND Corporation n.d.).

Delivery Team: Team Members who complete product tasks from the Sprint Backlog during a Sprint to deliver a product, also known as the Delivery Team. They are the individuals in the Agile Team who are committed to creating any aspect of a usable Increment in each Sprint.

Descriptive analytics: The study and consolidation of historical data; data and questions that are focused on the past provide hindsight on what already happened.

Diagnostic analytics: Reviewing past performance to determine what happened and why. Businesses use this type of analytics to complete root cause analysis.

Delivery risks: Risks that may affect our ability to meet our objective of providing results or assurance by a certain time.

Emphadamant: A portmanteau of two words: emphatic + adamant. This word is used to denote when a person expresses oneself in a manner that displays copious emphasis over an issue or topic while being firm and unwavering in their convictions.

Epics: Loosely defined ideas or large user stories.

Generally Accepted Auditing Standards (GAAS): Standards that guide external financial audit work.

Generally Accepted Government Audit Standards (GAGAS): Standards that provide the foundation for government auditors to lead by example in the areas of independence, transparency, accountability, and quality through the audit process.

Government Accountability Office (GAO): The body that created the Generally Accepted Government Audit Standards (GAGAS), also known as the Yellow Book.

IIA Standards: Standards for the Professional Practice of Internal Auditing, issued by the Institute of Internal Auditors, that guide internal audit work.

Institute of Internal Auditors (IIA): The recognized global authority and standards-setting body that sets expectations for the performance of internal audit activities and internal auditors.

International Professional Practices Framework (IPPF): The IPPF is the conceptual framework that organizes authoritative guidance promulgated by the IIA.

Institute of Internal Auditors' International Professional Practices Framework (IIA IPPF): A set of mandatory and recommended guidance for the internal audit profession, also known as the Red Book.

Increment: A product deliverable, usually a small portion of the overall product, also known as a Sprint.

Internal audit: An independent, objective assurance and consulting activity designed to add value and improve an organization's operations. It helps an organization accomplish its objectives by bringing a systematic, disciplined approach to evaluate and improve the effectiveness of risk management, control, and governance processes (Institute of Internal Auditors 2017a).

Kaizen: A Japanese term meaning "change for the better" or "continuous improvement." It is a Japanese business philosophy regarding the processes that continuously improve operations and involve all employees. Kaizen sees improvement in productivity as a gradual and methodical process. In Scrum, a Kaizen, or Process Improvement, is the goal of the Sprint Retrospective event (Hargrave 2020).

Kanban: A method for defining, managing, and improving services that deliver knowledge work, such as professional services, creative endeavors, and the design of both physical and software products. It may be characterized as a "start from what you do now" method – a catalyst for rapid and focused change within organizations – that reduces resistance to beneficial change in line with the organization's goals. The Kanban Method is based on making visible what is otherwise intangible knowledge work, to ensure that the service works on the right amount of work – work that is requested and needed by the customer and that the service has the capability to deliver (Anderson and Carmichael 2016).

Machine learning (ML): Detection, correlation, and pattern recognition generated through machine-based observation of the human operation of software systems along with ongoing self-informing regression algorithms for machine-based determination of successful operation leading to useful predictive analytics or prescriptive analytics capability (see Predictive Analytics and Prescriptive Analytics, discussed below) (IEEE Standard 2755-2017).

Optimization analysis: The process of finding optimal problem parameters subject to constraints. Optimization algorithms heuristically test a large number of parameter configurations in order to find an optimal result, determined by a characteristic function (also called a fitness function) (Lean Methods Group 2019).

Participatory Auditing: Requires the involvement of the audit client's direct participation in the audit. Instead of being the unwilling auditee, the audit client is part of the audit team from the start of the audit project, if they choose to be. Our Agile audit framework embeds Participatory Auditing. The audit client is part of the Agile audit team from day one.

Predictive analytics: The analysis for forecasting future outcomes based on patterns in past data.

Prescriptive analytics: Builds on predictive analytics by including actions and making data-driven decisions by looking at the impacts of various actions.

Product Backlog: A compilation of user stories, epics, and themes that provide a list of requirements and deliverables for a product.

Product Goal: A product is a vehicle to deliver value. It has a clear boundary, known stakeholders, and well-defined users or customers. A product could be a service, a physical product, or something more abstract (Schwaber and Sutherland 2020).

Product Owner: The guardian of the Product Backlog, who defines the priorities for the product and Delivery Team and approves the increments and products for delivery.

Product Backlog Refinement: A whole-team activity led by the Product Owner. The ongoing process of adding detail, estimates, and order to the items in the Product

Backlog. Not an official Scrum Event, but a highly recommended practice. Usually consumes no more than 10% of the capacity of the team (Scrum Inc. 2020).

Red Book: The IIA IPPF.

Risk universe: A listing of risks, also called a risk register or risk inventory.

Robotic desktop automation (RDA): The computer application that makes available to a human operator a suite of predefined activity choreography to complete the execution of processes, activities, transactions, and tasks in one or more unrelated software systems to deliver a result or service in the course of human-initiated or -managed workflow (IEEE Standard 2755-2017).

Robotic process automation (RPA): A preconfigured software instance that uses business rules and predefined activity choreography to complete the autonomous execution of a combination of processes, activities, transactions, and tasks in one or more unrelated software systems to deliver a result or service with human exception management (IEEE Standard 2755-2017).

Scrum: An Agile framework to support teams in complex product development. Scrum is a lightweight framework that helps people, teams and organizations generate value through adaptive solutions for complex problems. In a nutshell, Scrum requires a Scrum Master to foster an environment where: A Product Owner orders the work for a complex problem into a Product Backlog; the Scrum Team turns a selection of the work into an Increment of value during a Sprint; the Scrum Team and its stakeholders inspect the results and adjust for the next Sprint; and repeat. Scrum is simple. Try it as is and determine if its philosophy, theory, and structure help to achieve goals and create value. The Scrum framework is purposefully incomplete, only defining the parts required to implement Scrum theory. Scrum is built upon by the collective intelligence of the people using it. Rather than provide people with detailed instructions, the rules of Scrum guide their relationships and interactions. Various processes, techniques and methods can be employed within the framework. Scrum wraps around existing practices or renders them unnecessary. Scrum makes visible the relative efficacy of current management, environment, and work techniques, so that improvements can be made (Schwaber and Sutherland 2020).

Scrum Master: A facilitator for the Agile/Scrum project who champions Agile, encourages the right behaviors, and removes roadblocks and obstacles to help the team remain efficient in completing the sprints. The Scrum Master is a servant leader for the Scrum Team and is responsible for making the process run smoothly, for removing obstacles that impact productivity, and for organizing and facilitating the critical meetings (Cprime 2020).

Sprint: A short, timebound project within which the team members will complete an increment of work to deliver products.

Sprint Backlog: Specific, focused list of tasks, determined by the Delivery Team to complete an Increment.

Sprint terminations: Discontinuing a Sprint after it starts.

Story point: The estimate of the difficulty to complete a user story.

Structured data: Data that is organized according to a predetermined structure, such as a database.

Team: Considered to be a group of people who follow a shared goal (Ferreira Peralta, Nuno Lopes, Gilson, Renato Lourenco, and Pais 2015).

Unstructured data: Data that has no identifiable structure, such as text, audio, video, all mobile activity, social media activity, surveillance imagery including GPS, and facial recognition.

User story: A statement of what is needed from a product, from a user's perspective. A user story always takes the form "As a [who] I want [what] so that [why]."

Variability: The extent that data points diverge from the mean and from each other. Variability is typically measured by range, mean, variance, and standard deviation.

Variety: The sources of data captured.

Velocity: A measure of the rate of progress during an Agile audit. It is a measure of the amount of work a team has completed during a single Sprint, and it is the key metric in Scrum.

Veracity: The quality and accuracy of the data.

Visualization: The ability to translate vast amounts of data into readily presentable graphics and charts that highlight insights gleaned from the data while being easy to understand and interpret by the end user.

Waterfall life cycle: A succession-based process where one step or phase of a project must be completed before moving to the next until the entire project is complete.

Yellow Book: A document produced by the U.S. Government Accountability Office (GAO) that guides and provides standards for government audit work.

Appendix A: Product Backlog Template

User Story	Risk Certainty/ Uncertainty	Value (Client's Value)	Dependency	Data Needed	Resource Required	Effort

By Raven Global Training, LLC

Appendix B: Agile Audit Example

Let's begin an Agile audit of remediation activities for the following audit finding. This Agile Audit time lapse is one week.

 ## SECURITY/ACCESS CONTROLS: DEFICIENCIES IN THE USER PROVISIONING PROCESS FOR TERMINATIONS

Weaknesses in the user provisioning process can lead to a risk of unauthorized user access. Per review of the user provisioning process, we observed that 18 terminated employees had an active account within SAP. Per further inquiry, it was noted that the termination notification reports from HR to the SAP security team did not capture all action types for terminated employees (e.g., deactivated contractors). Therefore, SAP security did not remove these users from the SAP system.

The Agile Audit Team includes the following:
- Product Owner (PO): IT Audit Division Director
- Scrum Master (SM): Audit Accounting Team Manager
- Delivery Team (DT): Auditor A (the original IT auditor who noted the finding), Auditor B (the auditor completing remediation review), Auditor C (the audit manager for HR functions), Audit Client SAP (the systems administrator for SAP)

Day 1

10:00 a.m.: Sprint Planning Meeting (2 hours) – The Agile team collects in a conference room. The PO shares the written finding on a projector screen and states that while the finding was identified in the SAP audit, other sensitive and critical systems with similar problems for terminated employees exist. The PO wants the Agile audit to include the HR notification reports for all critical systems. The SM articulates the *user story* as "As an HR manager, we want to notify all critical systems of terminated employees and contractors, so they can remove the terminated user and ensure the security of the systems." Auditor A clarifies the issue was limited to the SAP system. Auditor C describes the current notification process and reports. Auditor B asks several clarifying questions. The DT lists items for the *Definition of Ready*, including a list of all critical systems, an initial walkthrough confirmed by the current HR contact for notification reports, list of current HR system termination codes, and a daily meeting location secured for 10:30 a.m. The *Definition of Done* includes confirmation of 18 original exceptions removed from SAP; confirmation that the notification report includes all other termination types; workpapers reviewed by Auditor A; Sprint Review held; and Sprint Retrospective scheduled. The Agile team decides the *project canvas* is not required for this engagement. The SM uses a rolling whiteboard to create the *taskboard/Sprint Backlog*. Items in the "To-Do" column include: confirm location, perform walkthrough, obtain notification report, obtain termination codes, obtain critical system listing, and data analytics testing of critical system terminations. Additional information sharing and items are added to the taskboard by the DT. During the meeting, the SM confirms the daily meeting location and moves the task item to "Done."

12:00 p.m.: Auditor B confirms walkthrough with HR contact.

12:30 p.m.: Auditor B obtains the critical system list and moves the item to "Done." Auditor B reviews prior workpapers for the related audit and queries the issues database for similar issues.

2:00 p.m.: Auditor B performs the walkthrough and obtains termination codes and notification reports during the walkthrough. The HR contact and Auditor B obtain the population of any worker who has not logged in to the network for 30 days or more, who does not have a current access card, and those identified on the current termination report. HR and Auditor B cross-reference the three reports and conclude that the current termination report is 100% accurate. Auditor B documents the walkthrough and population verification in the automated workpaper system, and HR reads the workpaper as documented.

4:30 p.m.: Auditor B flags the workpaper for peer review.

4:45 p.m.: Auditor A completes workpaper review.

Day 2

8:30 a.m.: Auditor B reviews the critical system list, requests the access reports for each system from the IT audit team via email, and adds the task to the taskboard. Another task for "confirm 18 original" is added.

10:30 a.m.: *Daily meeting.* SM asks about the IT audit request to confirm that it should be in scope. A member of the IT audit team is observing the meeting. Auditor B states that yesterday, they completed the walkthrough and confirmed the completeness of the termination report. Today, they will verify that all terminated employees are removed from all critical systems. No obstacles are impeding the audit.

10:45 a.m.: Auditor B approaches the IT auditor after the daily meeting to confirm that the requested access reports can be obtained before 1 p.m.

12:30 p.m.: Auditor B receives access reports, moves the related taskboard item ("data analytics of terminations") to "In Progress," and identifies two critical systems that have employees listed on the terminated report. Auditor B confirms that SAP does not have the original 18 and moves the associated taskboard item to the "Done" column. Auditor B discusses the exceptions with the IT auditor to confirm their understanding and obtain the system administrator's name. Auditor B prepares the SAP workpaper and submits it for peer review.

2:00 p.m.: Auditor A completes peer review of SAP workpaper and approaches Auditor B to document the removal date of the 18 workers. Auditor B asks, "Does that help add value to the result?" Auditor A says it would help the audit to know that the updates were made within a reasonable time after the original issue and provide a level of comfort that all updates are timely. Auditor B said that there was one termination five days prior, and that person was not on the SAP report. The workpapers were updated to include this notation while discussing with Auditor A, and the workpaper was approved. [*Notice that the additional documentation of "the 18-worker termination date in the system" was unnecessary. The desired comfort level was achieved with a more recent example. Thus, time was saved from having to research the original 18.*] Auditors A and B agreed to add a "Reviewed" column to the taskboard to ensure the review of all workpapers is complete as per audit policy.

4:00 p.m.: Auditor B contacts the system administrators via phone for the two critical systems with terminated employees. Meetings are scheduled to review the exceptions, and the administrators receive an invitation to the daily meeting, as they are now part of the Delivery Team.

Day 3

9:00 a.m.: Auditor B and the HR contact conducts a meeting with the first system administrator. The auditor shares the termination roster and the data analytics used to identify the exceptions. The system administrator pulls the manual notification reports provided by HR. Both conclude that the terminated user was not on the notification report. HR reviews the report date, and from memory states that there was an update made to the notification reports around the date of the terminated users. Auditor B adds the taskboard item "Determine the cause for error on notification report." The HR contact is then assigned this item.

10:30 a.m. *Daily meeting.* HR contact states that today they are researching the notification report error for the critical system. Auditor B provides their update. The SM requests a level of effort to complete, and, based on HR and Auditor B's responses, SM is confident the audit will be completed on time.

11:00 a.m.: HR contact and Auditor B discuss the notification report's update that resulted in the error. There was a new termination code added that was not included in the notification report for two months. Once identified, the code was added; however, new notifications were not sent for the two months. HR and Auditor B agreed that any new codes added should be manually verified on the notification reports. The workpaper documented this, and the related corrective action was noted.

1:00 p.m.: Auditor B and HR conduct a meeting with second system administrator providing the details on the termination roster and data analytics. There were two terminated employees in the critical system, and they were also on the notification report. In this case, the three parties agree that the system administrator failed to remove the terminated users. The workpaper documented this, and Auditor B determined that further testing and determination of the root cause of the failure was out of this engagement scope and added an item to the *Product Backlog* for IT. Auditor B submitted the workpaper for peer review.

2:30 p.m.: Auditor B adds notification report exception to the taskboard for discussion.

Day 4

10:30 a.m. *Daily meeting.* Auditor B stated yesterday that they completed a review of exceptions with system administrators and added an item to the Product Backlog to review in a future audit. The PO interrupted briefly before the SM reminded the PO that any additional questions could be addressed after the meeting. The SM also reminded the team that the project was due before the Sprint Review the next day at 2:00 p.m. Auditor B continued stating that today they would clear any review notes when provided by Auditor A and provide the written notice and correction action for the issue tracking database. Auditor A stated that today they would review all open workpapers.

11:00 a.m.: Auditor B added "Bug – notification report updates" to the taskboard and placed it in the "In Progress" column.

11:10 a.m.: Auditor B and HR contact draft the bug for inclusion in the issue-tracking database.

11:35 a.m.: Auditor B receives review notes from Auditor A on the second critical system's termination errors. Auditor B provides the needed responses and creates a user story for the newly added backlog item as requested.

12:00 p.m.: Auditor B prepares the agenda for the Sprint Review.

Day 5:

10:30 a.m.: *Daily meeting.* All tasks were moved to "Done."

10:35 p.m.: Auditor B verifies the completion of the *Definition of Done.*

2:00 p.m.: *Sprint Review* meeting held. Auditor B stated that the original 18 terminations were corrected, provided an overview of the notification report error, highlighted that all tasks were completed, and provided the user story for the new Product Backlog item. During the next *Product Backlog Refinement* meeting, the item would be prioritized.

3:00 p.m.: *Sprint Retrospective* meeting was held with a discussion on what went well and what could be better on the next engagement.

3:30 p.m.: *Product Backlog Refinement* meeting.

Bibliography

Adams, J. 2014. "Managing Risk: Framing Your Problems." Boeringer Ingelheim Alumni Seminar." Cologne, Germany, June 28.

Agile Alliance. 2001. *Manifesto for Agile Software Development*. Accessed January 2, 2019. https://www.agilealliance.org/agile101/the-agile-manifesto/.

Alexiou, S. 2017. "Agile Audit Practice." *ISACA Now* [blog], April 10. Accessed June 20, 2020. https://www.isaca.org/resources/news-and-trends/isaca-now-blog/2017/agile-audit-practice.

Anderson, David J., and Andy Carmichael. 2016. *Essential Kanban Condensed*. Seattle, WA: Lean Kanban University Press.

Banasiewicz, Andrew, D. 2009. *Risk Profiling of Organizations*. Bristol, RI: Erudite Systems Books.

Beck, Kent, Mike Beedle, Arie van Bennekum, Alistair Cockburn, Ward Cunningham, Martin Fowler, James Grenning, Jim Highsmith, Andrew Hunt, Ron Jeffries, Jon Kern, Brian Marick, Robert C. Martin, Steve Mellor, Ken Schwaber, Jeff Sutherland, and Dave Thomas 2001. *The Agile Manifesto*. Accessed June 1, 2014. http://agile-manifesto.org.

Blake, J. 2004. "Project Managing the SDLC: Using Milestones to Align Project Management and System Development Lifecycles and Report Project Success." *PMI Global Conference*. Anaheim, CA: Project Management Institute.

Cambridge Dictionary. 2020a. "Framework." *Cambridge Dictionary*. August 8. Accessed August 8, 2020. https://dictionary.cambridge.org/us/dictionary/english/framework.

Cambridge Dictionary 2020b. "Methodology." *Cambridge Dictionary*. August 8. Accessed August 8, 2020. https://dictionary.cambridge.org/us/dictionary/english/methodology.

CareerExplorer by Sokanu. 2020. "Are Auditors Happy?" https://www.careerexplorer.com/careers/auditor/satisfaction/.

Catlin, Raven. 2020. "Agile Auditing in Remote Environments." Webinar. Raven Global Training, LLC, Virginia.

Catlin, Raven. 2014. Agile Auditing Seminar. Raven Global Training, LLC, Roseland, NJ.

Cazaly, L. 2017. *Agile-ish: How to Create a Culture of Agility*. AgileNZ.

Chambers, Richard. 2017a. "Seven Signs You Might Be a Jurassic Auditor." *IA* [blog], October 16. Accessed November 6, 2019. https://iaonline.theiia.org/blogs/chambers/2017/Pages/Seven-Signs-You-Might-Be-a-Jurassic-Auditor.aspx.

Chambers, Richard. 2017b. *Trusted Advisors: Key Attributes of Outstanding Internal Auditors.* Altamonte Springs, FL: Internal Audit Foundation.

Chambers, Richard F. 2019. *The Speed of Risk: Lessons Learned on the Audit Trail.* Lake Mary, FL: Internal Auditor Foundation. Accessed February 5, 2020.

Cockburn, Alistair. 2019. "Post-Agile Thoughts." *Heart of Agile* [blog], April 22. Accessed August 9, 2020. https://heartofagile.com/post-agile-thoughts/.

Committee of Sponsoring Organizations of the Treadway Commission (COSO). 2013. *Internal Control – Integrated Framework.* Durham, NC: American Institute of Certified Public Accountants.

Consultancy.eu. 2020. *"Half of Companies Applying Agile Methodologies & Practices."* May 7. Accessed August 8, 2020. https://www.consultancy.eu/news/4153/half-of-companies-applying-agile-methodologies-practices.

Cprime. 2020. *"What Is Agile? What Is Scrum?"* October 30. Accessed October 30, 2020. https://www.cprime.com/resources/what-is-agile-what-is-scrum/.

Davenport, Thomas H., and Jeanne G. Harris. 2017. *Competing on Analytics: The New Science of Winning.* 2nd edition. Boston: Harvard Business Review Press.

Davidson, B. 2012. *Mind Maps: Master Mind Mapping in Under 90 Minutes.* Shaffer Enterprises and Marketing Ltd.

Denning, Stephen. 2018. *The Age of Agile: How Smart Companies Are Transforming the Way Work Gets Done.* New York: AMACOM.

Duhigg, Charles. 2014. *The Power of Habit.* New York: Random House.

Dumas, Marlo, Marcello La Rosa, Jan Mendling, and Hajo Reijers. 2013. *Fundamentals of Business Process Management.* Heidelberg: Springer.

El-Erian, Mohamed A. 2010. "Navigating the New Normal in Industrial Countries – International Monetary Fund." Washington, DC: The Per Jacobsson Foundation. Accessed August 7, 2020. https://play.google.com/books/reader?id=OdYvolUO8RUC&hl=en&pg=GBS.PP2.

Evans, James, R. 2016. *Business Analytics: Methods, Models, and Decisions.* 2nd edition. Upper Saddle River, NJ: Pearson Education, Inc.

Ferreira Peralta, C., P. Nuno Lopes, L. Gilson, P. Renato Lourenco, and L. Pais. 2015. "Innovation Processes and Team Effectiveness: The Role of Goal Clarity and Commitment, and Team Affective Tone." *Journal of Occupational and Organizational Psychology* 88: 80–107.

Frick, Don M. 2004. *Robert K. Greenleaf: A Life of Servant Leadership.* Berrett-Koehler Publishers. Accessed November 11, 2020. https://www.greenleaf.org/robert-k-greenleaf-biography/.

Goasduff, Laurence. 2019. "Gartner Forecasts Global IoT Enterprise Drone Shipments to Grow 50% in 2020." Gartner press release, December 4. Accessed August 25, 2020. https://www.gartner.com/en/newsroom/press-releases/2019-12-04-gartner-forecasts-global-iot-enterprise-drone-shipmen.

Hargrave, Marshall. 2020. "Investopedia" Accessed February 1, 2021. https://www. investopedia.com/terms/k/kaizen.asp

Heldman, Kim. 2005. *Project Management Professional Study Guide.* Indianapolis, IN: Wiley.

Howell, Robert T. 2001. "Fostering Self-Directed Team Members." *The Journal of Technology Studies* 27 (1/2): 51–53. Accessed November 10, 2020. https://www. jstor.org/stable/43604701.

IEEE. 2020. "About IEEE." Accessed August 18, 2020. https://www.ieee.org/about/ index.html.

Institute of Internal Auditors. 2017a. *International Professional Practices Framework (IPPF).* Altamonte Springs, FL: The Institute of Internal Auditors Research Foundation.

Institute of Internal Auditors. 2017b. "Understanding and Auditing Big Data." April 17. Accessed August 15, 2020. https://na.theiia.org/standards-guidance/Member%20 Documents/GTAG-Understanding-and-Auditing-Big-Data.pdf.

Institute of Internal Auditors. 2019a. "2019 North American Pulse of Internal Audit: Defining Alignment in a Dynamic Risk Landscape." Accessed August 12, 2020. http://contentz.mkt5790.com/lp/2842/263452/2019-1826%20IIA%20 Pulse%20Report-online%20CX%20March2019.pdf.

Institute of Internal Auditors. 2019b. "OnRisk 2020: A Guide to Understanding, Aligning, and Optimizing Risk." http://contentz.mkt5790.com/lp/2842/275148/ OnRisk-2020-Report_0.pdf.

Institute of Internal Auditors. 2020. *OnRisk 2021: A Guide to Understanding, Aligning, and Optimizing Risk.* Global Survey, Lake Mary, FL: The Institute of Internal Auditors, 38.

International Organization for Standardization. 2018. *ISO 31000:2018, Risk Management.* Geneva, Switzerland: ISO.

Kotter, John P. 2012. "The Key to Changing Organizational Culture." *Forbes,* September 27. https://www.forbes.com/sites/johnkotter/2012/09/27/the-key-to-changing-organizational-culture/?sh=de6fddd55094.

Lam, James. 2014. *Enterprise Risk Management: From Incentives to Controls.* 2nd edition. Hoboken, NJ: Wiley.

Lamaire-Harvey, Bernice M., and David A. Harvey. 2020. *"RPA Internal Controls Support Audit Readiness." Journal of Government Financial Management.*

Lean Methods Group. 2019. *Data Analytics Glossary.* Accessed November 13, 2020. https://leanmethods.com/resources/articles/data-analytics-glossary/.

LeMay, Matt. 2018. *Agile for Everybody: Creating Fast, Flexible, and Customer-First Organizations.* Sebastopol, CA: O'Reilly Media Inc.

Mathis, Bryan. 2013. *Agile Project Management for Beginners: Mastering the Basics.* CreateSpace. Kindle Edition.

Merriam-Webster, Inc. 2020. "Governance." Accessed August 16, 2020. https://www. merriam-webster.com/dictionary/governance.

Moore, Geoffrey A. 2014. *Crossing the Chasm.* 3rd edition. New York: HarperCollins.

Nussbaumer Knaflic, Cole. 2015. *Storytelling with Data: A Data Visualization Guide for Business Professionals.* Hoboken, NJ: Wiley.

Oxford Dictionary. 2020a. *"Efficacy." Oxford English and Spanish Dictionary*. Accessed August 7, 2020. https://www.lexico.com/definition/efficacy.

Oxford Dictionary. 2020b. *"New normal." Oxford English and Spanish Dictionary*. Accessed August 7, 2020. https://www.lexico.com/definition/new_normal.

Parente, Susan. 2019. "The Grateful Agile Leader." Center for Grateful Leadership, November 25. Accessed September 24, 2020. https://gratefulleadership.com/the-grateful-agile-leader/.

Patterson, Kerry, Joseph Grenny, Ron McMillan, and Al Switzler. 2012. *Crucial Conversations: Tools for Talking When Stakes Are High*. New York: McGraw-Hill.

Project Management Institute. 2017. *A Guide to the Project Management Body of Knowledge (PMBOK® Guide)* – Sixth Edition. Newtown Square, PA: Project Management Institute.

Poisson, D. 2020. "A Machine Learning Primer for Auditors." February 11. Accessed August 20, 2020. https://www.linkedin.com/pulse/machine-learning-primer-auditors-david-poisson/?trackingId=.

Pratchett, Terry. 2010. *I Shall Wear Midnight*. Discworld book 38. HarperCollins Publishers.

PricewaterhouseCoopers. 2017. "Staying the Course toward True North: Navigating Disruption." April 1. Accessed August 8, 2020. https://www.pwc.com/id/en/publications/assurance/state-of-the-internal-audit-profession-2017-april-2017.pdf.

RAND Corporation. "Delphi Technique" Accessed February 1, 2020. https://www.rand.org/topics/delphi-technique.html.

Raven Global Training, LLC. 2020. "Agile Auditing Definition." Unpublished work. Virginia, August 1.

Reding, Kurt, Paul Sobel, Urton Anderson, Michael Head, Sridhar Ramamoorti, Mark Salamasick, and Cris Riddle. 2009. *Internal Auditing: Assurance and Consulting Services*. Altamonte Springs, FL: The Institute of Internal Auditors Research Foundation.

Ries, Jeffrey. 2018. *Lean Startup: The Complete Step-by-Step Lean Six Sigma Startup Guide*. Jeffrey Ries.

Rigby, Darrell K., Jeff Sutherland, and Hirotaka Takeuchi. 2016. "Embracing Agile." *Harvard Business Review*, May.

Sampet, Jomjai, Naruanard Sarapaivanich, and Paul Patterson. 2019. "The Role of Client Participation and Psychological Comfort in Driving Perceptions of Audit Quality." *Asian Review of Accounting* 27 (2): 177–195. Accessed November 11, 2020. doi:10.1108/ARA-09-2017-0144.

Schwaber, Ken, and Jeff Sutherland. 2017. *The Scrum Guide: The Definitive Guide to Scrum: The Rules of the Game*. Attribution Share-Alike license of Creative Commons. https://www.scrumguides.org/docs/scrumguide/v2017/2017-Scrum-Guide-US.pdf.

Schwaber, Ken, and Jeff Sutherland. 2020. *The Scrum Guide, The Definitive Guide to Scrum: The Rules of the Game*. November 18. Accessed December 10, 2020. https://www.scrum.org/resources/scrum-guide.

Scrum Alliance. 2015. "Scrum Alliance: Scrum Values." April 13. Accessed June 1, 2020. https://www.scrumalliance.org/about-scrum/values.

Scrum Alliance. 2020. "Certification Types and Tracks." Accessed September 28, 2020. https://www.scrumalliance.org/get-certified. Scrum Guides.org. 2020. "Changes between 2017 and 2020 Scrum Guides." November 18. Accessed December 12, 2020. https://scrumguides.org/revisions.html.

Scrum Inc. 2020. "Welcome to Scrum inc's Glossary." Accessed December 5, 2020. https://www.scruminc.com/scrum-glossary

Stedman, Craig, and Linda Rosencrance. 2019. "Hadoop." TechTarget, October. Accessed August 25, 2020. https://searchdatamanagement.techtarget.com/definition/Hadoop.

Steinberg, Richard M. 2011. *Governance, Risk Management, and Compliance: It Can't Happen to Us – Avoiding Corporate Disaster While Driving Success.* Hoboken, NJ: Wiley.

Stippich, Warren W., and Bradley J. Preber. 2016. *Data Analytics.* Altamonte Springs, FL: Internal Auditors Research Foundation.

Sutherland, J.J. 2019. *The Scrum Fieldbook: A Master Class on Accelerating Performance, Getting Results, and Defining the Future.* New York: Currency.

Sutherland, Jeff, and J.J. Sutherland. 2014. *Scrum: The Art of Doing Twice the Work in Half the Time.* New York: Crown Business.

Taulli, Tom. 2020. *The Robotic Process Automation Handbook: A Guide to Implementing RPA Systems.* Monrovia, CA: Apress. Accessed August 20, 2020.

Tuckman, Bruce. 1965. "Developmental Sequence in Small Groups." *American Psychological Association Psychological Bulletin* 63(6).

Tukey, John W. 1980. "We Need Both Exploratory and Confirmatory." *The American Statistician* 34 (1): 23–25.

Umlas, Bob. 2007. *This Isn't Excel, It's Magic!* 2nd edition. New York: International Institute for Learning.

Umlas, Judith W. 2013. *Grateful Leadership: Using the Power of Acknowledgment to Engage All Your People and Achieve Superior Results.* New York: McGraw-Hill.

U.S. Government Accountability Office (GAO). 2014. *Standards for Internal Control in the Federal Government.* Washington, DC: GAO. Accessed November 8, 2020. https://www.gao.gov/assets/670/665712.pdf.

U.S. Government Accountability Office (GAO). 2018. The Yellow Book. July. Accessed August 20, 2020. https://www.gao.gov/yellowbook/overview.

Wikipedia. 2019. "Robot *(Lost in Space)*." May 1. Accessed September 23, 2020. https://en.wikipedia.org/wiki/Robot_(Lost_in_Space).

Williams, Roy. 2012. "Data Volumes." Center for Advanced Computing Research at the California Institute of Technology, January. Accessed November 10, 2020. https://www.eecis.udel.edu/~amer/Table-Kilo-Mega-Giga---YottaBytes.html.

Wright, Rick A. Jr. 2019. *Agile Auditing: Transforming the Internal Audit Process.* Lake Mary, FL: Internal Audit Foundation.

Index